Aliens on Our Shores

An Anthropological History of New Ireland, Papua New Guinea

1616-1914

Paula G. Rubel and Abraham Rosman

Development Resources Press

Pasadena, California

© Paula G. Rubel and Abraham Rosman, 2021

Published by
Development Resources Press
P.O. Box 94859
Pasadena, California 91109
www.devresbooks.com

Rubel, Paula G., and Abraham Rosman
Aliens on Our Shores; An Anthropological History of New Ireland, Papua New Guinea 1616-1914

Includes Bibliography, Index

Library of Congress Control Number: 2021933794

1. History – Papua New Guinea 2. Ethnology – New Ireland, Papua New Guinea 3. Missionaries, South Pacific 4. Explorers, South Pacific 5. Capitalism, expansion of 6. German colonialism 7. Cannibalism, Papua New Guinea

ISBN 978-0-9906337-5-4

Cover Image: Two images combined, both by Isaac Gilsemans, from Abel Tasman's Journal: A View of the Murderers' Bay (1642, cropped, from Alexander Turnbull Library, New Zealand: https://tiaki.natlib.govt.nz/#details=ecatalogue.191814) and New Ireland Canoe. Cover Design: Rita Toews

Contents

PREFACE 1
1. INTRODUCTION 9
2. NEW IRELAND BEFORE THE "ALIENS" ARRIVED 35
   Prehistory and Languages 36
   European Explorers' Reports 38
   Material Culture 41
   Social Organization 44
   Warfare, Cannibalism, and Peace-making 49
   Ceremonial Life 51
   Gender Relations 59
   Discussion 62
3. EUROPEAN IDEAS ABOUT NON-EUROPEAN OTHERS . 67
   "Wild men" and "Noble Savages" 70
   Shifts in Thinking After the Scientific Revolution 75
   The "Other" in Popular Fiction 80
   Discussion 82
4. EUROPEAN VISITORS TO NEW IRELAND DURING THE
   AGE OF EXPLORATION 85
   Isaac Le Maire and Willem Schouten 86
   Abel Janszoon Tasman 92
   William Dampier 98
   Phillip Carteret 104
   Louis Antoine de Bougainville 106
   Evidence of New Irelanders' Views 109
   Discussion 111

5. BETWEEN BEACH AND SHIP: THE DEVELOPMENT OF EXCHANGE WITHIN THE LIMINAL AREA 113
   The Duperrey Expedition 114
   M.J. Dumont d'Urville 118
   Increased Frequency of Contact: Whalers and Traders 121
   Castaways 126
   Whalers' Reports 129
   Discussion 134

6. NEW IRELANDERS ENCOUNTER CAPITALISM 141
   Trading Stations 143
   New Irelanders' Responses to Trading Stations 152
   Traders' Behavior 153
   Punitive Expeditions 154
   Competition Among Aspiring Colonial Powers 156
   Pacification of Rebellious Natives by Violence and Other Means
   158
   Efforts to Conclude "Treaties" 160
   French Traders in Southern New Ireland 161
   Discussion 164

7. BLACKBIRDING: SHANGHAIING NEW IRELAND WORKERS FOR THE PLANTATIONS 173
   First-hand Accounts of Labor Recruiters 174
   Europeans' Differing Official Positions on Labor Recruitment
   181
   Discussion 187

8. CHRISTIANITY COMES TO NEW IRELAND: ESTABLISHMENT OF MISSIONARY STATIONS 191
   The Methodist, Reverend George Brown 193
   Christianity and Gender Roles 205
   Reverend Benjamin Danks 207

    Fijian Teachers 210
    Reverend Rickard 213
    German Annexation Changes the Missionary Approach 214
    Discussion... 215

9. PACIFICATION AND ADMINISTRATION: THE
    IMPOSITION OF GERMAN RULE 219
    Continuation of Punitive Expeditions 220
    Misunderstanding New Irelanders' Conflicts.......................... 225
    Shifts in Local Power Relations 226
    Changes in the Colonial "Pacification" Approach 228
    Creation of a Territorially-based Administrative System 230
    Continuation of Village Warfare in the South......................... 231
    Road Construction 234
    Discussion... 235

10. COPRA: VILLAGE TRADE AND THE ESTABLISHMENT
    OF PLANTATIONS 239
    Richard Parkinson: The First Plantation Manager 241
    Plantation Laborers from Elsewhere 243
    Different Types of Plantations.. 244
    Sabotage by Laborers and Local Populations......................... 248
    Trade and Payments.. 251
    Friction Between Traders and Villagers 254
    Regulation of Competition Between Traders 256
    Discussion... 257

11. THE EXPANSION AND SPREAD OF CHRISTIANITY
    DURING THE GERMAN COLONIAL PERIOD 261
    The Methodists 262
    Translating Christian Texts 265
    Boarding Schools.. 269

Indigenizing the Church 270
Ligeramaluoga's Story 271
Catholicism 272
Confrontations Between Methodists and Catholics 278
Discussion 280

12. CONSOLIDATON OF COLONIAL CONTROL: 1884-1914 287

Populations Relocate from Mountains to Coastal Settlements 288
Increasing Numbers of Men Working for Europeans 291
European-owned Plantations, Large and Small 292
Tension in New Irelanders' Relationship with the Colonial Government 293
Chinese Traders 297
Health Services 299
Infrastructure Development 299
The Last Anti-Colonial Uprisings 300
The End of German Control 302
Discussion 304

13. CONCLUSIONS 307

APPENDIX A. THE ARCHEOLOGY AND LINGUISTICS OF NEW IRELAND 323

APPENDIX B. DEED OF LAND PURCHASE ON NEW IRELAND, MAY 5, 1885 337

APPENDIX C. THE POPULATION OF NEW IRELAND BEFORE 1914 339

BIBLIOGRAPHY 341

INDEX 365

ABOUT THE AUTHORS 369

Figures

Figure 1. Tatanua Mask, from the Authors' Collection 56
Figure 2. Two Tatanua Masks from New Ireland, exhibited in the Australian Museum, Sydney 57
Figure 3. Dukduk Dancers in the Gazelle Peninsula, New Britain, 1913 58
Figure 4. Woodcut Broadside Illustrating the Discoveries of Amerigo Vespucci. Augsburg, 1505 69
Figure 5. New Ireland Canoe, drawing by Isaac Gilsemans, from Abel Tasman's Journal, 1643 98

Maps

Map 1. The South Pacific, Papua New Guinea, Australia, New Zealand 5
Map 2. Melanesia, Micronesia, Polynesia 6
Map 3. Papua New Guinea 7
Map 4. New Ireland and New Britain, Papua New Guinea 8
Map 5. Languages of New Ireland 39

Tables

Table 1. Plantation Statistics for 1906-1907 for New Ireland 246

PREFACE

This is the last book written by Paula Rubel and Abraham Rosman. It was completed in 2018. Both have since died, Paula Rubel in 2018, and Abraham Rosman in 2020. As their former student and their friend, I offer this manuscript with some light editing, to bring their huge scholarly effort.

The authors present this book as an "anthropological history." It provides detailed descriptions of the first 250 years of contact between New Irelanders and European explorers, traders, missionaries, and colonists. The purpose of these descriptions is to understand how encounters probably were understood by New Irelanders themselves. Context for interpretation is provided by archeological and ethnographic information on social structure and culture, and by the authors' own comparative perspective.

Aliens also devotes attention to the European cultural context, describing the long-standing, widespread cultural stereotypes of "Others" -- both positive and negative -- that framed explorers' perceptions of people in the New World and elsewhere and helped them to justify their own actions as "civilizing" the New Irelanders.

This book probes several important questions. Who exactly were the New Ireland people that the European explorers first met in the 17th century? What were New Irelanders' initial reactions to armed strangers in trading ships? Who controlled the interactions at specific steps in the history of contact, and how did they do so? What was the role of technology (guns, metal, cloth), new trade goods (tobacco, hoop iron), European money, or shell currency? How and when did European traders, plantation owners, missionaries, and conquerors start to change New Ireland political and economic life?

These and other themes are explored in ways that emphasize New Irelanders' agency in their relationships with European outsiders. Stories of specific incidents reveal subtleties of mutual misunderstanding and their consequences for New Irelanders during their long, eventually futile, struggle for control over the contact situation. While describing violence and domination in graphic terms, the authors manage to avoid seeing New Irelanders as mere "victims" of the Europeans.

In this book Professor Rosman and Professor Rubel create a bridge between analysis of traditional exchange systems -- their long-standing, principal research focus -- and more conventional political economics. They describe in detail the various ways that capitalism eventually penetrated New Irelanders' long-standing systems of labor, leadership, and determination of economic value, eventually changing day-to-day village life in significant ways. They emphasize the point that New Irelanders came to the relationship with their own ideas of how society was organized, and fit the European newcomers into their own pre-existing framework of moieties, allies, and enemies.

The focus in *Aliens* is on history. Ethnographic studies are used to interpret New Irelanders' probable perceptions of encounters and to understand their reactions to the Europeans. The authors were not long-term researchers of New Ireland social and cultural life, although they did some fieldwork in 1987, with funding from the National Science Foundation and the Guggenheim Foundation. Their social and cultural analysis depends mostly on the work of other anthropologists and reports by European traders,

PREFACE

missionaries, and government officers before 1914. The reader seeking further information on New Irelanders' social life and culture may wish to consult some of the many ethnographic studies not included in the bibliography: for example, the works of Nicholas A. Bainton, Dorothy K. Billings, Brigitte Derlon, Richard Eves, Michael Gunn, Stephen A. Jackson, S. Kuchler, and Karen Sykes.

In her book, *Unstable Images* (University of Hawai'i Press, 2005), Brenda Johnson Clay offers supplementary insights into Western missionaries' and early ethnographers' perceptions of New Irelanders. Her analysis overlaps with Rubel's and Rosman's for four decades, as she continues the history of cultural and political encounters beyond World War I with a focus on the nuances of Westerners' discourse.

I am not a specialist in this area of the world, so my editorial efforts may well have overlooked some social and cultural details. Further revisions may be needed. Meanwhile, I hope you will appreciate and learn from this 250-year voyage as much as I have.

I wish to thank the following people for help with this project: David Rubel for help with illustrations, Dr. Maxine Weisgrau for help with bibliography, Dr. Nicholas Bainton for his help with checking terminology, Rita Toews for cover design, and Brenda van Niekerk for e-book formatting.

Suzanne Hanchett, Ph.D.
Pasadena, California
February 2021

ALIENS ON OUR SHORES

MAPS

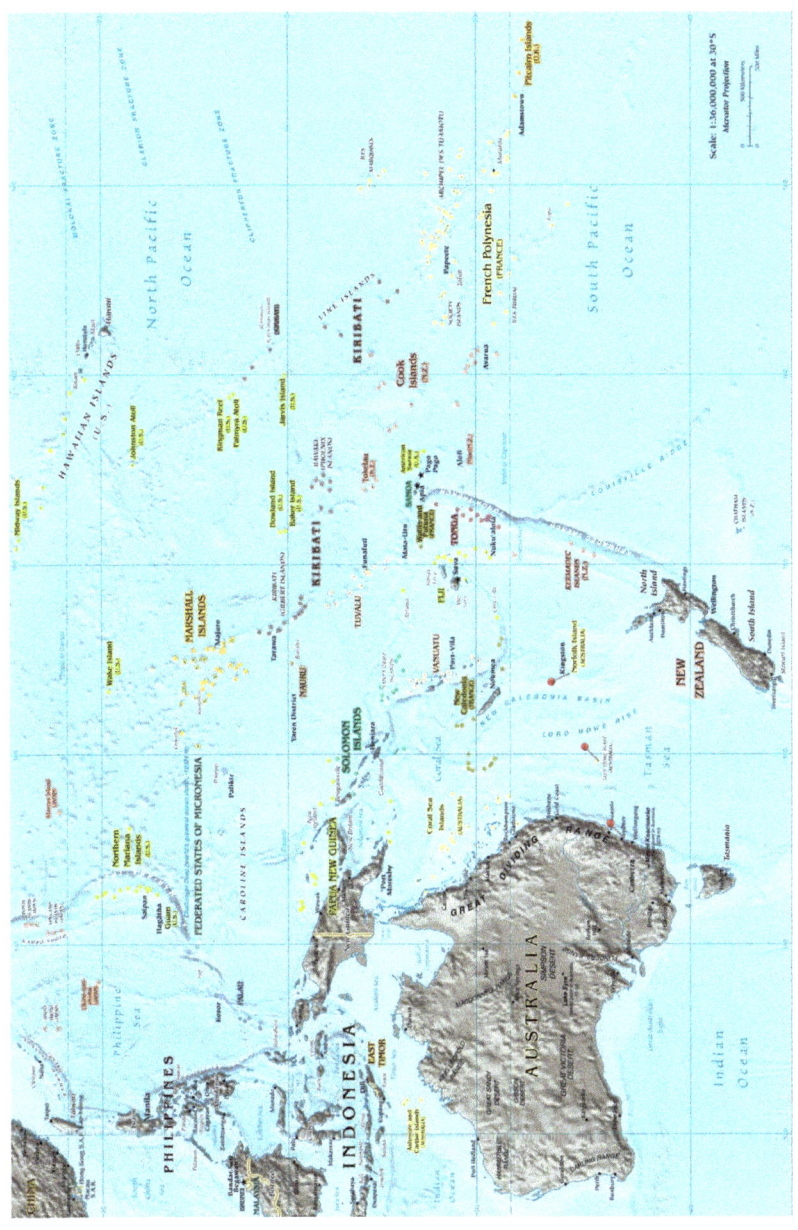

Map 1. The South Pacific, Papua New Guinea, Australia, New Zealand (Source:

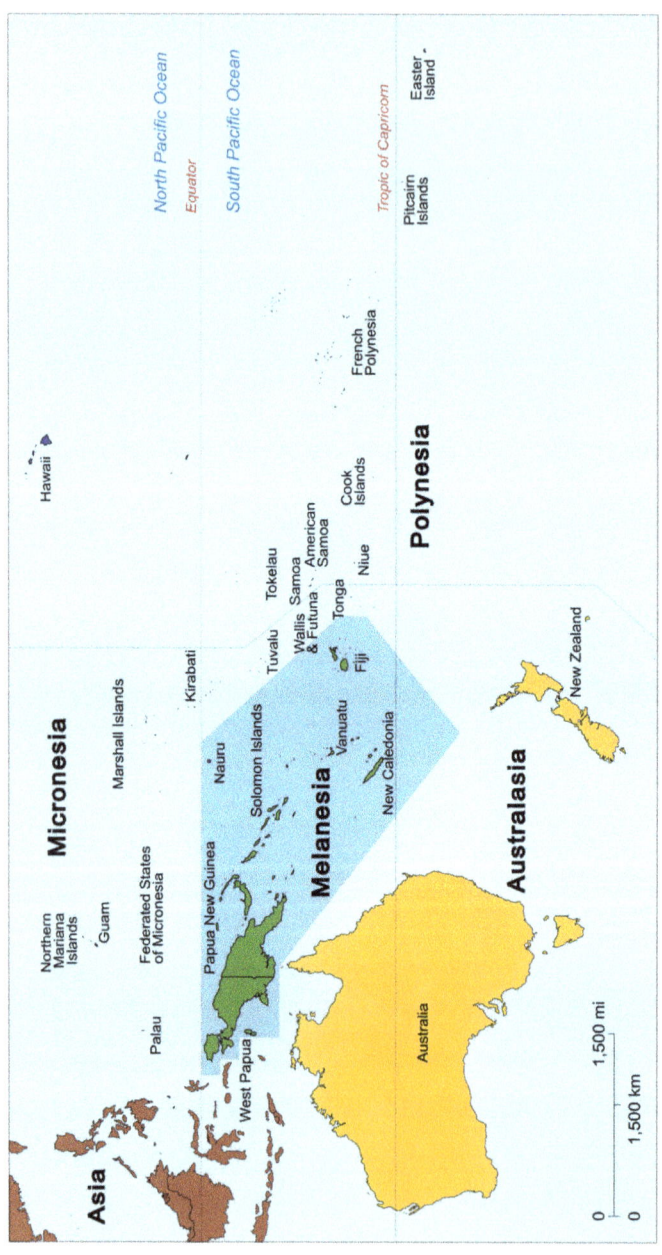

Map 2. Melanesia, Micronesia, Polynesia (Source: https://upload.wikimedia.org/wikipedia/commons/thumb/5/59/Oceania_UN_Geoscheme_Map_of_Melanesia.svg/1200px-Oceania_UN_Geoscheme_-_Map_of_Melanesia.svg.png)

MAPS

Map 3. Papua New Guinea (Source: Library of Congress, https://www.loc.gov/resource/g8160.ct001593/?r=-0.19,0.279,1.075,0.597,0)

Map 4. New Ireland and New Britain, Papua New Guinea (Source: http://www.mappery.com/maps/New-Ireland-and-Kavieng-Map.mediumthumb.png)

1. INTRODUCTION

"Call me Ishmael" is the way Melville began *Moby Dick*, to tell the reader that he would see events as they enfold through the eyes of the storyteller, Ishmael, the wanderer. We do not have a New Ireland Ishmael to tell the story of what happened when Europeans came to New Ireland. Nor do we wish to create a fictitious New Irelander to tell us his or her tale, since we do not intend this to be a work of fiction but rather one of historical anthropology. To us the line between fiction and historical anthropology is an important boundary. What we propose to do is to tell the story of the encounters between Europeans and New Irelanders as these events would have appeared to New Irelanders, using European accounts of these interactions and later ethnographic works. This is a work of history. However, some today speak of historical narratives as just another form of "storytelling." (Ankersmit in Rosenau 1992: 66) Though we will deal with hunting great whales, explorers, castaways, blackbirders, "cannibals" and vengeful missionaries, colonial officials, planters, and the islanders they encountered, the stuff of which the fiction of Melville, Robert Louis Stevenson, and Jack London was created, these events and those who peopled them will be considered differently here. The explorers, whalers, castaways and missionaries who are the central characters were real individuals: the outsiders, aliens who arrived on New Ireland shores through several centuries.

We will try to tell the tale as a New Ireland Ishmael would have told it[1]. The changes, often profound, brought about in the life of the New Irelanders, and their responses as agents to the intrusion of these "colorful and exotic" outsiders, will occupy center stage in our account. This perspective, as we shall discuss below, was used by Dening in his work on the Marquesas and Richter in his discussion of the American Indians of northeastern North America.

Western society has its own conceptualization of history which, in fact, has changed through time. Western history is chronological and is dependent on a linear view of time. (Cohn 1981: 227) For many historians, this European view of time which developed into "history" was formed at the beginning of the Renaissance, when budding nation states sought to construct a past. The units of historical accounts were nation states and history became largely political history. (Cohn 1981:246) Although people had been living there for many millennia, New Ireland enters history as the West constructed it, in seventeenth century explorers' accounts. The description of the "discovery" of New Ireland, encounters with the New Irelanders by Le Maire and Schouten became a minor episode in the history of the expansion of the Dutch state and its search for new markets. In contrast, New Irelanders and many other Oceanic peoples view history as repetitive and cyclical with one generation replacing an earlier one, with ceremonies celebrating this transformation.

We intend to focus on the interaction and framework of understandings which developed between New Irelanders and the succession of European outsiders who visited and later came to colonize the island from the first recorded encounter in the seventeenth century by Le Maire to the beginning of the twentieth century, more specifically to the end of German colonial rule in 1914.

The historical record of this interaction was compiled by Europeans, representing their point of view, and utilizing their stereotypic misconceptions of the people they were encountering. It includes travel accounts by explorers,

INTRODUCTION

sea captains hunting whales, traders, colonial papers, archives, and the records of colonial officials. We recognize and will take into consideration that these Europeans' behaviors must also be understood by reference to their particular cultural and historical time frame. We also recognize that "history" is a selective rather than an objective representation of the "facts" of what really happened. As Douglas notes,

> ...Knowing indigenous pasts and identifying indigenous agency [can be accomplished] through critical readings of colonial texts. 'Colonial text' is shorthand for all kinds of 'texts' produced about indigenous people by Europeans...from their first contact...such texts were ideologically 'colonial', in that their authors sought to 'possess' – symbolically and intellectually, if not actually – to exploit, transform or control indigenous people. (1998:23)

We will try to construct a picture of the New Ireland point of view over these several centuries of history. Comprehending the "...performances of the indigenous participants [requires entering] a world that is distant in time and alien in culture." (Lutz 2007:1, 32) In each contact between Europeans and New Irelanders from the very first one, "Each side was left to guess what the message [was that] the other was trying to convey. Each side continually revised its attempt to communicate, looking for signs of recognition of the other...each side was looking for signs of recognition from the other...each side was looking for cross-cultural clues about meaning and motivation...[but] misunderstanding was communicated as well as meaning." (Lutz 2007: 33)

Ethnographic information about New Ireland culture from a later time will be used to try to understand the behavior of New Irelanders as recorded by the Europeans, and the meanings of the messages New Irelanders were trying to convey to the latter. The cultural and sometimes spiritual symbols of both parties also must be considered. We recognize that the ethnographic information we will be using often was collected and analyzed within a colonial context which must, of course, be taken into consideration. Further, earlier ethnographers collected and analyzed their data within a succession of different theoretical frameworks developed within anthropology. These must be considered when using their material. Interestingly, the comparison of these different texts reveals many cultural similarities that remained, though the New Irelanders were being impacted by a changing contact situation.

For the most part, this ethnographic information does not consider agency, which has become important in anthropology today. Agency refers to the individual's point of view, the choices made by that individual, and his or her ability to create or alter the collectively shared social structure and ideas. As Douglas notes, "In my formulation, 'agency' embraces and transcends 'action' to include actors' desires and volition. …it refers to a general human capacity for action, choice, self-representation and deployment of strategies, always historicized in terms of circumstantial and structural possibilities and constraints." (1998:20-21)

European explorers in the 17th and 18th centuries approached the islanders of the unknown Pacific, in this particular instance, New Ireland, with a set of highly ambivalent, paradoxical ideas. The explorers were at first sometimes unsure about the very humanity of those they met. Were they human or animal? At first, "primitive" people were said not to have language, but to grunt and whine. Their nakedness seemed to indicate that they were less than human. Like apes, they wore no clothing. Was not the use of clothing a significant representation of culture and therefore of humanity? Some Europeans considered clothing as important as language.

INTRODUCTION

Yet nakedness itself also seemed to have another meaning: it also represented innocence. From this point of view, these "savages" were seen as truly noble in stature, and their nakedness reminded European travelers and explorers of an Age of Innocence, of Greek gods, and Adam and Eve. This was a sharp contrast for them to the corruption of their contemporary European world, with its hypocrisy of wigs, powder and elaborately frilled clothing which totally hid the body, presenting and displaying it in a complete culturally "clothed" manner. As we shall see later, some female travelers were quite taken with the manly figures of the unclothed New Irelanders. The Europeans approached these Others, about whom they knew nothing, with their cultural stereotypes, wary and ambivalent of those they considered "savages" and prepared for armed defense if necessary

As in other parts of Oceania, the indigenous population had their own customary ways of dealing with strangers. The New Irelanders were cautious in approaching the Europeans and their ships. They had no comprehension of them, their clothing, shoes, hats, or skin color. Yet, even in their bewilderment, they were prepared to deal with them. The New Irelanders' cultural conceptions organized their behavior towards the Europeans, who suddenly appeared on the scene. We will try to interpret the meanings of their responses to Europeans, their gestures, actions in arming themselves, and so on, to the extent that these cultural categories can be explained by later ethnographic information. We will consider how the New Irelanders must have perceived these encounters, and examine the ways in which their cultural categories, indeed their lives, were transformed by their experiences. They were prepared either to fight the Europeans, or to exchange with them, as they did with voyagers from other more distant islands. However, due to misunderstandings and the lack of knowledge of each other's cultural meanings, the early encounters between Europeans and New Irelanders often ended badly and in violence, as well shall see.

In describing the nature of first contact on the Northwest Coast of North America, Lutz notes all of the different aspects of it – the danger, the possibility, the question of how to respond, the message to be conveyed, the gestures to be used, what to offer, and the ambiguity of the situation. (Lutz 2007:7) Our focus here will be upon the actors whose actions "…as symbolic artifacts …may leave decipherable traces in colonial and other texts…and include actors' desires and volition… choice, self-representation and deployment of strategies…." (Douglas 1998:20,21) Lutz also notes, further, that, "Something was always exchanged on first contact. Often the exchange included goods, but it always involved attempts at communication …Typically, the parties would speak to each other without any comprehension; then they would turn to gesture." (2007:7) Further, these first contact events are seen as performances, the retelling of which created and recreated the meaning of these events to those who had not witnessed them. (Early contacts have become a subject of great interest and there is a burgeoning literature on the subject. *cf.* Dening 1996, Lutz 2007.)

Accounts of events and experiences may be passed on either in the form of oral tradition or in written documents as "history." It is important to recognize that history as well as oral tradition are cultural products. History or the record of the passage of time is always culturally construed as in the descriptions of New Irelanders in explorers' accounts. They present events from the point of view of the recorders and reflect many cultural factors. As Hill notes, there is for Western accounts, a "…need for a critical, reflexive awareness of sociological and historical research as a personally mediated and historically situated activity …. [In contrast, for the indigenous population,] oral and nonverbal formulations…can show how indigenous societies have experienced history and how they struggle to make sense of historical processes…." (1988:3) Written records such as imperial representations of the colonized and the colonizers are frozen in time; but oral accounts which are retold over and over again, are always reformed in the retelling by the culture of the re-teller's own time. They may end up as legends and myths which then take on a sacredness that the original account did not have.

A number of people have considered the relationship between oral traditions and written documentary history and the utility of examining them in tandem. In his analysis of the attack on a blackbirding schooner by Kwaio warriors from Malaita, Keesing notes, "...The oral historical accounts complement the archival record and give meaning and motive and political comprehensibility to an otherwise flat record of the labor trade in which `the natives' are always objects, never subjects." (1986: 288) In this case, the oral tradition which Keesing uses consists of several accounts as well as an epic narrative chant. The advantage of using oral tradition alongside written documents is also noted by Day, who states, "…The validity of the oral tradition is enhanced by its goodness of fit with the historical data. But the phenomenon which struck me was the frequency with which the traditional statements solved puzzles created by the partial coverage of the documents and the frequency with which the data of history and the data of tradition taken together form a congruous and more believable whole." (1972: 100; see also Neumann 1992)

Every culture has some notion of past events, their own indigenous view of history. Hill notes that one must "…explore indigenous ways of interpreting history…contextualizing historical interpretations within situations of contact….." (1988:2) Sahlins points out that Polynesian societies like the Maori have what he calls "heroic history," which focuses upon heroes and their great deeds, privileging them historiographically, in keeping with the Polynesian emphasis on preserving lengthy genealogies, which are used to justify the exercise of power in the structure of chiefdoms. (Sahlins 1985) However, in New Ireland, where political systems are based on Big Men and not chiefs as in Polynesia, memories of distant ancestral figures are hazy and not accorded great importance; and genealogical information is very shallow, going back only several generations. In these kinds of societies, heroes are remembered for the short duration of oral history, but not beyond. Cultural heroes, if they are present, are found only in mythology.

There is no written New Ireland perspective on the first two hundred years of their encounters with Europeans. Oral history seems to be easily transformed into myth on New Ireland; and oral traditions, as far as we know, do not seem to have been encoded by New Irelanders in the form of epic narrative chants, as was commonly the case in Polynesian societies and in other parts of Melanesia -- as evidenced by the Kwaio chant collected in the Solomon Islands by Keesing. (1986) Historical events may sometimes be remembered by being incorporated into myths.

Hill notes the way in which the "interpenetration in varying degrees and in various combinations of myth and history [can occur, and] myth can become a part of history…." (1988:5) Lutz describes how the first arrival of the Europeans at Port Simpson, British Columbia became part of a story with supernatural components, in which Europeans become associated with the spirit world in a mythic context. (Lutz 2007: 29ff.) Albert has pointed out how a myth being told among the Lak in the southern part of New Ireland reflects the historical event of the Marquis de Rays' ill-fated expedition to this area in the nineteenth century. (Albert n.d.) Lak society encountered the Marquis de Rays expedition, and the result was the incorporation of these events into a Lak myth.

The New Irelanders, except for some oral history recently recorded, have not left us their accounts of their interactions of those foreigners who came to their islands. The New Ireland perspective on encounters with Europeans must be read primarily from the traces of their actions in European accounts. However, one must recognize that these accounts represent a biased, "colonial" mentality. These accounts, and historical information about the culture of their time, represent European perspectives on events, and reveal the conceptual ideas they had about savages. Each of the explorers, as shall come out of their accounts, differed in their perceptions of the New Irelanders, affected by their own personal, and cultural situation and the historical period in which they lived. Islander perceptions, strategies, and indigenous conceptualizations, particularly with regard to their encounters with Europeans, can only be derived from later ethnographies or by careful examination of the framings of New Irelanders by Europeans.

Wachtel has analyzed and used records composed by native observers, such as the Mayan chronicle *Chac Xulub Chen*, to analyze the European conquest of Peru and Mexico. This chronicle is an account of an Indian chief as well as orally transmitted folk accounts. Wachtel notes, "It has been my constant concern to reverse the traditional view from Europe, and to look at events through the eyes of the conquered native people." (1977:207) The pre-existing structures in each of these cultures led to contradictory interpretations of the conquest. Wachtel observes, "For the victors therefore, history appeared rational: but the vanquished experienced it as irrationality and alienation." (1977:209)

The temporal frame of reference for late 19th century anthropologists was an evolutionary one. At the beginning of the twentieth century, Boas turned from evolutionary thinking to a historical frame of reference, which in the absence of historical records depended on trait distribution. The succeeding major anthropological paradigm, structural-functionalism, placed such an emphasis on synchronic study and ethnographic detail, that history was completely divorced from anthropology. In the absence of written records, the small-scale societies which were the focus of anthropology at that time, especially in England, were seen as having only "conjectural histories."

The ethnohistorical perspective began to be developed in the United States in the 1970s and continues to be important today It may be defined as "a kind of historical ethnography – one which studies culture of the recent past through oral histories, through the accounts of explorers, missionaries, and traders; and through the analysis of such data at land titles, birth and death records and other archival materials." (McPherson 2009: 4) Today, history has now become an integral part of anthropology. As a consequence, many new perspectives, which are relevant to our endeavor have been developed in what is now entitled historical anthropology.

Until recently, scholarly histories of colonial and former colonial areas were written only from a Eurocentric perspective, emphasizing those events of concern to Europeans. Historical scholarship was "positivist," meaning that it was seen as objective and "…as a finite body of truth about a fixed real past contained transparently in documents." (Douglas 1998:2) But history is not the past, it is the past which has been transformed into something else. The past can only be known through the products -- records of all kinds -- called by

INTRODUCTION

Douglas, "the relics and debris, the words, objects, landscapes, images… which have been left behind and which have been successively interpreted by scholars whose work is a …creative engagement with such relics...." (1992:99) As Dening noted, "Reflexive history insures that the interpreting is discernable in the interpretation...." (1996:127) Reflexivity means that one recognizes the discursive choices one is making when one "makes" a history.

As we noted earlier, Dening and other historians of Oceania, in particular Australian historians, began to develop an "island-centered" point of view during the last century -- one focusing not on the colonizers but on the islanders' perspective. They recognized the need to move from a Eurocentric view of the historical process to one which analyzes the situation from both points of view, though obviously that of the European is much more fully documented. (Davidson 1966: 10) Maude's work on beachcombers and castaways (1964) and Corris's on blackbirding (1968, 1973) represent this "island-oriented perspective" and have been useful in our thinking about New Ireland, where blackbirding occurred. Richter, in his work on Native Americans and Europeans in North America, talks about a shift in perspective, "…to try to view the past in a way that faces east from Indian country… [so that] Native Americans appear in the foreground and Europeans enter from distant shores." (2001:8) His methodology is much like the one we will use here, when he indicates that, "…It helps to consider what written sources and oral traditions from later periods tell us about native ways of conceptualizing relationships with outsiders." (Richter 2001:14) In the focus on reciprocal exchanges of goods, and the importance of spiritual forces, North America and Oceania represent parallels. On a larger scale, Wolf's *Europe and The People Without History* represents the same perspective.

This meant, as Douglas notes, reading "...against the grain in an effort to reveal indigenous presences...." (In Buschmann 2007:118) This shift in focus parallels the emphasis that historians of the western world are now placing on "subaltern individuals," socially marginal individuals, and their ways of life. What were the ways in which they opposed and resisted those who possessed power and dominated, be they colonial or government officials? The Australians also discussed the need for historians to acknowledge, as anthropologists had, the factor of reflexivity and the way in which historians favored one epistemological position over another. Interestingly, there are now "counter-ethnographies," which are "studies that constitute distinctive, particular inquiries into the colonizer's culture; that in playful, subversive ways reflect colonial anthropology back on itself...." (Buschmann 2009 118) Sometimes, the indigenous people themselves reflect on the colonizers as in the African sculpture which depicts colonial officials in a pompous manner.

According to Dening, "The ethnohistorian's prime concern is with the description of illiterate [sic] societies by literate observers at the time when contact between the two had not changed or destroyed the illiterate society. On every continent, this period of contact and change has been caught in the journals and letters of explorers, administrators, traders and missioners [sic]." (1966: 25) Dening notes that this data is selective in nature, reflecting the interests, biases and experiences of the describers. He also recognized the need to overcome the Eurocentric point of view and provide the native point of view on these encounters which must be pieced together from this material. The way in which the Marquesans viewed the intrusion of Europeans into their island world is the central theme of Dening's book, *Islands and Beaches*. He is concerned with the behavior "facing" the Europeans and how the latter viewed the locals. (Dening 1980: 19-20)

INTRODUCTION

In his work on the Marquesans, Dening recognized a "middle ground" which existed between them and the Europeans. As Davis characterized it, "Domination and resistance were still essential to understand the past, but the American historian Richard White could then go from there to map a 'middle ground' in which diplomacy, trade and other forms of exchange took place between Native Americans and the English who settled in their native land." (2006:11) White, in his history and analysis of European and American Indian contact in the Great Lakes, 1650 – 1815, sees contact as productive of a common mutually comprehensible world. (1991) As White notes, "The process of accommodation…involves cultural change, but it takes place on what I call the middle ground…the place in between…cultures, peoples, and in between empires and the nonstate world of villages." (1991:x) The conceptualizations used here aptly describe what was happening between the Europeans and New Irelanders in the nineteenth century.

Natalie Zemon Davis discusses four strategies which sum up some of the ideas we have discussed involving moving Europeans from the center of contact stories. In the first, European attitudes and images of non-European peoples are seen as elaborations of European categories. Second, both indigenous people and Europeans are recognized as actors and reactors, in particular in terms of resistance and domination. Third, the "middle ground" recognized by Richard White in which shared and contested meanings which focus around exchange and mixture must be recognized and examined. Fourth, one must look at cultures in contact simultaneously in terms not only of the signs of common experience, but also the existence of concrete cultural differences. (Davis 2001, cited in Lutz 2007 :5)

Ethnohistorians have recognized the importance of being aware of the cultural lens which the traveler or explorer brings with him and of the influence of the author's rhetorical devices and the literary form of the writing of the account in evaluating the ethnographic information it presents. (Brettel 1986) The traveler's own cultural perspective directs his or her attention to some things, often to things that are strikingly different from what is found in his or her own culture and away from others. On the other hand, other characteristics such as gender relations which are of great importance in a culture, may go unnoticed and overlooked.

As Douglas notes, "… 'Natives' cannot be known outside of their engagements with literate 'strangers': because the recording, discovery and archiving of the debris of native pasts were artifacts of encounters with strangers for whom such collecting betokened identity… decentered colonial history…denotes that colonial texts are crucial resources to be exploited in writing histories about Islanders… and one must know the authors and the discourses which shaped them… [making] space for identifying the imprint of indigenous agency …(Douglas 1998:15) Defert makes the point that travelers' accounts "…must be reread as organized knowledge, coherent and efficient and produced by the tactics of domination which can be identified." (1982:12) Representations of indigenous pasts, in brief, are always partial.

Defert's point needs to be qualified with respect to New Ireland. Though the Europeans had superior power because of their arms and sought to employ "tactics of domination," colonial subjugation did not arrive in New Ireland until the 1880s. In the earlier period travelers and explorers were not describing a conquered people. Although these European explorers and travelers visiting New Ireland in the nineteenth century came with a colonial mind-set.

At an earlier period in anthropology, social structure and culture were seen as relatively unchanging entities, and "societies" were studied as if they

INTRODUCTION

were fixed unchanging entities. Under this period when structural-functionalism held sway, societies were analyzed in terms of how they functioned. During the same time period, a similar theoretical perspective was adopted in linguistics. Saussure had argued that synchrony and diachrony must be kept apart in linguistic analysis. Nineteenth century linguistics, dominated by the discovery that Sanskrit was ancestral to the Indo-European language family, proposed that languages constantly changed over time. However, to analyze how any particular language functioned at a point in time, one had to set aside ideas about language change, or diachrony. He used chess as an example. Knowing that the game of chess had originated in India and moved through Persia into Europe gave the chess player no advantage in playing the game. Today, we would recognize that Saussure's dictum is too extreme. In language, synchrony and diachrony are much more inter-twined; and irregularities are constantly introduced into a language. Languages constantly erode those irregularities to produce present-day forms. This comparison is instructive in thinking about the interrelation of culture and history. From the initial contact of New Ireland culture with agents of Western culture, significant changes such as economic changes were occurring and continued. At the same time, however, the distinctive type of social structure which governed the life of New Irelanders continued to reproduce itself through its rites and ceremonies.

Today's anthropology turns structural-functionalism on its head. Culture has become a set of "contested codes," "polyphonic representations," or heterogeneous alternative voices. From a view of culture as a monolithic, perduring representation, we have moved to culture as continually being reinvented and recreated. Each generation is seen as continually reformulating the past. History is always culturally ordered, and cultural meanings are historically ordered, with each practical enactment of them having the potential for reordering or transforming these cultural meanings. (Sahlins 1985) Moving from an "essentialist" mode of thinking, culture has become pluralist and a construction. Parallel to this, are "The New Model Anthropology" and "The New Melanesian Ethnography." These labels reference recent anthropological work in Melanesia as being "…qualitatively different from earlier work." (Bolyanatz 2000:9) What is being emphasized is the anthropologist as one who records the divergent responses and points of view of the population, emphasizing process not essentialism, taking nothing about the group for granted. (Bolyanatz 2000: 9-10) However, as we shall see, according to the European accounts, the responses of the New Irelanders to Europeans remained much the same for over a century and a half.

What is the current status of concepts like custom, tradition and culture in anthropological usage? "Tradition" has become the selective utilization of cultural material continued or resurrected from the past, to be used as a political weapon within a colonial or postcolonial context. (See Linnekin 1983) Custom is more problematic. In Hobsbawm's view, custom is "living, genuine and flexible." When custom becomes "kastam" in Neomelanesian, it has become politicized and transformed into a reformulated tradition, as defined above. Interestingly, "kastam" is also the word the Usen Barok of central New Ireland "...use for their traditional culture." (Wagner 1991: 329)

The various emphases on creativity, manipulability and inventiveness of culture, as well as the possibility of recreating it, while understandable in the present postmodern, postcolonial environment, have detracted from characteristics of culture which still make it useful as a conceptual tool. Culture as a way of life is structured though the structure may change, and much of the world still reproduces itself through focal institutions and

INTRODUCTION

ceremonies which qualify as total social phenomena in the Maussian sense. Andrew Strathern considers the *moka* as a focal institution in this sense for the Melpa today. (1991:209) Biersack, in her introduction to *Clio in Oceania,* points out how the *moka* ceremony and the Barok *kaba* ceremony discussed by Wagner contrast with a ceremony like the Fijian *kerekere,* discussed by Thomas. (Biersack1991) The *kerekere* is a politically motivated "kastam," a ceremony being manipulated today for political purposes. Melpa *moka* is not "externalized" and "objectified," but instead is an institution which reproduces as it actualizes a structure with its own distinctive features. Each performance is a new creation, not a replica of previous performances, yet certain structural features represent its continuity, though *moka* partners and their political motivations continually change. In our investigation, we will discuss the way in which New Ireland ceremonies like the *malanggan* ceremony, which commemorates the death of several clan members, are focal institutions which demonstrate continuity as well as change.

With the appearance of post-modernism, history itself is being challenged, just as is the concept of culture. According to Rosenau, "Skeptical post-modernists can hardly be called history-friendly. They contend that history is logocentric, a source of myth, ideology, and prejudice, a method assuming closure." (1992: 63) In postmodern thinking, the importance of history is solely to be found in its impact on the contemporary. The problematic nature of history today has placed it in the throes of redefinition. "...Social historians seek to hear, represent, and perhaps share authorial authority with voices -- women's, peasants', workers', the colonized -- rendered inarticulate by textual bias; for some, the morally and politically charged question 'Who owns the past'? has become insistent, despite -- or perhaps because of -- inequalities of power and access which continue to privilege Western scholarship." (Douglas 1992:86) Today, historians creating their texts are making choices regarding narrative techniques and analytical form. (Hunt 1989:20)

The anthropologizing West, at first, treated Melanesian societies as if they were caught in a time warp, locked in a timeless, traditional present -- the ethnographic present -- as if they were the isolatable, exotic authentic Other, a primitive remnant of our own past, but dialectically opposed to Us. Anthropologists studied, represented, and gave the societies they studied "authenticity" and tried to fit them into the preconceptions of texts produced by a professionalizing discipline. (Carrier 1992) This "essentialist" view, which highlighted the opposition between Us and "pristine" Them, created "isolates," and ignored the broader connections between villages and between islands which continued from the time Melanesia was first peopled more than thirty thousand years ago. It also did not pay attention to the Western colonial and post-colonial governments which had an impact on this area from the time Europeans explored what was for them *terra incognita.*

Keeping all of this in mind, we have taken the New Ireland region as the focus of our history. That entity includes more than the main island of New Ireland and the various outliers like New Hanover, Tabar, Tanga and Lihir. The networks of exchange relationships which circumscribe this area also encompass the Duke of York Islands, parts of New Britain, particularly the Gazelle Peninsula, Nissan and Buka. (See Maps 3, 4, 5.) These interconnections began in the period of the first settlement of this area, continued through the colonial period, and are still operative today.

Aliens on Our Shores attempts to situate New Irelanders in a diachronic context, a time frame which will enable us to understand what happened as successive waves of "aliens" arrived on New Ireland shores. Western impact

INTRODUCTION

on Melanesian societies has been highly variable. What we have endeavored to do here is to present a picture of the way in which the inhabitants of New Ireland responded to the visits by explorers, and after them whalers interested in trading supplies, missionaries, and later conquest by the government of the German colonial administration. As Western contact became more frequent, New Irelanders continued to try to maintain control over their lives. This was despite increasing missionary pressure to convert to Christianity and German pressure to submit to the colonial administration and become "civilized" copra cash-croppers. Expanding their engagement with the Western capitalist system, the military force of the colonial government, and the missionary establishment which sought to convert and "civilize" them will reveal how they tried to control their own destiny with greater or lesser success. It will enable us to understand how New Irelanders as agents always tried to respond opportunistically to what was happening to them. Though the German colonial government and the missionaries saw the changes they were trying to introduce as "rational," to the New Irelanders they were irrational and often incomprehensible.

We will see the ways in which New Irelanders continued to try to control the nature of their interaction with the West, the options they had and the decisions they made. We will see how they tried to co-opt the Europeans to further own New Ireland ends. We will see the increasing difficulties the New Irelanders had in doing this until they lost their political autonomy, were encompassed within the German Imperial realm and were drawn into the world economic system in the form of the copra trade.

As we have noted above, the texts available for this exploration are, by and large, those that have been framed by Western explorers, whalers, government officials, traders, planters and missionaries. We will be using ethnographic information to inform these texts. We recognize that today such ethnographic texts are contextualized within a discipline which has of late been subject to "reinvention," "reflexivity," and the critical examination of everything from field methods to text construction. As Douglas notes,

> We cannot take for granted that…the ethnographic present of anthropologists are unproblematically linked to indigenous pasts, given the creeping encompassment of world systems, and the varied, ambivalent, often traumatic local engagements with external contacts, [and] colonialism…. Ethnographies provide crucial clues for identifying and systematizing ethnohistorical inscriptions…the inadvertent, partial, shadowy traces of local agency, relationships and settings… Colonial texts need creative not literal readings. Their representations of past indigenous worlds are always narrow and deformed but, in some cases,…they are virtually all there is." (1998 161,162)

Even more specifically, social anthropology as pursued in the southwest Pacific for the past 75 years has been referred to as "this special anthropological brand of Orientalism [which takes] … 'primitive' societies to be static, self-contained, self-reproducing: a series of experiments in human and societal possibility [which] it was anthropology's task to catalogue, characterize, and analyze in terms of their internal functional logic." (Keesing 1992:186-187)

Anthropologists have always recognized that understanding involves recognizing some sort of order in a more chaotic reality. What first persuaded Tylor that there was something called culture was that human cultural behavior did exhibit some degree of regularity which enabled human individuals to communicate with one another and understand one another's

INTRODUCTION

behavior. Over time, there has been a great fluctuation in regard to the level of generalization and abstraction used to make anthropological conclusions.

In contrast to the perspective of cultural relativism embraced by some anthropologists, we consider New Ireland and neighboring islands as a region, and we will use a comparative approach in this work in order to bring out characteristics which are common to this region. We are aware of the need not only to situate our historical sources within their proper cultural setting, but the necessity of also locating the ethnographic texts we will use in their own theoretical and historical framework.

.Despite the current problematic view of ethnographic texts, there is much consistency regarding many core aspects of village organization in New Ireland in the various texts about New Ireland societies. This gives us some degree of confidence in the reconstructed picture of New Ireland culture which we will be using to inform our historical texts. This construction of New Ireland society enabled us to better understand aspects of behavior in New Ireland responses to European intrusion, giving us a further degree of confidence in it. Douglas, in support of this methodology, has pointed out that history is a "…creative process of interpretation" having only "relics of the past," documents of "engaged human perception" whose reading and translation require a grasp of "actors' idioms and communication" which can be "…derived in part from later ethnographies and from people's present notions about their past, which may resonate with, and help give meaning and pattern to more fleeting glimpses in contemporary [of the period] texts." (Douglas 1992:87) Historical ethnography is a construction by the anthropologist, an outsider's perspective in which the native point of view is not neglected but rather is used to construct.." a suggested version of a possible reality which did not willfully ignore or contradict the native's point of view." (Silverman and Gulliver 1992:18)

The nature of the local New Ireland scene and its connections to the wider world will be described as these have changed through time. Our story will deal with the growing penetration of the world system and how global processes of capitalism, state formation, and economic relate to local culture and history. Following some of the more recent theoretical points of view of historical anthropologists, we will also be concerned with how the local New Ireland scene also serves to provide a picture not only of local "evolving" practice through time, but also the connections with the wider world and its "landscapes of power." (Kalb et al.. 2006: 4) It has been suggested that a focus on "critical junction," that is, relations though time, relations in space, relations of power and dependency and the interstitial relations between economics, politics and social relations, should be the focus for understanding any human collectivity. (Kalb et al.. 2006:2-3) Each of the incidents in which New Irelanders are engaged with the aliens who arrive on their shores is an example of micro history. Stories of encounters are examples of "thick descriptions" to be followed through time, and through space, as they connect with the larger cultural economic and political universes of which they were a part. (Kalb et al. 2006:15)

During the Age of Exploration, European voyagers set sail with the idea of charting unknown seas and unnamed continents. Those explorers who touched down on New Ireland set out on their voyages for a variety of specific reasons -- for commercial purposes such as finding new lands for trade, to discover the as yet unknown Southern continent or other new lands, or even to investigate the possibilities of establishing penal colonies. Almost uniformly, they stopped at New Ireland only to replenish supplies, not to explore the

INTRODUCTION

island. A few inquisitive individuals did venture into villages to find out what the people were like. From them, we have something approaching ethnographic description.

The interaction in the first instance was framed by the Europeans in terms of exchange. They wanted fresh supplies and were willing to give to the New Irelanders in return what they considered trifles. New Irelanders' responses, as described by Europeans, indicate that they recognized the Europeans wanted to exchange and responded according to their own cultural conceptualizations and their own notions of exchange. The resulting conjuncture of European and New Ireland exchange perspectives continued as developing intercultural communication. The exchange of "stuff" for fresh supplies remained the basic purpose of European-New Irelander encounters for more than 200 years. A distinctive pattern of exchange eventually developed which became a "structure in its own right." As we shall see in the coming chapters, over a long period of time, what developed between New Irelanders and Europeans was "a middle ground" of new and different behaviors and actions

The Europeans' reasons for undertaking the voyages need to be distinguished from the purposes of writing and publishing of the accounts of the voyages. Sometimes an account was written by the voyager himself and then published, as was the case with Bougainville. In other cases compilers such as Hawksworth put together and published edited versions of the journals of several voyages (such as those of Carteret, Cook, Byron, and Wallace). Sometimes the accounts of the voyages were published to justify the expenses provided by backers or to raise money for future exploration and voyages. Accounts often were translated into several languages, since there was a ready audience for them.

It is clear from the motives of the explorers, whose accounts we will analyze, that their encounters were for instrumental purposes; and they made no attempt in their accounts of their "voyages and discoveries" to present the New Irelanders in an empathetic fashion as fellow human beings. In fact, one might argue that, probably in order to overemphasize the danger in which they found themselves, they often harped upon the "savageness" of New Irelanders to their readers.

Traders and missionaries, and later plantation owners and government officials, who began to arrive in New Ireland in the latter part of the nineteenth century had different relations with New Irelanders than earlier European visitors. Most of them spent a great deal of time in the Bismarck Archipelago living on trading posts, missionary stations, plantations and government stations. Their interactions with the local people were much more extensive than those of others during the earlier period; and a lingua franca referred to at the time as Pidgin English became the usual mode of communication between the two groups. They visited New Ireland villages and made an attempt to understand the culture, in order to convert New Irelanders to Christianity or to exploit them economically. Clearly, their motives for being there and all these other factors need to be taken into consideration in evaluating their accounts

The absence of written records and the shallowness of New Irelander's own historic memory provide no indigenous perspective on the first 200 years of encounters[1]. Oral traditions are not encoded by New Irelanders in the form of epic narrative chants, as is commonly the case in Polynesian societies or in the case of the Kwaio chant referred to earlier. Some oral history has been collected by Brouwer and Alpert when they did fieldwork in New Ireland in recent years. We also gathered information of this type when we did fieldwork in New Ireland in 1987, and we have incorporated it into this volume.

INTRODUCTION

The New Irelanders responded to the intrusive aliens in many ways, often co-opting them for their own ends. At the beginning of our narrative of New Ireland-Western engagement, the New Irelanders are living in autonomous, independent villages, conducting elaborate ceremonial rituals which had as their aim the regeneration of society. Though a Hobbesian state of war characterized intervillage relations, villages conducted ceremonial exchange and intermarriage when they were not at war. By the end of our narrative, New Irelanders had been drawn into the world market system, and had lost their political independence, becoming subject to an all-encompassing German colonial government.

The traders who first came were agents of that broadening world system seeking raw materials and new markets. They had come to other parts of the Pacific, such as Hawaii, Samoa, Fiji and Micronesia, somewhat earlier. Labor recruitment in the form of blackbirding was part of this same expansion. The establishment of plantations and colonial rule soon followed. When a government post was set up at Kavieng in 1900, New Irelanders became completely subjugated to German colonial rule, though even at this point political leaders tried to utilize the German colonial administrative structure for their own political ends.

We will be concerned with how the New Irelanders perceived the ever-intruding world system, how they responded to it, and the ways in which the structure of exchange which developed with early travelers and explorers eventually became transformed into a New Ireland version of the world market system. We end our book with the termination of German colonial rule over New Ireland in 1914. At this point, Australian forces drove out the German colonial government and occupied New Ireland. In both Western and New Ireland time frames, this is a more or less arbitrary point at which to end our account. However, by this point New Ireland structures had come completely under the domination of colonialism and Christianity; and New Ireland had been encompassed by the world system.

NOTES

1. There is one picture of New Ireland from the late nineteenth century, that of Ligeramaluoga (1932), a native New Irelander. However, it is much shorter, not as extensive as those manuscripts left by al Hasan al-Wazzan also known as "Giovan Lioni Africano" also known as Leo Africanus, which has been described and analyzed by Natalie Zemon Davis. (2006)

2. NEW IRELAND BEFORE THE "ALIENS" ARRIVED

The major thrust of this work is upon the ways in which the New Irelanders tried to control their own destiny in the face of inroads from outsiders of other cultures. We must first understand who the New Irelanders were and the nature of their culture at the beginning of European contact. To help us comprehend New Irelanders' responses when Europeans appeared, that is, the way in which the New Irelanders "read" the encounters, we will try to reconstruct New Ireland culture as it existed before contact. To understand what the life of New Irelanders was like when Europeans came to their shores, we will use several centuries of accounts by European explorers, travelers, traders, missionaries and government officials. European visits were sporadic during the first centuries of contact. We will also use ethnographic descriptions from the late nineteenth century and early twentieth century. Later accounts present a picture which include the changes wrought by increasing European influence. We will take into account all of the caveats which we spelled out in the previous chapter.

Our reconstruction is framed by a particular theoretical perspective. We see culture as structured. Some aspects of culture, such as social structure, and ideas about time constitute an underlying structure which usually changes relatively slowly. Other aspects constitute surface phenomena which are more easily subject to change. It is the latter which may be "heterogeneous" and "contested." Dual organization and matrilineal descent, for example, constitute part of the underlying structure of northern New Ireland culture and have continued to be significant as organizing principles of New Ireland life up to the present. On the other hand, the substitution of hoop iron for stone in tools early in the nineteenth century was a change in surface phenomena bringing about other important changes in the economy, but which did not affect the underlying structure.

Prehistory and Languages

The archeological record reveals the beginnings of human occupation of New Ireland at least 33,000 years ago. (Allen *et.al*.1989; see Appendix A for a more extended account.) The first settlers were probably hunters, shellfish gatherers, and reef as well as deep sea fishermen. Traces of their culture -- crudely knapped flake stone tools -- are to be found in shell middens in caves or rock shelters. The presence of obsidian from other islands in New Ireland sites dated at 19,000 years before the present (b.p.) demonstrates the early existence of regional trade. As we shall see, this trade continued to be important up until the beginning of the twentieth century. Such large-scale trading and exchange networks were common throughout this part of Oceania. In addition to the Bismarck Archipelago, there were the trading networks in the Vitiaz Straits, and the Massim area. The languages these first settlers of New Ireland spoke has not been ascertained. However, between 10,000 and 15,000 b.p. speakers of languages belonging to the East Papuan phylum were displaced from the mainland of New Guinea and moved into the Bismarck Archipelago as a second wave of inhabitants, according to Wurm (1982: 236).

Approximately 4,000 years ago, Proto-Oceanic speakers from a different language family with a cultural complex, labeled luluai appeared in the Bismarck Archipelago, having a great impact on the people of New Ireland and their culture. The Lapita people settled on small islands off New Ireland and New Britain: such as Watom, Mussau and Ambittle. Though no "classic" Lapita sites have been found on New Ireland itself, Lapita culture obviously had great impact on New Ireland, since most of its languages today are Proto-Oceanic, not Papuan.

The Lapita people "...had an economy based jointly on gardening and fishing. The major root crops and tree crops of contemporary Oceanic economies, other than sweet potato and cassava, were represented: yam, taro, breadfruit, coconut. A variety of fishing techniques were exploited, including nets, lines, basketry traps, and plant poisons." (Pawley and Green 1984: 128-130) They had stilt houses and nucleated villages located on beaches. Though rank differences and chiefs were present in most of Polynesia, which the Lapita people also settled, the archeology does not reveal whether or not rank was present among the Lapita people at the time that they occupied the Bismarck Archipelago.

The diagnostic feature for the Lapita cultural complex is distinctive dentate-stamped pottery with geometric motifs. Archeologically, it is frequently found in conjunction with a simpler ware which may have applique designs, incised designs, or be completely undecorated. Sites on New Ireland from this period contain pottery which is similar to this simpler ware.

What was the relationship between the pottery makers of New Ireland proper and the Lapita people, since no Lapita sites have been found on New Ireland? Downie and White note, "...We are inclined to think that New Ireland pottery is a local development, perhaps by some kind of 'stimulus diffusion' from Lapita style pottery makers." (Downie and White 1978: 799) We hypothesize that the sites on New Ireland contemporaneous with Lapita are those of the descendants of earlier waves of settlement, probably Papuan speakers, who were in contact with, trading, exchanging, and influenced by the Lapita people. They adopted much of the cultural repertoire of the Lapita people, including their language, the keeping of domesticated pigs, the manufacture of pottery, and perhaps their form of social organization. The political relationship between the Lapita people, who may have had chiefs, and the inhabitants of New Ireland at this time is unclear. The Lapita people, no doubt, were aliens to the Papuan-speaking New Ireland population[1].

The New Ireland region is one of considerable linguistic diversity. There are 18 different languages spoken on New Ireland and the off-islands. (Map 5) Kuot, the only Papuan language probably spoken on New Ireland, represents a stock isolate, the sole remnant of the East Papuan phylum, spoken by those who first occupied the island. All the other languages belong to the Proto-Oceanic branch of Austronesian and are divided into three sub-groups: 1) Madak, 2) Northern New Ireland, and 3) Patpatar-Tolai.

European Explorers' Reports

There is no information about New Ireland life between the archeological period and the seventeenth century. What was life like on New Ireland when the first European aliens arrived in the seventeenth century? The first encounters between New Irelanders and Europeans are described from a European point of view. The Europeans focused on the nakedness of the New Irelanders. Male body decoration also captured the attention of many Europeans. As we shall see, this was an important aspect of New Ireland ceremonial structure. The Dutchman Schouten was the first European to report an encounter. It occurred in 1616. The East Coast men who came out to meet him were described as entirely naked. (Schouten 1619d: 60) Somewhat later he described other New Irelanders, probably from the offshore islands of Tanga or Lihir, as "black Indians," who "...seemed to be better and friendlier people than the other for they covered their privie members with leaves....." (Schouten 1619d: 63)

NEW IRELAND BEFORE THE "ALIENS" ARRIVED

From later accounts we know that when ceremonially greeting strangers, it was important for New Ireland men to be freshly decorated. In his encounter with men from Feni Island, off the New Ireland coast, in 1832, Thomas Beale, a surgeon on a British whaling vessel, noted that on the first day they were "...entirely naked, merely having their bodies coloured with various devices.... [The next day] we found that many of our friends had been very industrious during the night, for they appeared with their faces and parts of their bodies freshly and curiously painted....." (Beale 1839: 322)

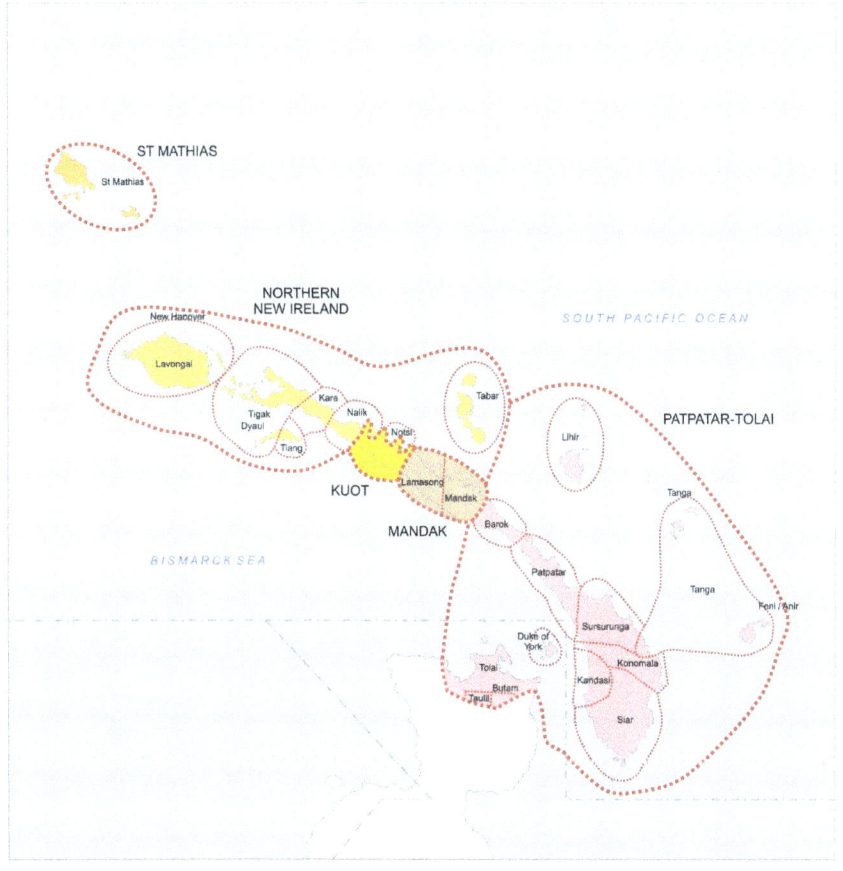

Map 5. *Languages of New Ireland* (Source: Wikipedia, based on Susanne Küchler, 2002. Malanggan: Art, Memory and Sacrifice. Taylor and Francis.)

Mrs. William Kent, who encountered New Irelanders in 1803, described how the men wore their hair, noting, "Their bushy hair is cut in the form of a Helmet. The center part from the Neck to the forehead loaded with a red powder resembling brick dust. The hair on each side cut close to the head and on one of the Sides is a thick plaister of a Yellow Composition and on the opposite side one of White, with long peaks to touch the corners of their eyebrows." (Kent 1803, 4:30-31)

New Ireland men probably always dressed their hair in some type of painted coiffure and usually had some form of body decoration. Travelers from other islands who came to engage in ceremonial exchange were greeted with this attire. As in many other parts of Melanesia and Papua New Guinea, body decoration was an integral part of the presentation of self, and was a form of art. Body decoration represented the solidarity and strength of the group and masculine power. Richard Parkinson, in the 1890s, describes this elaborate male hair-do worn at "death feasts" on Tabar. According to Parkinson, the *tatanua,* or "helmet" mask, worn only at *malanggan* mortuary ceremonies, was an imitation of this male coiffure. It also exemplified New Ireland concepts of male beauty. In addition to the coiffure, other features considered physically desirable in a man were a wide, projecting nose, pierced earlobes which hang as low as possible, side whiskers rubbed with lime, and a big mouth with sound teeth. (Parkinson 1926 [1907]) This was the hair-do worn to greet Europeans visiting, up to the middle of the nineteenth century. (See, for example, Fyshe, February 1838 PMB 375.)

Formal greetings took the form of a mock attack. Reverend Brown, visiting Rataman village, on the east coast, in 1876 describes how, "Suddenly some twenty or thirty men, painted with ochre and lime as for war, armed with spears and tomahawks, rushed out from the backs of the houses. With spears poised, and brandishing their tomahawks, they made towards us, shouting as though about to fight or kill every one of us.... They rushed close up to us, making their spears quiver and shake as they held them only a few feet from our faces, as though they were about to hurl them at us. Then with a loud yell they turned and ran back almost to the place from which they started, but only to return again as before." (Brown 1908: 161-162) The "attacking" villagers then crowded around Brown and welcomed him. This form of greeting also accompanied exchanges in many parts of New Ireland and the off islands. It is impossible to tell what the intentions of the New Irelanders were from accounts of explorers and travelers with this greeting. Were they welcoming strangers prepared to exchange or attacking them? In the Massim of southeastern New Guinea, among groups of the Northwest Coast of North America, and in other parts of the world, exchanges also included warlike attire at the beginning, as well as gestures of challenge and competition.

Material Culture

The settlement pattern, as it can be reconstructed, consisted of villages that were composed of hamlets. Villages were politically autonomous, though they had various kinds of relationships with other villages even those on other islands. Villages were located in the interior as well as near the coast. Coastal villages were rarely on the beach; rather, they were usually a mile or so inland, at locations which could be better defended. (Keppel 1853: 208, Brown 1908: 110, Hernsheim 1983:56) Only fishing hamlets were found on the beach itself. Coulter described a village he visited in 1835. It was located two miles inland from the southeast coast. He reported, "The huts of the natives were built, or rather formed, in clusters, of about fifteen or twenty, and situated on eminences on convenient distances, so that, in case of attack, a shout or signal of any kind could be easily made with effect." (Coulter 1847: 260) The village described was a large one, composed of hamlets dispersed along ridges in defensive positions, with a ceremonial plaza, on which stood a large men's house.

Coulter and others described semi-subterranean houses with thatched roofs of palm tree branches, constructed over pits three feet deep. (See also Keppel 1853: 208.) These small houses were dwellings for women and children, who seem to have lived separately from men. Each village had at least one men's house, where the men spent most of their time, often sleeping there; and some villages had several men's houses. The interior of a men's house, at Kudukudu in the Patpatar language area, for example, was rectangular and forty feet in length and "Along the sides and across one end were fixed low sleeping benches of the young men.... Along the battens were hung the jawbones of the men and pigs which had been eaten there, and on one batten I counted thirty-five human lower jawbones, some blackened with smoke and others only slightly discoloured, showing that they had not hung there very long." (Brown 1908: 164)

The economic orientation of the New Irelanders was primarily horticultural, though shellfish gathering, fishing and pig raising were also important. They cultivated crops such as yams, taro, coconuts, bananas (plantains), sugar cane, arrowroot and betel nut, which Europeans observed New Irelanders chewing. Gardens, cultivated by the slash and burn method, were located at some distance from the village. Men cleared the brush, felled the trees, and burned over the plots. They then fenced in the plots to protect them from the pigs. Women came in to weed, plant and subsequently to harvest. (See Powdermaker 1933.) As Keppel noted when he visited New Irelanders' gardens, "We were astonished... at the order that prevailed where no one appeared to rule. Each section of the village seemed to have its allotted portion. Parties arrived, cut and carried their vegetables away in perfect quiet." (Keppel 1853:208-210)

Each section was probably gardened by the members of a hamlet. A daily supply of vegetables was harvested by each family and carried back to the village by its members. Domesticated pigs, which were most valued for ceremonial exchange, and fowl were kept. Pigs were allowed to run free to forage, returning in the evening to be fed by the women. Wild pigs and marsupials were hunted, but hunting does not seem to have been a significant part of the economy, except in the mountainous area in the extreme south.

Much of the protein in the diet came from shellfish and the varieties of fish to be found in the lagoons continuing the pattern found archeologically. Ethnographic data indicates that women were the gatherers of shellfish, while men fished in the lagoon and from the reef, using nets, spears, poisons and traps. Fishing for sharks seems to have been the only form of deep-sea fishing done beyond the reef. The unique method of shark fishing on New Ireland, described by a number of observers, was not found elsewhere in Melanesia[2].

"Shell money" was used as a medium of exchange throughout the region. Valuable shells were exchanged for pigs, canoes, fishing nets, and magical spells of various kinds. These various items had fixed equivalents in shell money. They were also presented at different kinds of life cycle ceremonies. Various kinds of shell valuables, made of different kinds of shells, were used in different parts of the New Ireland region[3]. Shell valuables were an important aspect of inter-island trade. Frequently, the shells were found in one area, taken to a second area where shell discs were made, and then exchanged to be used in a third area. In addition to the many trading relationships between communities on different islands, there was also trade in various commodities between coastal communities and those in the interior.

Given the importance of the maritime aspects of the economy and inter-island exchange, it is understandable that canoes and their manufacture were important to New Irelanders. The 18th century English explorer Carteret observed one canoe made from a single log, with an outrigger, which he estimated at between 80 and 90 feet long, almost as long as his ship, without sail but rowed with paddles, and containing 33 men. (Carteret 1965, Vol.1: 191; see also Morrell 1832: 452-455.) There were two other kinds of canoes: ocean-going plank canoes, known as *mon,* and much smaller outrigger canoes which could hold one to three men. Fyshe, an American whaler, thought the carving on New Ireland canoes was as good as that of any artist in America. (See Figure 5, in Chapter 4 below.)

Social Organization

Because visitors had little close contact with New Irelanders and observed little of the fabric of their society, the fact that New Irelanders traced descent matrilineally was not noted until the 1890s[4]. The social structure was basically the same throughout the New Ireland region, although there were variations. Clans were based on matrilineal descent. Each hamlet was associated with a clan or matrilineage. These kinship units usually owned hamlet sites, gardening land, and ritual property such as *malanggan* sculpture designs. They had their own burial grounds, which often served as locations for ceremonies. Each matrilineage or clan, if sufficiently large, was associated with its own men's house and was associated with its own totemic item.

Exogamous matrilineal moieties were found from the southernmost part of the island northwest, to the Notsi-speaking area including Lesu. Features of the social structure were recorded by Mouton, a trader and planter during the last part of the 19th century. He noted, "Now I will call one totem eagle and the other totem hawk [the English translations of the New Ireland names of the two moieties]. The children are taking the totem of their mother, if the mother is an eagle the father will be a hawk and so the children will be of the eagle totem, therefore no eagle can marry an eagle he must marry a hawk and vice versa." (Mouton 1974 [written 1911]: 101) The names of the moieties throughout the area are Sea Eagle and Fish Hawk, though the birds are referred to by different terms depending on the language spoken in the area.

Moieties are a manifestation of a structure of dual organization. Continuing exchange of women through marriage between clans in opposite moieties, another manifestation of the same structure, is favored. However, from the Nalik-speaking community of Fatmilak north to the tip of the island, named moieties were absent, and there was only a multiplicity of exogamous matrilineal clans. Despite the absence of moieties, marriage rules in this northern area were also a manifestation of a structure of dual organization. Chinnery, working in northern New Ireland, notes, "...In some places, I was informed, the multiple clans are definitely divided into two intermarrying divisions. Even the natives themselves told me on more than one occasion that `such and such' a clan was `brother' to `such and such' a clan." (Chinnery 1929: 14) Fisoa, a Nalik-speaking village, "has three clans, two of which are 'brother' clans which do not intermarry…, [giving] the system in Fisoa much the same mode of operation and relationship implications as a dual organization." (Groves n.d.: 2-3)

Marriage with a classificatory cross cousin or cross-cousin's daughter was preferred; and this occurred throughout New Ireland, whether or not moieties were present[5]. In several areas there is a specific preference for sister exchange. The transgenerational pattern of marriage -- with cross-cousin's daughter -- produces a more complex version of the structure of dual organization, one in which moieties exchange their classificatory "daughters" rather than their "sisters." These marriage rules are all features of the structure of dual organization. Both polygyny and polyandry were practiced. (See Powdermaker 1933, Chinnery 1929, Wagner, 1986.) With uxorilocal residence, polygyny could only take place if a man married sisters or clan sisters, a practice which did indeed occur. Kinship terminology in all the different language groups of New Ireland is of the Dravidian or Iroquois type.

Post-marital residence took the form of a continuum, from uxorilocality to avunculocality, the two forms of residence typically found with matrilineal descent in other parts of the world. It varied in relation to the nature of political leadership, as we will see below. Uxorilocal post-marital residence, in which the couple lived with the wife's matrilineage in her hamlet after marriage, was the only residence pattern found in Lesu; but it was also practiced as an alternative in many other parts of New Ireland. While most men lived uxorilocally on Tabar, a man becoming politically important continued to live in his own matrilineage's hamlet with his wife and family. Among Barok speakers, post-marital residence seems to have been fairly equally divided between uxorilocality and avunculocality. (Jessop 1977: 111) Uxorilocality for one or two years after marriage was preferred among the Mandak, but there was a strong pull upon a man to return to his own matrilineage after that. The consequence of men returning to live on their own matrilineage land after marriage and a short period of uxorilocality is a form of avunculocal residence, if viewed in terms of the developmental cycle of a family or lineage. Avunculocality was the rule of post-marital residence on Tanga.

The nature of political leadership in New Ireland, which co-varied with post-marital residence, also formed a continuum. At one end there was a weak, rather undeveloped form of big man structure, associated with uxorilocal residence, as found in Lesu. Older men, possessing strength of personality, wealth, oratorical ability and magical knowledge exerted their influence and acted as political leaders of the clan. They were known as *orong*, or old men of influence. When they died their positions were not inherited. A clan needed an *orong* to speak on its behalf at initiation, marriage, and mortuary rites. The *orong* sponsored, planned, and organized these rituals. The man aspiring to leadership had divided interests. He lived in his wife's hamlet with her matrilineage, but he returned to his own matrilineage for the vital rites of passage of his sister's children and for the *malanggan*, mortuary rituals of his clan.

At the other end of the continuum was Tanga, which had the most complex form of political leadership, one associated with avunculocality. The *kaltu dok* (or *kahltu dok*) headed the sub-clan, acted on behalf of the group, and passed on his position to the sister's son he had selected earlier to succeed him. The heir, chosen because of his abilities, and not as a result of primogeniture, was formally invested with his mother's brother's name after the latter's death. One *kaltu dok* was recognized from the various sub-clan leaders as head of the entire clan. A *kaltu dok* organized and controlled the ritual activity of the clan. He had the power to restrict the use of certain resources for a time -- resources such as, fishing from a particular reef and the gathering of tree crops -- in order to accumulate foodstuffs for feasts and ceremonial rites. He also was responsible for organizing the building of the plank canoes used in overseas voyages. An important clan or sub-clan leader, who was recognized as "a born leader of men," a cunning warrior, a skilled organizer of feasts and a person of great wealth, could achieve the special position of *ka: ltu taufi* by erecting a sacred house. Bell calls such men "chieftains," and indicates that they each would have to have been declared *kaik ta: rawen*, or sacred children, at birth, to go through a special ceremony at adolescence known as *dafal*, and, having become chief, to have a lower incisor extracted during the mortuary rites for his predecessor. The house of the *kal: tu taufi* was taboo to women and most men, reinforcing the leader's position. In Tanga, though men were born in their fathers' matrilineage settlements, all went to live on their own sub-clan lands after marriage. In those settlements one of those who was a sister's son to the *kaltu dok* would eventually be chosen by him to be his successor. (Bell 1933, 1935a, 1946)

The forms of political organization in other areas of New Ireland fall somewhere along this continuum. A likely political leader on Tabar would remain at his matrilineage settlement after marriage (assuming that his father was living uxorilocally). Through acts such as sponsoring the manufacturing of a communal fishing net and directing fishing activity as well as other economic endeavors, he demonstrated that he was worthy of being chosen by them to represent the matrilineage, to hold their *mis* (treasured shell money), and to be the sponsor of their rituals. (Groves 1934)

The functions of leaders, or *orong*, among the Barok-speakers were the same as among the Mandak and Lesu, but differences existed in the way in which men became *orongs*. Among the Barok, in contrast to Lesu, and Tabar but similar to Tanga, there was a category of "sacred child," *ararum*. Boys in this category were preselected to become leaders. Later in adolescence a boy who had been made a sacred child could receive the training to become a *winawu*, one who had the task of giving the prescribed final speeches at Barok mortuary rites and at other feasts. A *winawu* was a likely candidate to become an *orong*.

The presence of "sacred children," who were set apart from the rest of the population, and who eventually might become important leaders, might have given early European visitors the impression that New Irelanders had "chiefs." Reverend George Brown, from his first encounter with New Ireland political leaders in the Patpatar-speaking area, referred to them as "chiefs," though he noted that, "…The chiefs had little or no power over them [the people]. When we gave a few little presents to the chiefs, there was quite a scramble for them, and they had no little difficulty in saving any for themselves." (Brown 1908: 126) Brown made some general observations about the position of chiefs in New Ireland, indicating that, "There is no special protection to the chief owing to his position. If he should be guilty of any crime he must fight in his own defense as any other man." (Brown 1910: 254)

Warfare, Cannibalism, and Peace-making

In many parts of New Ireland, in addition to the person in the *orong* position, every clan also had a man who led the group in time of war. This man had to have a reputation as a fierce warrior and to know the necessary war magic. The warrior, called *umri* in Barok and Patpatar-speaking communities, was given special training. During this time and before battle he kept apart from women, since it was assumed that they could sap his strength. In pre-contact times, warfare was endemic throughout the New Ireland region. As Coulter observed, "In New Ireland the chiefs of the various tribes and districts are continually at war, and, though their wars are not of a very devastating character, yet they require a constant supply of men and equipments...." (Coulter 1847, vol.1: 275)

Each village operated as an independent political unit in warfare. Villages had traditional enemies, who were often their nearest neighbors. Still other villages at some distance from them were their traditional allies.

Thus, a checkerboard pattern of enemies and allies covered New Ireland. This pattern was observed by Coulter when he went ashore and was caught up in intervillage warfare in 1835. In Tanga, on Boieng Island, the clans also formed the same checkerboard pattern. Neighboring clans were traditional enemies, despite the fact that wives came from those clans. (Bell 1934) With the practice of avunculocal post-marital residence, however, wives could come from enemy groups. Clans at some distance were united as allies and blood brothers with whom they could not intermarry. Allies on one side and enemies on the opposite side formed a system of unnamed moieties. In other parts of New Ireland, where uxorilocal post-marital residence was the norm, taking spouses from enemy groups did not occur, and would not make sense, since a man would then be living among his enemies.

Many Europeans visiting New Ireland mention cannibalism. Slain enemy warriors were always quartered, cooked and ceremonially eaten by the victors. Romilly described in detail how the bodies of six slain warriors, who were killed a the battle which he witnessed, were prepared and cooked for eating. The process of cleaning and scraping the human bodies was identical to the preparation of a pig for cooking at a ceremony. The packets of cooked flesh were ceremonially distributed. "The thigh and shin bone were preserved intact. They are used for making handles to spears. These spears are not meant for fighting, but are profusely ornamented, and are usually kept in the houses devoted to their carved images." (Romilly 1886:57) Ligeremaluoga (1932) notes that the thigh was always the chieftain's portion. Enemies' skulls were hung in the men's houses, as we noted above. According to Brown, "They called it incestuous (*kuou*) anyone who killed or ate any portion of a person of the same class [moiety] as himself...." (1910: 28) Rules concerning cannibalism seemed to parallel in part the rules of exogamy.

Traditional enemies had a continuing relationship. At one point in time, they might be at war with one another, and at another time at peace, when they would be exchanging women and valuables.

In addition to rules about warfare, there were rules about how to make peace. The first rite of peace-making in Lesu was the exchange of *tsera* (shell money in Notsi) between the warring parties, followed sometime later by an exchange of feasts. (Powdermaker 1933: 42-43) Bell describes a similar process for peace-making between traditional enemies in Tanga. When the leader of one clan decided to make peace, he announced that he would distribute pigs with shell money on them for each man killed by his clan. If the enemy clan agreed, both clans armed themselves, and the two leaders met. Pigs with *am fat* (Tangan shell money) were distributed, and a feast was held indicating that a truce between the two groups existed. (Bell 1934)

Ceremonial Life

Throughout the New Ireland region, rituals and ceremonies occurred at the same stages of the life cycle, including pregnancy, birth of a first child, naming, and death, though their content varied among the different groups. Mortuary rites were always the most elaborate. This was true not only for New Ireland, but also for a much wider area of island Melanesia. In New Ireland the structure of rituals always involved two sides or moieties, if they were present, which exchanged food and other goods and services.

In addition to ceremonies in which men were the principal participants, there also were separate women's ceremonies, in which the entire ritual event was organized and carried out by women. At women's ceremonies, the women of opposite sides not only exchanged goods, but they might also playfully fight or perform mock copulation. According to Coulter, "…They were at perfect liberty to say anything they pleased with impunity, to deal out affectionate praise on the men they loved, or abuse on the suitors they disliked." (1847, vol.2: 8)

Feasts and exchanges were also held to mark one or another of the stages of a child's maturation, such the appearance of a child's first tooth. These were held for individual children, and were not clan-wide events. Boys' and girls' initiations were held in conjunction with mortuary rites. Where mortuary rites were celebrated by *malanggan* ceremonies, boys' circumcision was part of those rites. Throughout most of New Ireland, female initiation, like male initiation, was also part of mortuary rites[6]. The entry into seclusion of female initiates was observed by Rev. Rooney who stated, "I was just in time to witness the ceremony of caging one of the girls. The poor little thing loaded with necklaces and belts of red, white, and blue beads looked very frightened. On the morrow she was to be tattooed in the New Ireland fashion, i.e., have all kinds of patterns carved on her body. One part of the ceremony was a fight between females of the Marmar and Pikalaba clans [moieties, or, as Rev. Brown refers to them, 'two exogamous classes'], seemingly for the possession or custody of the captive." (reported in Brown 1910:108) The mock fighting between women would seem to indicate that entry into seclusion was a women's ceremony. (See also Brown 1910: 105-107, Brown 1908:212ff, and Rickard in Brown 1910: 107-108.)[7]

Among the Mandak, girls' seclusion and initiation, known as *La Davan*, was associated with *malanggan* rites. On the day the girls ceremonially emerged, they were decorated and conceptually became *malanggan* images. (Brouwer 1980: 182-183; see also Clay 1986:233.) The Barok also had girls' initiation rites, including seclusion and the emergence of the initiates during the mortuary ritual. (Ligeremaluoga 1932: 13-14, see also Wagner 1986: 203.) Only on Tanga was the *dafal* initiation rite separate from mortuary rites. (Bell 1936)

Marriage was not an occasion for elaborate ritual in most New Ireland societies, though bride price and a return payment by the bride's side took place at feasts. Marriage was marked by the couple eating together, not by their having sexual relations for the first time. There was sexual freedom before marriage and in some places also after marriage[8].

Death was the point of greatest ritual elaboration throughout the entire New Ireland region. The ceremonies and rituals to mark other occasions, such as birth, pale in comparison. Funerary rites for a single individual were held immediately after death. In areas where there were moieties, members of the opposite moiety and of the same sex as the deceased washed the corpse in the sea and brought it to the deceased's dwelling house. All individuals who were buried had to be interred in land owned by their natal sub-clans. With uxorilocal post-marital residence, a man's body would be carried back to his natal village after death. (See Ligeremaluoga 1932:53 on the Barok.) In Tanga, with avunculocal residence, a woman's body would be carried to be buried in the cemetery belonging to her natal sub-clan. (Bell 1933) During funerary rites, sexual abstinence was observed by an entire village, and for a longer time by close relatives of the deceased. However, sexual joking between moieties sometimes occurred at funeral feasts. Among the Barok, according to Ligeramaluoga, sexual license took place at the *go-gorop*, the final day of the initial cycle of funerary feasts. (1932:59; see Wagner 1986:196.)

Since succession to leadership on Tanga occurred at the death of a sub-clan head, rites were more elaborate for that individual since they also involved formal recognition of the accession of the new leader. The corpse of the former sub-clan head was exhumed after burial and the skull, jaw and limb bones placed in a basket in the rafters of the men's house[9]. At the final funeral ceremony, the successor to the deceased chief mounted the roof of the funeral house with the bones of his predecessor and ceremonially assumed the deceased's name and position. On Tanga, the ritual referred to as *arel sigit* commemorated the dead of a clan. It involved dance performances and a large-scale pig exchange.

Among the Lak of the Siar region of New Ireland, the last stage of the funerary rites for an individual was characterized by the construction of a shell sculpture to represent the deceased. The Lak, however, did not seem to have a large-scale mortuary rite for their clan dead.

In addition to individual funerals, most people in the New Ireland region periodically held elaborate focal ceremonies which com-memorated those clan members who had recently died, to "finish them off." The girls' and boys' initiations described earlier were associated with these mortuary rites. Such rituals symbolized the formal replacement of the deceased by a new generation, to ensure the continuity of the sponsoring sub-clan or clan. They were also the occasions when leaders either assumed power, asserted power, or competed with one another for political power.

Within the region, there were differences in these focal ceremonies. The *malanggan* rituals, which were held from the middle of the island north, involved the manufacture and display of elaborate carvings[10]. This ceremonial cycle involved one clan inviting other clans as guests. At the ceremony, guests were fed and were given large numbers of pigs. Hence a clan preparing for a *malanggan* had to greatly increase its productive capacity. In the early stages of the *malanggan* a "Y"-shaped tree trunk was erected as an entry way to the yard around the men's house, as among the Barok. The *malanggans*, representations of clan spirits which honored the initiates and the deceased, were then secretly carved by specialists.

Myths and stories describe how *malanggan* designs, owned by clans, were taught to individuals by bush spirits (*gas*) while they dreamed. The owner would tell the story of the *malanggan* to the carver, and the carver visualized the sculpture, sometimes in a dream. At the climax of the rites, the *malanggan* sculptures, which the women were forbidden to see up to this point, were then displayed, and the initiated boys emerged from their seclusion. The girls probably also ceremonially emerged at the same time. At this point, the *malanggans* had supernatural power and were considered dangerous. *Tatanua* masks, the most prominent, were imbued with special supernatural power and were used in subsequent dances. (See Figures 1 and 2.) The wearers of such masks at performances had to abstain from sexual intercourse for four to six weeks in order for their own powers to be at their height. The next day the women performed a dance in the *malanggan* enclosure, followed by a night of sexual promiscuity where there was only a taboo against intercourse with a member of one's own moiety After this, there was a week of sexual abstinence, when men and women slept in separate houses. Sometime later, the *malanggans* were destroyed without ceremony.

In the central Barok-speaking area, the major mortuary rite was the *kaba* ceremony. The *kaba* itself is a section of a tree which is dug out with its roots attached, cleaned and inverted and then planted upside down where the *kaba* ceremony was to be held. Figures of humans, sharks and lizards were then carved on the *kaba*. The opposite moieties feasted each other, set up two platforms to hold taro, and competed with one another in decorating their side of the *kaba* tree with strings of shell money. The night before the final feast of the *kaba* Ligeremaluoga describes how "...the visitors join in the hilarious celebrations. They beat the drum, and have every jollification they know, and there is sexual license also." (1932: 14)

At the feast marking the culmination of the *kaba*, young boys who had been made *ararum* (sacred children) earlier sat on the platform behind the young man, standing atop the pigs, who was in training to become a *winawu* (ritual specialist) At the base of the tree sat the *dawan*, young girls being initiated. The young man pronounced the invocation of the *kaba* ("need of an *orong*") and made his first speech. One of the most important themes of the *kaba* is the connection between "finishing the dead" and political leadership. As Wagner puts it, " ...The *winawu* speaks on top of the pigs which are then cooked `on top of the deceased', at the *kaba*. In a significant sense, the kaba is about *orong,* and the need of *orong* rather than about the containment of the dead and their power." (1986: 207, see Ligeremaluoga 1932.)[11] The *kaba* is clearly about the reproduction of society, as a new generation produced by initiation rites replaces a generation now deceased. In addition, competition and interaction between the two moieties was also a central theme. (Wagner 1986: 207)

Figure 1. Tatanua Mask, from the Authors' Collection (photo by David Rubel)

Figure 2. Two Tatanua Masks from New Ireland, exhibited in the Australian Museum, Sydney (© Doranne Jacobson, International Images)

For the Patpatar-speaking area there are few details regarding the final mortuary ceremony, though chalk figures seen in men's houses by nineteenth century visitors seem to have had something to do with mortuary rites. Parkinson noted that, in the Laur district of New Ireland, chalk figures had been made to commemorate the dead. The figures were kept in a special hut which women could not enter. After a certain time, they were removed and destroyed by the men.

Mortuary rites in the central and southern parts of New Ireland were sometimes associated with cult performances which enabled men to have access to supernatural power. Young men were initiated into these cults during a period of seclusion. Though some cults like the *dukduk* seem to have been present in some places at the time of contact, others are specifically post-contact phenomena. Women were completely excluded from all aspects of men's' cults. Among the Lak, the *tubuan*, a masked figure also called *dukduk*, appeared on the occasion of the death of a man belonging to the cult. (Albert

1987) Though the Lak did not have the *dukduk* cult prior to contact, it was clearly present on the southern coast of New Ireland in 1823 when Bloiseville, the naturalist from the Duperrey expedition visited the village of Likiliki. He was met on the beach by a dancer holding a spear and completely masked in the characteristic *dukduk* regalia. (See Figure 3.) The d*ukduk* cult was also found in the Duke of York Islands and among the Tolai of New Britain in the nineteenth century. Errington (1974) believes it spread to the Duke of York Islands from New Ireland.

Figure 3. Dukduk Dancers in the Gazelle Peninsula, New Britain, 1913 (Source: Wikipedia, https://en.wikipedia.org/wiki/Duk-Duk)

On Tanga, the ritual referred to as *arel sigit* commemorated the dead of a clan. It involved dance performances and a large-scale pig exchange. The *Sokopana* cult, a men's cult found on Tanga, was also connected to mortuary rites. This cult spread to Tanga after the beginning of the German colonial administration from Nokon, in the Sursurunga-speaking area, where it was called *tamberan*. The ancestral ghosts of the clan, whose cries were produced by the bull-roarer and reeded instruments during the ritual, were said to gather and feast with initiates at the special ceremonial ground of the society, which was imbued with clan ghosts. Generally speaking, in the Bismarck Archipelago ceremonies of the type which we have described here were readily adopted from one group to another.

Gender Relations

The reproduction of society and ideas about gender relations were central to New Ireland society. Earlier accounts provide few insights on these central ideas and symbolic meanings. Therefore, they must be hypothesized using twentieth century ethnographic sources. Two separate components were involved in the reproduction of New Ireland society. The first component consisted of the birth of children and the initiation of boys and girls into adult males and females. Ceremonies celebrating birth were organized and managed by women. In contrast, men controlled the cultural creation of adult men and women from boys and girls through the process of initiation. The second component, death and mourning, may seem to be the antithesis of reproduction. However, the initiation ceremonies associated with mortuary rites, at which boys and girls replaced the deceased, as well as the accession of a new leader, which frequently accompanied mortuary rites clearly represent the other aspect of the reproduction of society. Thus, the separate and complementary activities of both men and women were required to reproduce New Ireland society

New Ireland conceptualizations of gender and relations between the sexes were consistent with this division. Each sex was involved in its own sphere of activities, in which its powers were strong and effective. It was believed that contact with the opposite sex on certain occasions, particularly in the form of sexual intercourse, would weaken those powers and cause harm. At other times it was absolutely necessary for men and women to come together.

Some of the activities which men performed required that their productivity, strength, and power be at their height. Magic and solicitation of the supernatural were employed on these often-dangerous occasions. These male activities included warfare, fishing, hunting wild pigs, capturing sharks, gardening, and ritually powerful activities like the *malanggan* mortuary rite and men's' cult activities. Women had to be kept away from these undertakings, and their dangerous influence through sexual intercourse avoided, or the effect of the magic would be blunted.

The female counterpart to male activities, which required abstention and even avoidance of contact with men, was the period from conception to the weaning of a child. Conception was believed to be due to the coming together of semen and vaginal secretions or maternal blood after several acts of intercourse, during which the substances gelled to form the fetus, which was then nourished by the mother's blood. When a woman became aware of her pregnancy, sexual intercourse ceased, and the child was nourished solely by the mother's substance. The ban on sexual intercourse continued after the birth of the child until the mother stopped nursing and the child was weaned. Sexual intercourse was seen as harmful to the early development of children, since they belonged to the mother's clan.

Women's conduct at ceremonies which they orchestrated at birth and at the exchange of bride price, demonstrated their assertiveness and involved the mockery and caricature of males. New Ireland female independence was seen by Coulter in the early nineteenth century. He saw the women mock as well as praise their men at the women's dances he observed.

Funerary and mortuary rites and the initiation rites associated with them involved an alternation between sexual abstinence for a period of time and subsequent ceremonial sexual license across moiety lines. Sexual abstinence and sexual license were like two sides of a coin, characterizing two modes of the relationship between the moieties. Sexual abstinence represented a turning inward towards one's own sex to enhance one's magical powers turning inward towards one's own clan representing a denial of inter-moiety relations. Ceremonial sexual license on a number of ritual occasions, like spouses feeding each other at a marriage, the exchange of food, and mock fighting, were symbolic expressions of the relationship between moieties. Through sexual intercourse and through the performance of services for one another at initiation, the two moieties thus helped to reproduce each other and the total society.

At times, the theme of sexual relations joins opposite moieties to each other was expressed by women engaged in mock intercourse with women of the opposite moiety, or by men of the opposite moieties performing the same kind of behavior. Such mock sexual intercourse and lewd performances occurred as part of birth and death rites. On the occasion of the birth of a first child, some women of the opposite moiety would dress as men and perform dances in which they engaged in mock "copulation" across the moiety lines. (Clay 1975: 138) Parkinson describes male transvestism in a dance in connection with mortuary rituals in which one male masked dancer portrays a woman who succumbs to the courting of another male dancer. (1926: 142) These forms of transvestism, reminiscent of Iatmul performances in *naven* ceremonies, illuminate the cross-cutting divisions of male-female relations and moiety relations.

Both sexual license and sexual abstinence are ultimately related to the division between mother's side and father's side, which is simply another way of describing the dual organization expressed in the moiety structure. However, each moiety partakes of the qualities of both mother's side and father's side. In order to reproduce one another's groups and society at large, the men of one moiety must engage in sexual intercourse with the females of the opposite moiety, and *vice versa*. There is an important conceptual distinction between the food and other things one gets from the paternal side and that which one gets from one's own maternal side. Whatever comes from the father's group, though it may be conceptualized as nurture, eventually has to be reciprocated, while this is not the case for mother's group, where things are shared. This, of course, is equivalent to saying that, with dual organization or moieties, there is one kind of relationship with one's own group and a different relationship with one's father's group in the opposite moiety. One copulates with the opposite moiety, competes with them, fights with them, exchanges food and services with them, and one even eats their dead bodies if they are enemies.

Therefore, eating, cannibalism and sexual intercourse are symbolic equivalents. Within their own group, men cooperate with members in many undertakings but may compete for leadership. Men also have taboos of avoidance toward their sisters and clan sisters and cannot copulate with them or any other moiety member. One cannot marry within one's own moiety, nor with brother clans. One cannot eat the dead bodies of members of one's own moiety if they are slain in battle.

Discussion

This is probably what life on New Ireland was like when the first European aliens appeared on New Ireland shores, as can best be reconstructed from European and American sources. The account of the Christian convert

Ligeremaluoga represents the only New Ireland voice on these matters, unfortunately. It is very clear that many of the basic premises of New Ireland society would have seemed very strange to the Europeans who tried to understand them. Similarly, the New Irelanders would not have been able to comprehend the Europeans.

Using this reconstruction of New Ireland culture and society, we will try to understand the behavior of New Irelanders in their encounters with Europeans over the centuries, and to comprehend their perspectives on these encounters. In the next chapter, we will first explore the cultural frameworks and the ideas about Others which the Europeans brought to the encounters.

NOTES

1. Concerning the origins of Lapita, Pawley has hypothesized that the Proto-Oceanic branch of Austronesian developed its characteristic features in the Bismarck area, in association with "classic" Lapita culture, and then quickly spread south and east, diversifying as it spread. However, Kirch notes, "These findings and comparisons do not support the hypothesis of an indigenous Bismarck Archipelago 'homeland' for Lapita. This is not to deny that Lapita populations in the Bismarcks adopted some cultural traits from the older 'Papuan' populations that they encountered." (Kirch 1988b:336)

2. Fyshe provides a description of shark-fishing, noting, "I was highly amused at seeing them catch sharks.... They have a cane which is strung [with] several tops and bottoms of the cocoa nut shell, this they shake up and down in the water, and if a shark is within a mile of them, he will surely make his appearance close to them. They then move the canoe towards the shark holding out a stick on which is hung several fish. As soon as he sees

them, he makes for them as fast as he can. They are then hauled up and a snare is prepared through which the fish are again put into the water. When the shark follows the fish they are pulled in towards the canoe and Master shark gets his head in the noose and as soon as he is in far enough they haul tight and he is fast. They then haul him up to the side of the canoe and while one holds his head tight another dives under him and at the same time that two are hammering him about the head with clubs." (Fyshe, February 1838, PMB #375) This method of shark fishing was limited to the northern half of the island. An additional implement was used: "...a wooden float [with] ...wings... like the blades of a ship's propeller." (Parkinson 1926 [1907]: 258-259) An illustration of New Irelanders in a canoe, which accompanies the account of Tasman's visit to New Ireland, shows the propeller.

3. Each language community had its own term for these shell valuables. In the Notsi language area, strings of shell discs, which were made in Lavongai and traded to Lesu, were known as *tsera*. Red *tsera* was twice as valuable as white. (Powdermaker 1933) Tanga, for example, had two forms, one called *am fat*, made in Tanga of giant clam shell, and the other *kemetas*, small bead-like discs strung on twine, made on New Ireland and then traded to Tanga by way of Lihir. The Tangans then traded *kemetas* for plank canoes made on Tabar. (Bell 1935b)

4. This discussion of New Ireland social structure is based almost entirely on twentieth century ethnographic accounts.

5. In some groups, a man was expected to marry his classificatory cross-cousin. In others this marriage was prohibited, and marriage with real or classificatory cross-cousin's daughter was preferred. (Chinnery 1929:18,19,23,24)

6. Girls' initiation ceremonies are not reported in 20th century ethnographic literature but are described in 19th century accounts, which provide the basis for our description of these ceremonies.

7. The connection between female initiation and mortuary rites is further demonstrated by the similarity between decorations used in seclusion huts and *malanggan* sculpture. Hernsheim, visiting the Tigak-speaking area, noted: "When the mats were removed I found that the side-walls of the house consisted entirely of carved and painted ornaments, all in red, white and black....When some of the ornaments were removed, I saw a small girl of about ten years sitting in the house." (Hernsheim 1983: 56-57, 122-123) Along the northwest coast, near Latangai Island, Rev. Brown purchased "elaborate wood-carvings, some of them being representations of the hornbill (*Buceros ruficollis*), and others representing iguanas eating snakes... put up in houses where certain young girls are kept confined for some months or years at the commencement of puberty." (Brown 1881: 217) These motifs were used in *malanggan* sculptures.

8. In Lesu, both men and women regularly had sexual intercourse outside of marriage but they could never eat with their "lovers" (Powdermaker's term), only with their spouses. After having sexual intercourse, a man would give shell money to his female "lover" which she would turn over to her husband. (Powdermaker 1933: 152,244) This practice of allowing sexual access outside of marriage contradicts some definitions of marriage.

9. This exhumation is reminiscent of Trobriand mortuary practice.

10. The following generalized description of the *malanggan* ceremony is based upon information from Lesu (Powdermaker 1933, Lewis 1969), and

also from the Mandak (Brouwer 1980) and Tabar-speaking areas. (Groves 1934-35, 1935-36; Fergie 1985)

11. Despite the details from Wagner and Ligeramaluoga regarding the *kaba* ceremony, the relationship between the ceremony, its sponsorship, and succession to political leadership remains unclear. In Ligeramaluoga's account, the focus is on *orong*, glossed as chief or chief's child, and the *kaba* ceremony is clearly tied to succession. Ligeremaluoga does not mention *winawu*. In Wagner's account, an *orong* sponsors the *kaba* ceremony. However, in his description, it is the *winawu* who seems to take central stage rather than the *orong*, though the new *winawu* utters the expression "Asiwinarong," "need for an *orong*." It is not clear from Wagner's account whether *winawu* and *orong* are two different positions held by different individuals, or the *winawu* also the *orong*. (Wagner 1986:168, 171) To further complicate the picture, Jessop (1977) states that *orong* are not made but make themselves and the boy who becomes *winawu* at the *kaba* ceremony may not necessarily become an *orong*.

3. EUROPEAN IDEAS ABOUT NON-EUROPEAN OTHERS

New Irelanders never lived their lives in isolation, cut off from other people. As the archeological record shows, they were constantly in touch with people from other islands from the time they arrived on New Ireland. When they engaged foreigners like the Europeans, it naturally was in terms of their own culture, and the ways in which one customarily dealt with strangers and outsiders. Beginning in the 17th century, Europeans, very different kinds of visitors, intruded upon New Irelanders, bringing their own ideas and material objects. Though the items and cultural images which Europeans brought were, at first, largely resisted by the New Irelanders, the latter developed their own ideas about Europeans and who they were.

We must understand the nature of the "intellectual baggage" the Europeans brought with them which organized their actions, if we are to understand the New Irelanders' responses to encounters with Europeans. Explorers, who began to visit New Ireland in the seventeenth century, were imbued with ideas of Others -- ideas held in Europe long before the Age of Exploration. During the Middle Ages on voyages and expeditions to Ethiopia, India, and Cathay, Europeans encountered people who were very different from themselves but who, by and large, had cultures which were equally complex. Those with state organizations, like the Ottomans and the Chinese, had sufficient power to completely control the encounters. Columbus's voyages to the New World introduced a different type of Other not met on these earlier trips. Many of the New World peoples were similar to the people whom Europeans were to encounter in seventeenth century New Ireland.

When reports of European discoveries began to circulate in Europe at the end of the fifteenth century, they seem to have excited only a few people. (Ryan 1981: 521ff; Elliot 1970: 10ff) The reason may have been that the discoverers, and those who read their reports, assimilated this new information into their preexisting categories and did not sufficiently recognize the distinctive character of the cultures of these newly discovered Others. The classical traditions of Greece and Rome had become an important focus of scholarly interest during the Renaissance; and they, together with Biblical tradition, provided a framework by means of which "Europeans assimilated exotic peoples into their own universe of discourse." (Ryan 1981: 521)

Since the Bible provides a myth of the creation of all humanity, if the people in the newly discovered lands were human and capable of conversion, then they would have to be fitted into the Biblical genealogy. The framework of the Bible was used to attempt to link the people of the New World genealogically to one or another of the sons of Noah. (Ryan 1981: 532-533) The people of the New World were also thought to possess an archaic form of Christianity, truer to God's intention. Ryan shows how de Acosta saw traces of this tradition among the Aztecs, Garcilaso de la Vega saw it among the Inca, and the French missionary Mauraile de St-Michelle saw it in the Caribbean peoples. (Ryan 1981: 535)

Classical antiquity provided one model by means of which Europeans comprehended the people of the New World. Peter Martyr (Pietro Martyr d'Anghiera, 1533), Gonzalo Fernandez de Oviedo (1548), Bartalome de las Casas (1552), and de Acosta (1598) all made frequent reference to the similarity of the Indians of the New World to the pre-Christian peoples of the Classical Greek and Roman world. (Ryan 1981)

One of the earliest European depictions of the people of the New World is a German wood-engraving from 1505, which circulated through Europe during the early 16th century. (See Figure 4.) The caption was reputedly culled from reports of Amerigo Vespucci and notes,

Figure 4. Woodcut Broadside Illustrating the Discoveries of Amerigo Vespucci. Augsburg, 1505 (Source: Feest 2014:298, after Colin, 1988, p. 392, figure 5)

> This figure represents to us the people and island which have been discovered by the Christian King of Portugal or by his subjects. The people are thus naked, handsome, brown, well shaped in body, their hands, necks, arms, private parts, feet of men and women are a little covered with feathers.... No one has anything but all things are in common. And the men have as wives those who please them, be they

mothers, sisters or friends, therein make they no distinction. They also eat each other even those who are slain, and hang the flesh of them in the smoke. They become a hundred and fifty years old. And have no government. (Eames 1922, quoted in Hulme and Jordanova 1990)

This caption encapsulates many of the ideas which Europeans entertained about the inhabitants of the New World during the sixteenth century. The focus is on nakedness, cannibalism, communal ownership, absence of incest taboos and the lack of "government." These European conceptualizations were not based on observation. Rather, they were the inverse of the way Europeans thought about themselves.

"Wild men" and "Noble Savages"

These characteristics could be read ambiguously, enabling Europeans to cast the people of the New World in a negative light as a Wild Man, or in a positive light as the Noble Savage. For example, the characteristic of "nakedness" which, as will be seen later, was one of the first things which Europeans noted in descriptions of New Irelanders, can be interpreted in opposite ways. On the one hand, Europeans saw nakedness as meaning that the people were so uncivilized that they felt no shame at revealing their private parts to others. On the other hand, this same nakedness signified the simple, naive innocence of a people living in a Golden Age people, who had never fallen from grace. This was the way Adam and Eve had appeared initially.

Communal ownership of property and the absence of government also have both negative and positive connotations. On the negative side, the Europeans saw a people whom they considered to be at such a low level of civilization that no social hierarchies existed to separate the highest from the lowest, no laws were present by which people could be governed; and no man therefore could possibly better himself. However, the absence of government and private property also could be seen as revealing the natural goodness of man, who could live harmoniously with no need for any form of government. The lack of government additionally was interpreted as giving a degree of freedom in comparison to the constraints of their own repressive European governments. Europeans like Montaigne saw the natives of the New World as representing "natural man" with a positive connotation, and accepted the incest and cannibalism which they imputed to these people as part of that larger construct.

The idea of the Noble Savage can be traced as far back as the Biblical Garden of Eden. It encapsulates the concept of man as naturally good before his fall from grace. (Baudet 1965: 10-11) Since everything found on earth was created by God, the Noble Savages were also God's creations. Though not specifically mentioned in the Book of Genesis, they were seen as remaining behind when we, the descendants of Adam and Eve, were prevented from returning to the Garden of Eden. Throughout history, beginning with the Greeks and Romans, there has been a continuing search for a simpler, more moral and forthright existence someplace else here on earth, or in a Utopia. When the New World was discovered, these qualities were projected by some onto its inhabitants in an attempt to explain and understand them. They thought they had found the Noble Savage in the New World. (Elliot 1970: 25) Baudet (1965: 11) explains the persistence of the idea of the Noble Savage as deriving from man's continual dissatisfaction with the repressive constraints of his own culture throughout history.

Sixteenth century discussions of the people of the New World juxtaposed their qualities of simplicity and innocence with the "monstrous" trait of cannibalism. Both Columbus and Vespucci, in their first reports, described the people as physically beautiful, noble in character, and innocent, though both also reported the presence of cannibalism. Montaigne, having read accounts of the inhabitants of Brazil, ironically concluded, in his essay "Of the Caniballes," that despite the practice of cannibalism, these people demonstrated their natural goodness -- a central characteristic of the Noble Savage. (1965 [1580]) Clearly, Montaigne condoned cannibalism only because it was part of their "natural existence." He found the "civilization" of his own time artificial, a bastardization of natur,e and much more reprehensible than the natural state of the "cannibals." If the Noble Savage was naturally good, exhibiting the traits of simplicity, truthfulness, loyalty, and consequently fertility and abundance, then its eighteenth-century European counterpart was baroque and complex, deceitful, cunning and duplicitous, and naturally immoral.

The concept of the Noble Savage was frequently used in alternation with the Wild Man. White sees the concept of the Wild Man as defining humanity, but in a negative way. We as humans represent everything that is good; and the Wild Man is everything that we are not. (White 1972:4-5) White notes that in the Old Testament the great rebels "...are depicted as wild men inhabiting a wild land, above all as hunters, sowers of confusion...." (White 1972: 14) The Wild Man of the Old Testament was a heretic who defied God's law.

The Greeks distinguished between barbarians, meaning anyone who did not speak Greek, and civilized men. This was in accordance with "...the tendency of the Greeks and Romans to describe as 'barbarians' all those people whose language, customs and religious practices differed from their own." (Elliott 1970: 46) Aristotle characterized barbarians as natural outcastes -- tribeless, lawless, heartless -- over whom it was right that Greeks should rule.

(White 1972: 20) Montaigne had also noticed this same tendency for Europeans to call "barbarian" those with customs different from their own.

The concept of the Wild Man became very prominent in Europe during the Middle Ages. Men of the time "...conceived barbarians and wild men to be enslaved to nature, to be, like animals, slaves to desire and unable to control their passions; ...as passionate, bewildered and hostile to 'normal' humanity -- all of which are suggested in the Latin words for wild and wilderness." (White 1972: 2) The various ideas which clustered around the concept of the Wild Man included cannibalism, barbarism, savagery, paganism, bestiality, blackness, hairiness, degeneracy, sexuality, and a solitary existence in the forest. As we will see later, some of these conceptualizations were used by Europeans to characterize New Irelanders.

The first appearance of the word "canibales" in a European text occurs in Columbus's Journal. (Hulme 1986: 16, see also [Nov. 23, 1492] Columbus 1960: 68-69) In his letter to Queen Isabella, Columbus notes, "Thus I have found no monsters, nor had any report of any, except in an island 'Carib', which is the second at the coming into the Indies, and which is inhabited by a people who are regarded in all the islands as very fierce and who eat human flesh." (Hulme 1986: 42) The word "Carib" subsequently was transformed into "canibales." The 1505 illustration and caption, shown in Figure 4, were inspired by Columbus's description, represented the peoples of the New World as cannibals. And this image was widely disseminated throughout Europe. Hulme notes that the purported anthropophagi of the West Indian Canibales or Caribs fitted "them for the role of archetypal savages [so] that cannibalism soon came to displace the classical word." (Hulme 1986: 20)

The theme of bestiality was also a recurrent characteristic used by Europeans to describe the people of the New World. Referring to those whose customs were different from the Europeans' as beasts was a common practice. Frobisher, who encountered the Eskimos of Baffin Island in 1577, for example, opined that, "They live in Caves of earth, and hunt for their dinners or praye, even as the beare or other wild beastes do. They eat raw flesh and fish, and refuse no meat howsoever it be stinking." (in Hakluyt 1904: 370) While humans eat meals, Frobisher sees Eskimos "feeding" like animals. Frobisher also thought that they were "Anthropophagi or devourers of man's flesh."

If the inhabitants of the New World were more like beasts than men to the Europeans, then Europeans had to confront the question of whether they had the souls of men or of beasts. It was necessary for Pope Paul III to issue a bull in 1537 which declared that the Indians were not to be considered dumb brutes created for our service, but rather were true men capable of becoming Christians. (Elliott 1970: 43; Robe 1972: 47)

Still another characteristic associated with the concept of the Wild Man was sexuality. Ideas about the Wild Man's sexuality can be seen as closely related to his animal nature. Unlike a man, he cannot control his gluttonous need to eat or his sexual desires. Like a beast, the Wild Man is compelled to act upon his basic animal drives.

Analytically, the concepts of the Wild Man and the Noble Savage are abstractions in opposition to one another. However, in the reports of explorers such as Cortez, and others in Europe discussing and summarizing their accounts, like Montaigne, both concepts were frequently used together. Both conceptualizations have negative and positive aspects. The Noble Savage in his natural innocence lacks the self-consciousness which is necessary for the development of philosophy, government, and laws. The Wild Man has his positive side. He represents the qualities of freedom and passion, as opposed to control and reason.

Shifts in Thinking After the Scientific Revolution

In the seventeenth century, a new and significant way of thinking developed which had a strong impact on 18th century explorations in the Pacific. The publication of Newton's *Principia* and Locke's essay, "...which conceived the world of nature and of man as machine-like in its construction, governed by laws discoverable by man and, when known, immeasurably conducive to his advantage, this age raised the average traveler to an eminence he had never before enjoyed." (Frantz 1934: 15) The assumption was that travelers and explorers went on their voyages with these scientific ideas in mind.

In line with the thinking of this new era, the Royal Society published in 1665 a set of *Directions for Seamen bound for far Voyages* in which they were enjoined to keep an exact record of what they observed with respect to both natural phenomena and the people they encountered. Regarding the people, the Directions stated,

> Above the ignobler 'Productions' of the Earth, there must be a careful account given of the 'Inhabitants' themselves, both 'Natives' and 'Strangers', that have been long settled there; And in particular, their Stature, Shape, Colour, Features, Strength, Agility, Beauty (or want of it) Complexions, Hair, Dyet, Inclinations, and Customs that seem not due to Education. And as to their Women (besides other things) may be observed their Fruitfulness or Barrenness; their hard or easy Labour, &c." (Royal Society Philosophical Transactions 1665 I: 188)

In a way, this represents an early version of *Notes and Queries* -- a guide provided by the Royal Anthropological Institute in the second part of the nineteenth century. In this new mode of thinking about the Other, people were viewed in the same manner as other natural phenomena studied by scientists. They were described, depicted, and measured.

Though voyagers and travelers took the directions of the Royal Society very seriously, their viewpoint continued to be quite ethnocentric. As Frantz notes, "The voyager's typical outlook on man, whether in America or in the South Seas, Persia or East India, was that of a superior being scrutinizing inferiority." (Frantz 1934: 37) In France, as well as in England, ideas about science became important in the eighteenth century. However, they co-existed with earlier ideas. In 1751, Maupertuis, a philosopher and scientist who was a member of the Royal Society, outlined a plan for exploring the large southern continent which people still believed existed in the South Pacific. He remarked, "It is in the islands of that sea [the Pacific] that voyagers assure us they have seen wild men covered with hair and having tails, a species half-way between ourselves and the monkeys. I would rather spend an hour in conversation with one of them than with the greatest *'belle espirit'* in Europe." (quoted in Symcox 1972: 232)

During the latter part of the eighteenth century, expeditions were sent out with the explicit purpose of gathering scientific information about natural phenomena, as well as about the way of life of different peoples. As Peter Gay notes, "For the social scientists of the Enlightenment, travel reports were a valued source of information, a 'museum, in which specimens of every variety of human nature may be studied', and, with that, a basis for general theories." (Gay 1969: 320) Accounts of `primitive' peoples in other parts of the world provided the impetus for the development of evolutionary theoretical frameworks like those put forth in the middle of the 18th century by Turgot and Condorcet. Turgot developed the idea that human beings and their behavior were subject to natural laws, just like plants and animals. He saw culture as cumulative and transmitted from generation to generation, though he also recognized that cultural ideas could be diffused. These ideas are the precursors of concepts which later become central to cultural anthropology as it developed in the 19th century.

In addition to making careful observations, the scientific approach dictated that the traveler also should collect natural specimens -- plants, birds, animals, fossils and rocks. As part of this undertaking, human "specimens" and "artificial curiosities" were brought back to Europe. Bougainville and Cook each brought a Tahitian man back to Europe with them. These individuals were an added stimulus to the thinking of the reigning philosophers who had been inspired by accounts of life in the South Pacific.

Frost (1976) refers to the Pacific Ocean as "the eighteenth century's 'new world'." During the eighteenth century Enlightenment, when explorers began to pay serious scientific attention to the Pacific, the ideas of the Wild Man and the Noble Savage continued to be important. But the work of Rousseau and others had made conceptualizations of the Noble Savage the more prominent of the two by this time. As Howe notes, "Many of the French and English explorers in the Pacific, in particular, Joseph Banks, George Forster, and Louis Antoine de Bougainville, were steeped in both the current wave of neo-classicism and the cult of the Noble Savage. To their delight, many Pacific peoples appeared to be living examples of Rousseau's Savage, especially Tahitians whose lifestyle seemed to epitomize a pre-industrial, Arcadian purity." (Howe 1977: 138)

There is a contradiction between the objectivity which is expected of the scientist and naturalist and eighteenth-century conceptualizations of the Other as the Noble Savage. This is apparent in the "Observations" of Johann

Reinhold Forster and the account of his son George Forster. Both Forsters accompanied Captain Cook as botanists on his second voyage to the Pacific. In discussing their work, Spate notes, "The Forsters' work is shot through with ambivalence. The picture of the South Seas is often idyllic, but realism will break in: "…Though *le mirage tahitien* exerts its innocent spell, even in this happy isle the trustful philosophic heart is shocked and grieved to find inequality and corruption...." (Spate 1988: 201-202)

Scientists like the Forsters, Bougainville, and others during the late eighteenth century applied a natural history approach to human beings in the same manner that they used it to observe and describe plants and animals. The Forsters looked at Tahitians in the same way as they did the plants of Tahiti. However, the study of human behavior is always mediated through language. Even the early explorers of New Ireland, such as Schouten, understood this. They would gather lists of words on one island and try to use those words on other islands which they subsequently visited, only to discover that different languages were spoken there. As Marshall and Williams point out, Sir Joseph Banks, naturalist and Fellow of the Royal Society, tried to learn about the religion of the Tahitians, but he soon recognized that he would have to be much more conversant in Tahitian to learn about their religion. (Marshall and Williams 1982: 271)

For several reasons Tahitians came to exemplify the exotic Other encountered in the Pacific. First Wallis, then Bougainville, and then Cook visited Tahiti and, for the most part, were greeted in friendly and hospitable fashion. Bougainville and Commerson, the naturalist who accompanied him to the Pacific, both described Tahiti as a true Utopia and described Tahitian men and women as though they were Greek gods and goddesses. Even more effective in elevating the position of Tahitians to prominence was the bringing back to Europe by both Bougainville and Cook of Tahitian men. When Bougainville was anchored at Tahiti in 1768, Ahutoru, a "brother" of a chief, expressed his desire to join Bougainville's expedition. On the return voyage, Bougainville learned some Tahitian vocabulary and Ahutoru, some French. Ahutoru lived in Bougainville's home, was presented to Louis XV at Versailles, met the president of the French Academy, de Brosses, and Diderot. He became a favorite of members of the aristocracy. He never succeeded in learning much French, however. He died of smallpox off the coast of Madagascar on his way back to Tahiti.

Sir Joseph Banks, who tried to bring a Tahitian boy, Tupaia, back to England, clearly expressed the motives behind bringing South Seas Islanders to Europe. He noted in his journal, "I do not know why I may not keep him as a curiousity, as well as some of my neighbours do lions and tygers at a larger expence than he will probably ever put me to; the amusement I shall have in his future conversation and the benefit he will be of to this ship, as well as what he may be if another should be sent into these seas, will I think fully repay me." (Banks, in Daws 1980: 10) Though Ahutoru and Tupaia may have been regarded as scientific specimens, they were not really studied; rather, they were kept as objects of curiosity and amusement.

The Tahitians did not acquire a good knowledge of French or English, and their Tahitian language was not studied in any great detail by the Europeans. One may wonder why Voltaire, characterized as an early social scientist by Peter Gay, did not take the opportunity to converse with Ahutoru to gain information about Tahiti from him, instead of making up imaginary savages with whom he could debate social and moral issues.

Though Diderot may have met Ahutoru, his *Supplement to the Voyage of Bougainville* is based on an imaginary creation using Bougainville's account of his voyage as a starting point. Diderot saw Rousseau's natural man in the Tahitians described by Bougainville. In his opinion the moral code of the Tahitians followed natural law, which was far superior to that of "civilized nations." A Tahitian invented by Diderot chastises Bougainville for having proclaimed, "'This land belongs to us [the French]'. This land belongs to you! And why? Because you set foot in it? If some day a Tahitian should land on your shores and if he should engrave on one of your stones or on the bark of one of your trees: 'This land belongs to the people of Tahiti' what would you think?." (Diderot [1772] 1964: 188) Instead of getting information from Ahutoru on the Tahitian way of life, Diderot creates imaginary Tahitians whose words present Diderot's own point of view about Tahitian life. Diderot had the Tahitians denouncing the injustices of French colonialism before it had really developed in the Pacific.

The "Other" in Popular Fiction

Many writers read and incorporated into their writings the accounts of travelers and explorers regarding the inhabitants of the newly discovered places. Their literary works were influential, in turn, in shaping the cultural conceptions of the Other which later travelers and explorers brought to their own experiences. This is as true of Sir Thomas More's *Utopia* as it is of Rabelais' *Gargantua and Pantagruel*, and Shakespeare's *The Tempest*.

Writings about Utopias flourished during the sixteenth and seventeenth centuries, stimulated, no doubt, by the discoveries of the Age of Exploration. In his discussion of imaginary travel voyages to Utopias, Symcox (1972: 228) points out, "Details culled from real voyages were used to lend conviction to the political message." Utopias encapsulate a belief in an ideal society, "…an earthly Paradise far removed from the imperfections of our civilization. It was criticism of our society in particular and our culture in general." (Baudet 1965: 32) For example, Sir Thomas More's *Utopia*, written in 1516, reports the travels of Raphael Hythlodaye, who had sailed on Vespucci's last voyage, and whose account of the culture of Utopians includes information on their religion, marriage and the family, betrothal customs, mortuary rites, dwellings, apparel and other customs. The idea of "Utopia" as an ideal place where humans led a perfect life was important in shaping European concepts of the Other. For example, when Bougainville, and shortly thereafter Cook, arrived at Tahiti, their first impressions were that they had found a Utopia.

According to Adams, imaginary voyages as a type of literature were "…almost as popular in the eighteenth century as were the authentic travel accounts." (1980: 2) These fictional works drew heavily upon the journals of explorers and travelers returning from far-off places. This type of fiction is exemplified by Chateaubriand's *Atala*, a romantic love story about a Natchez chief, who, as an old man, recounts his life story to a French traveler. *Atala* went through five editions in its first year, 1801. (Thorsley 1972: 290) It is clear that the figure of the Noble Savage is being glorified in *Atala*. There were also fictionalized travel accounts, such as Daniel Defoe's *A New Voyage Round the World*, which, in the public eye, bore a close resemblance to real travel accounts, though Defoe never left his London living room. Novels such as *Atala* and fictional travel accounts stood side by side on book shelves with factual travel accounts. Europeans of the time developed their image of non-European Others from both these genres.

Shakespeare's play *The Tempest*, written in 1611, also shows the influence of ideas about newly discovered peoples of the New World. It, in turn, had an impact on the ideas Europeans had about Others. A central theme of the play contrasts Prospero and Caliban as analogues for the civilized

European and the subjugated "savage." Shakespeare was clearly influenced by reports coming back from the New World. As Cro notes, "... He repeats, almost word for word Peter Martyr's and Bembo's passages on the happy state of the American natives...." (Cro 1989:46, note 66) There is no doubt that he was also familiar with Montaigne's essay, "Of the Cannibals," which we discussed above. Shakespeare chose cannibalism as the archetypical savage trait and used it as a basis for the construction of the name of the "savage" Other, Caliban, an anagram of cannibal. The characteristics of Caliban identify him as an exaggerated form of the "Wild Man." (Greenblatt 1990:26) Caliban movingly replies to Prospero, who has taught him language in order to enable him to express himself, "You taught me language; and my profit on't is, I know how to curse. The red plague rid you for learning me your language!" (Shakespeare in Greenblatt 1990:25) In the dialectic between the Wild Man and the Noble Savage, the nobility of Caliban, the Wild man, emerges as he curses his master. Caliban continues to serve as a metaphor for subjugated people up to the present. "What is our history, what is our culture, if not the history and culture of Caliban?" proclaims the Cuban essayist, Roberto Retamar. (1989:14)

Discussion

During the Age of Exploration and Discovery in the New World and the Pacific, the dialectically linked themes of the Noble Savage and the Wild Man primarily served to order European conceptualizations of the Other. These ideas were also associated with the Bible, in that the Noble Savage resembles Adam and Eve before their fall. And the Wild Man was a heretic and sower of confusion. In their reports, the travelers and observers visiting these new lands couched their descriptions in both terms alternately, frequently resulting in contradictions. In the seventeenth century, the scientific approach was introduced as a counterpoint to these themes. Voyages of exploration were undertaken to observe natural phenomena and to collect specimens. The canons of observation were extended to humans of other cultures, but these served to distance the Other, who was viewed only as an object. Subscribing to the scientific approach did not assure that observers would no longer employ constructs like the Noble Savage.

In the nineteenth century, these central themes were shaped and transformed by the economic and social events of the times, though the concepts of the Noble Savage and the Wild Man could still be recognized in newer guises[1]. As increased industrialization produced greater and greater alienation in Europe and America, some continued the search for a simpler and more natural life. In the romantic writing of the nineteenth century, the metaphor of the castaway, as in Melville's *Typee* or Stevenson's idyllic South Seas, represented an attempt to find a more satisfying life beyond that of the great anonymous cities of Europe and America. In similar fashion, Gaugin's paintings of the late nineteenth century also represented a sort of Garden of Eden. This continued into the twentieth century. As Baudet points out, the most popular European writer of the early part of the twentieth century was probably Karl May, whose "Apache" chief Winnetou epitomized all that was Noble in the Savage.

However, and more significantly, the nineteenth century saw the full-blown development of imperialism and colonialism. It was the era of the great colonial empires -- not only of the Dutch, who had begun theirs two centuries before, but also of the French, the German and the British Empires. Based on occupation, exploitation, and conquest, colonialism demanded that those who were exploited be made to appear savage and brutish, rather than noble. At the same time, ideas about the evolution of human culture and society, first tendered in the late eighteenth century, became the central theoretical framework for the development of a scientific approach to the study of other societies in the emerging disciplines of sociology and anthropology. In the evolutionary schema of Tylor, Spencer and Morgan, the terms Barbarian and Savage, earlier associated with the concept of the Wild Man, reappear as labels for the earlier stages of a cultural evolutionary progression which had culminated in the industrial empires of the Victorian period.

NOTES

1. In a recent discussion of the "noble savage," LeBlanc (2003), an archeologist, notes that the absence of warfare, and the idea that humans lived in ecological balance, which he sees as characteristic of the idea of the "Noble Savage," are not supported by the archeological record. The remains of fortress walls and other evidence of frequent warfare throughout human history, and the nature of the exploitation of the environment in ancient times do not support these supposed characteristics of the life of the "Noble Savage."

4. EUROPEAN VISITORS TO NEW IRELAND DURING THE AGE OF EXPLORATION

European explorers began appearing in the Pacific after Magellan's early 16th century voyage. However, it was not until the 17th century that we have records of European landings on New Ireland. The impact these explorers and their ships had on New Irelanders can be gleaned from the accounts which they have left us. Using the ethnographic information presented earlier, we will reconstruct a picture of the impact of these European intruders on the various groups of New Irelanders which they encountered. Almost uniformly, the surprise, curiosity and the eventual fear shown by the New Irelanders as a result of the encounters, come through in the European accounts. In this chapter, we will see the ways in which, after the wonderment of the first encounter, New Irelanders and Europeans attempted to develop systems of communication and exchange. Both sides were motivated to conduct such exchanges because each side wanted things the other possessed. However, as we shall see, during the next two hundred years fear and mistrust prevented such exchanges from becoming institutionalized.

The great majority of the 17th century explorers' trips followed the route Magellan had taken across the Pacific from east to west in his voyage around the globe between 1519 and 1521. This was because the prevailing trade winds made it infinitely easier to cross the south Pacific travelling from east to west. In addition, explorers seeking new lands and opportunities for trade had to go beyond the area over which the Dutch East Indies Company had a monopoly, an area which extended to passage through the Straits of Magellan.

Isaac Le Maire and Willem Schouten

The first encounter between New Irelanders and Europeans recorded in European accounts occurred during the voyage of Le Maire and Schouten. Isaac Le Maire, an Amsterdam merchant and defiant competitor of the East India Company, formed a company together with Willem Corneliszoon Schouten, a renowned navigator and merchant, who had made three earlier voyages to the East Indies. Schouten's voyage with Le Maire was to be different, in that it was the first Dutch voyage across the Pacific, from East to West. (See Beaglehole 1966: 127.) Le Maire and Schouten developed a plan to find a passage through the archipelago which they thought lay south of the Strait of Magellan.

Le Maire, the supercargo, and Schouten, the skipper, left from Hoorn in June 1615 with the express purpose of finding new lands where they could pursue trade and commerce beyond the area of the Dutch East India Company monopoly. They were successful in finding a passage south of the Straits of Magellan. They named it after Le Maire. The rocky stretch of land to the south they named Cape Hoorn; and henceforth, rounding the tip of South America was known as rounding the Hoorn. Soon after, in the Pacific portion of the voyage, Le Maire died; and the expedition continued under Schouten. After visiting the Tuamotus and the northern fringes of the Tongan group (Tafahi), their course led them to the Solomon Islands. From there, they went in a northwesterly direction, sighting the island now called Feni, which lies off the southeast coast of New Ireland.

On June 25, 1616, the day after sighting Feni, which they named St. John's Island, Schouten wrote, "…We saw other land before us which was exceeding high, which we thought to be the poynt of Noua Guinea...." (Schouten 1619d: 60) In the primitive geography of this time, the Bismarck Archipelago was thought to be part of the island of New Guinea, which itself was considered to be part of Australia. Schouten was stopping at New Ireland to renew supplies. The crew lowered a shallop, a light open boat, and "there came 2 or 3 Canoes to it, with blacke Indians in them, all naked, ... which fiercely cast stones at our men with slings, but as soone as our men began to shoote at them they fled away." (Schouten 1619d:60) As they sailed along the east coast of New Ireland, they saw land, "pleasant to behold," and houses. When they anchored in a bay further along the coast, the people on shore lit fires and kept watch. That night, "…there came some Canoes close under gallery of our shippe, from whence wee threw them some beades shewing them all the friendship wee could, withal making signes unto them to bring us some Cocos nuts, hogs, oxen, or goates, if they had any...." (Schouten 1619d:61)

However, Schouten was frustrated in his attempt to obtain fresh supplies. The following morning, eight canoes came out to the ship, the largest of which contained eleven men. The men in the canoes were armed with "Assagayes or Clubs, wooden swords and slings." Schouten again attempted to trade for supplies, offering the men in the canoes "beades and other trash ["trifles" in Villiers translation, 1619e: 216], ...but they had another meaning, and all together began fiercely to sling with their slings, & other weapons thinking to master us, but we standing upon our guarde, shot with our muskets and great shot among them, and slew at least 10 or 12 of them. They left the great Canoe, and 3 others, and leaping into the sea, swam to land...." (Schouten 1619d:61) Schouten then lowered the ship's boat and pursued the fleeing men, killing some and capturing three prisoners. After one of the prisoners died, the other two were taken ashore with the intention of ransoming them for needed supplies. Schouten records, "…There the prisoners cryed to their fellowes to bring us hogs, Bananas and Cocos nuts, wherewith one Canoe came aboord, that brought a little hog, and a bunch of Bananas, wee set one of the men at 10 hogs ransome, the other that was sore hurt, we let goe in the Canoe… those men had 2 holes bored in their noses, on either side one, wherein they ware rings, strange to behold." (Schouten 1619d: 61-62)

Two days later, with the ship still anchored in the same place, "…There came certaine Canoes aboord our ship, but brought nothing with them, neither would they ransom their man, therefore we let him goe on shore againe. Wee thought those people to be Papoos, for all their haire was short, and they eat Betell and Chalke mingled with it…." (Schouten 1619d: 62)

Schouten continued up the east coast and encountered New Irelanders once again several days later off an island group which we now know to have been Tabar. In this instance,

> …Divers Canoes with blacke Indians came aboord our ship, who in signe of peace, as they entered, brake their Assagayes [slender spears] over their heads, they brought us nothing but desired something of us. They seemed to be better and friendlier people than the other for they covered their privy members with leaves and had better kind of Canoes, set out before and behind with some carved workes, they are very proud of their beades [beards] which paint with chalke and the haire of their heads also. Upon the three or foure Islands, from when those Canoes came, there was a great store of cocos trees: they brought us nothing, how earnestly soever we urged them that wee had neede of victuales…. (Schouten 1619d: 63)

The following day, "...There came 25 Canoes towards our ship, with many men, well armed: being the same people who the day before brake their Assagaies over their heads, an made a friendly shew unto us, but with intent to abuse us...." (Schouten 1619d: 63) These people tried to tow Schouten's ship to the shore by attaching their Canoes to the ship's anchor. When this failed," "...at last, they began fiercely to throw at us with stones, and other weapons, and thereby hurt one of our men, being the first that was hurt in all our voyage, but while they were busie to assaile us thinking they had got the upper hand, we shot among them with our Muskets and with our upper tyre [type] of Ordinance, and kild at least 12 or 13 of them, and hurt many more." (Schouten 1619d: 63)

The ship's armed shallop pursued the fleeing canoes and captured one canoe, killing two of the men in it, while "...The other yeelded himselfe prisoner, being a young man about 18 yeares old whom wee named Moses after our mans name that was hurt." (*ibid*: 64) This young man was kidnapped and taken away on Schouten's ship. A week later, "Moses" was still aboard the ship, communicating to Schouten that he could not understand the language of the people encountered on what Schouten labeled Vulcan's Island (probably Karkar, a volcanic island off the coast of Papua New Guinea). When Schouten finally arrived in the Dutch East Indies, his ship and its contents were impounded by the Dutch East India Company at Jakarta, Java, on November 1, 1616.

Schouten had compiled a word list from "Cocos" Island (Tafahi, in the Tongan group), which he endeavored to use in New Ireland, but without success. He also noted that the language of the New Irelanders was "cleane contrary" to that of the Solomon Islanders. Two word lists were collected in New Ireland. The first list, comprising 85 lexical items, was identified by

Friederici as being from the "Nokon" language, today called Sursurunga, and the bay in which Schouten anchored as being between Namatanai and Muliama. One item on the list, *tounsiet*, "bone spear," was ceremonially important, as we noted earlier. (Friederici 1912: 4) The second list is called the language of "Moyses," which Lanyon-Orgill (1960:50) thinks is the language of Moses Island, but there is no Moses Island. Friederici has identified this language as that spoken on the southwest coast of Tabar. The word list was obtained from Moyses, who it will be recalled, was taken aboard Schouten's vessel as a prisoner after the final clash at Tabar. These word lists collected by Schouten were a major scientific achievement.

In contrast to Schouten's dealings in the Tuamotus and in Tafahi, where he offered beads and knives and received ample foodstuffs in return, to the New Irelanders he only offered beads, which they clearly thought not worth the coconuts, yams and pigs which he desired. Not receiving what they wanted the first time, the New Irelanders behaved in a menacing manner when they returned to the ship the next day. Schouten reports that he sought to have a friendly encounter, but the New Irelanders responded to his overtures in an aggressive manner. Though Schouten desperately wanted fresh supplies, he was only willing to give things of little value in exchange for them. In the end he was determined to get supplies by any means, including holding captured men for ransom, the phrase which he himself used.

To the New Irelanders, the Europeans were not easily placeable into familiar cultural categories. They and their ship were so radically different in appearance and behavior, that they were surely put in the category of unknown stranger and perhaps enemy -- but certainly not, at this juncture, in the category of "people with whom we exchange. The New Irelanders came to the encounter armed. In fact, the first group that Schouten saw viewed him as hostile and immediately attacked his ship with sling stones. A fusillade of musket and cannon shot was in turn unleashed by Schouten. The Europeans thus appeared to the New Irelanders as dangerous, violent killers with weaponry beyond their imaginations. The power of Schouten's response had gone far beyond what constituted warfare in New Irelander terms. By his own account, one of

Schouten's men were hurt by a sling stone, but more than 25 New Irelanders died. The New Irelanders surely retold the story of this event many times over, and it probably spread to other parts of the island.

For the New Irelanders of the southeast coast, this was probably their first encounter with Europeans. However, for Schouten, this was not his first encounter with Others. At Tafahi, in the Tongan Islands, and in the Solomons, Schouten was able to barter goods for food, though both of these encounters also ended in violence. These earlier encounters, no doubt, provided the foundation for Schouten's expectations of how the New Islanders would respond to his behavior. The New Irelanders were unwilling to respond as the Tongans and Solomon Islanders previously had and provide supplies in exchange for "trifles."

Schouten's characterization of the New Irelanders as "Papoos" indicates his familiarity with previous accounts of the people of New Guinea. He dwells on the blackness, nakedness and ferocity of the New Irelanders. From this depiction of the New Irelanders and Schouten's interactions with them -- his apprehension that they would attack him, and the aggressive nature of his response to them -- one can conclude that he viewed the New Irelanders in terms of the various features characterizing Wild Men. In his text, he heightened the dangers faced by intrepid European explorers, creating an exciting narrative by portraying New Irelanders as fierce Wild Men. His readers thus got the impression that the inhabitants of this region, and not Schouten, were the Wild Men. Yet Schouten's interest in their language, as evidenced by the word lists, served to emphasize that they were human, like him. The word lists also demonstrated his scientific interest. As a result of the tremendous European curiosity about overseas voyages, by 1618, Dutch, French and German versions of the account of the voyage already had been published, indicating the rapidity with which such information was disseminated internationally.

Abel Janszoon Tasman

The Dutch continued to be interested in expanding their colonial empire, and soon after the voyage of Le Maire and Schouten, Anton van Dieman, then the Governor of the Dutch East Indies, sent two ships southeast from there to make another attempt to find the mysterious continent -- Terra Australis. The expedition left in 1642 under the command of Abel Janszoon Tasman.

Tasman, though literate, had come from a poor family from Groningen. By 1634 he was the skipper of a yacht in the general East Indian Service. His success as a skipper led to his being chosen by van Dieman "for the prospective discovery and exploration of the 'rich southern and eastern lands'; to which discovery he found himself 'strongly inclined'." (Beaglehole 1966:144) Frans Jacobszoon Visscher, a hydrographer and pilot, formulated the detailed plan for Tasman's voyage and sailed with Tasman as pilot and chief advisor. To assist him in his voyage, Tasman was given a Spanish description of the Solomon Islands, a vocabulary of words used by "the natives of those seas," and orders to follow Le Maire and Schouten's track along the north coast of New Guinea. (Beaglehole 1966: 144)

EUROPEAN VISITORS TO NEW IRELAND DURING AGE OF EXPLORATION

From New Zealand, which Tasman discovered and named, he sailed north, visiting the Tongan and Fijian groups, eventually entering the Solomons, where he turned to consult the Spanish description of the islands and the map of this area made by Le Maire and Schouten. Following this map, he passed Ontong Java, which he named for its resemblance to Java. He then passed Marken (Carteret Island), Green Island (Nissan) and S. Jans (St. Johns or Feni) islands, which Schouten had charted 27 years earlier. On April 1,1643, Tasman approached the East Cape area of New Ireland, which had been named Capo Santa Maria by an unknown Spanish explorer who left no account of his voyage. He thought he had sighted the coast of New Guinea because the separation between New Guinea and New Ireland was not yet known to Europeans. On April 2nd, Tasman began to sail along the east coast of New Ireland. He first encountered and named Anthonij Caen's Island (Tanga), then Garde Neijs Island (Gerrit Denys or Lihir). The next day he came upon some men in canoes fishing near another island, which he named Visschers island (Fishers Island, later Tabar), after his pilot and chief advisor.

Tasman gives detailed accounts of his encounters with New Irelanders. Describing this first encounter, Tasman stated,

> Towards noon we saw 6 prows ahead of us, three of which came paddling so near our ship that we let 2 or three pieces of old canvas, 2 strings of beads and two old nails drift towards them; they did not seem to care for the canvas and the other things, too, hardly excited their attention; but they kept pointing to their heads, from which we concluded that they wanted turbans. These people seemed to be very shy, and by their gestures afraid of shot; they did not come near enough for us to discern whether they were armed. They were very black and stark naked, having only their privities covered with a few

green leaves....Their prows had outriggers and each of them had 3 or 4 persons....At times [they] called out to us, to which we replied in the same way, though we did not understand each other, they paddled back to shore. (Tasman 1964 [1642]: 79)

The following day, while Tasman was still at Visschers Island, eight or nine canoes approached the ship's prow:

> ...They left off paddling, and called out to us; we could not understand them, but made signs for them to come nearer.... At length one of our quartermasters took off his belt, and held it up to them from afar. Upon this one of these prows came alongside our ship; we gave them a string of beads and our quartermaster also handed out his belt to them, for which all we got in return was the piece of the pith of a sago-tree which was the only commodity they had with them. Meanwhile, the other prows, seeing that their comrades received no hurt, also came paddling alongside. None of these prows contained any arms or anything with which they could have done us harm. We at first suspected they might be villains, who were intent on mischief and in search of booty, since they affected such timidity.... We called out to them the words Anieuw, Oufi, Pouacka, etc. (meaning coconuts, yams, hogs, etc.), which they seemed to understand for they pointed to the shore as if they wished to say: they are there." (Tasman 1968 [1642]): 80)

Sharp indicates that these words come from the Le Maire vocabulary of the Tafahi and Horne Islands languages. (Sharp 1968: 212, fn 1) It is curious that Tasman did not use the words collected from Moises by Le Maire and Schouten, since Moises was from Tabar.

Tasman further noted, "...We did not see them again. These natives are dark brown, nay almost as black as the blackest Caffre; they have hair of various colors, owning to the lime with which they powder it; their faces are smeared with red paint, except their foreheads. Some of them wore a thick bone through the lower part of the nose, about half the thickness of a little finger. For the rest they wore nothing on their bodies except some green leaves covering their privities. Their prows were new, trimly made up and adorned with wood-carving in front and behind, with one outrigger each; their paddles were not long or broad and pointed at the end." (Tasman 1968 [1642]:80)

In the first encounter with Tasman, the New Irelanders circled his ships at a distance, a measure of their great suspicion. Tasman, knowing about Schouten's earlier encounter and his shooting of New Irelanders, interpreted their behavior as an indication of their fear of being shot. It is very likely that the people from Tabar (Fisher's Island) whom Tasman encountered had heard about the encounter with Schouten 27 years earlier. Tasman, too, was suspicious, to the point of interpreting their timidity as deception rather than simply as fear. He viewed them as villains intent on mischief. It is clear that the New Irelanders and Europeans were attempting to communicate with one another, but they had no common language. In an attempt to obtain from the islanders the supplies that he needed, Tasman, in contrast to Schouten, initially offered gifts, including nails, assuming that they knew about iron. However, the New Irelanders still seem to have been unfamiliar with iron. On the second day, Tasman again gave presents, but all he got in return was some sago pith, the only thing the canoes were carrying. When the islanders pointed to their heads, Tasman thought they wanted turbans. Rev. George Brown noted later onthat this gesture, patting the top of the head with the hand, was a sign of welcome in northwestern New Ireland. (Brown 1910: 378)

On the following day, off the east coast of New Ireland, in another location north of the East Cape, twenty canoes approached and warily circled Tasman's ships beyond gunshot reach.

> They had nothing in their prows except in one of them three coca-nuts, of which we got one in exchange for a string of beads.... Another man had a shark (which in their tongue they called *Ilacxz*), which we also bartered against three strings of beads; a third again, had a dorado or dolphin, which one of our sailors exchanged for an old cap.... Finally, three or four of these people came on board of our ship, looked about them in great amazement and walked about the ship as if they were intoxicated; a curious circumstance, truly, for in their small prows they paddled about for miles out to sea, without any signs of sea-sickness, but in a large ship like ours they seem to get intoxicated by the motion caused of the swell of the sea. They had no arms with them, or anything which could have hurt us. They seemed to subsist by fishing for some of them carried wooden eel spears. (Tasman 1964 [1642]: 81)

Another narrative of the Tasman voyage, authored by Henrik Haalbos, a barber and surgeon, includes a description of a New Irelander who "...had got by barter an old jacket." (Haalbos-Montanus Account in Sharp 1968: 50) This indicates that other Europeans who had not recorded their voyages had previously passed this way.

Though at first suspicious, the New Irelanders from the mainland eventually boarded Tasman's ships. Like the people from Tabar (Fisher's Island), they came unarmed and showed great timidity. Their "wonderment" on coming aboard the ship indicates that they had never seen anything like it up close. The islanders seem to have been interested enough to exchange what they were carrying with them, like fish, but not sufficiently interested in what Tasman offered to go back to their villages and gardens and bring back the things that he wanted. They were certainly very curious about the Europeans and their ship. By the time that he reached New Ireland, Tasman had had a variety of experiences with Pacific Islanders, some, like at Tanga Tapu, involving successful exchanges and others, like the Maori, where unsuccessful exchange ended in armed conflict. (Beaglehole 1966: 152-153) What Tasman experienced in New Ireland fell between the hostility of the Maori and the friendly exchanges at Tanga Tapu.

From the descriptions of the New Irelanders which Tasman presents, he seems to put them in the category of savages, and this colored his behavior towards them. He emphasizes that their genitals are barely covered, and that they powder their hair with lime, paint their faces red, and put bones in their noses. The engraving accompanying Tasman's journal depicting these people represents a fanciful, romantic and more "noble" rendering, contrasting with Tasman's verbal description of the rude New Irelanders. (See Figure 5.)[1] Though the engraving is inaccurate in its romantic portrayal of the inhabitants, it is ethnographically accurate in depiction of the propeller used for shark-catching, as we discussed earlier.

Figure 5. New Ireland Canoe, drawing by Isaac Gilsemans, from Abel Tasman's Journal, 1643 (Source: Alamy stock print)

William Dampier

William Dampier was the next explorer to give an account of a visit to New Ireland. He was born in 1651 in Somerset, England, the son of poor tenant farmers, and he went to sea at the age of eighteen. After serving on several West Indies trading vessels in the Caribbean, he turned buccaneer. He shipped out across the Pacific in 1685 and remained in the South China Sea, gaining maritime experience for six years, and returned to England in 1691. Beaglehole notes that Dampier's book *A New Voyage Round the World*, published in 1697, "…was not merely an exciting and extraordinary account of adventure; it was also an exceptionally accurate, detailed and many-sided record of observation that can truly be called scientific...." (Beaglehole 1966: 169) Dampier met the Earl of Orford, Lord High Admiral of England, who asked him to suggest a voyage in England's interest. Dampier proposed exploration of New Holland and the remoter parts of the East Indies which, he argued, should produce a wide variety of commodities. (Beaglehole 1966:

169-170) The Admiralty agreed to sponsor such a voyage because of its important commercial possibilities.

Dampier sailed from England on January 14, 1699. He took the route around the Cape of Good Hope and along the west coast of Australia. He then turned eastward along the north coast of New Guinea to St. Mathias island. On Feb. 28, 1700, he encountered Wishart's Isle (Fisher's Island or Tabar). According to his account,

> …Seeing many smokes upon the main… [the] sides of hills had many plantations and patches of clear land which together with smoke we saw were certain signs of its being inhabited…. I was desirous of entering into commerce with the inhabitants…. a great many boats came from all adjacent bays. When they were forty-six in number, they approached so near us that we could see each other sign and hear each other speak though we could not understand them nor they us. They made signs for us to go in towards the shore pointing that way.... The natives lay in their proas around us; to whom I showed beads, knives, glasses to allure them to come nearer. But they would not come so nigh as to receive anything from us; therefore I threw some things to them viz a knife fastened to a piece of board and a glass bottle corked up with some beads in it which they took up and seemed well pleased. They often struck their left breast with their right hand and as often held up a black trunchon over their heads which we thought was a token of friendship wherefore we did the like and when we stood in towards their shore they seemed to rejoice but when we stood off they frowned yet kept us company in their proas still pointing to the shore….

[Sometime later] ... we had near two hundred in proas close by us and the bays on the shore were well lined with men from one end to the other where there could not be less than three or four hundred more. What weapons they had we knew not nor yet their design; therefore I had, at their first coming near us, got up all our small arms and made several put on cartouch boxes to prevent treachery. At last I resolved to go out again; which when the natives in their prows perceived, they began to fling stones at us as fast as they could, being provided with engines for that purpose: and therefore I named this place Slinger's Bay; but at the firing of the first gun they were all amazed, drew off and flung no more stones. They got together as if consulting what to do; for they did not make in towards the shore, but lay still, though some of them were killed or wounded and many more of them had paid for their boldness. (Dampier 1770, in Pinkerton 1886: 159-160)

An elaborate minuet is played out here in Dampier's encounter with the New Irelanders. The people of Tabar probably came out in great numbers because their earlier encounter with Tasman some fifty years earlier had been a positive one. Dampier appeared to have correctly guessed that touching the head was a sign of greeting. Though they picked up the objects thrown to them, Dampier failed in attempts to exchange, since they offered him nothing in return. Instead, they tried to lure him to come on shore. When he rejected their entreaties and turned to leave, they became angry and hurled stones at the ship with their slingshots. Like Schouten eighty years earlier, Dampier responded with a volley, which amazed the New Irelanders, leaving some dead and some wounded. From Dampier's description, it is apparent that hundreds of men gathered along the shore at the sighting of Dampier's ship.

The amazement of the New Irelanders at the firing of the gun would seem to indicate that there was no memory at this place of Schouten's earlier visit. Or, perhaps Dampier had landed in a place sufficiently far away from where Schouten had landed, that no word of the earlier visit by Europeans had penetrated.

Dampier then proceeded to Garret Dennis Island. (Lihir) He described the many villages and "plantations" and the large number of coconut trees. Though he did not go on shore, he described the island as very populous. He was taken with the physical appearance of New Irelanders, describing them as "…very black, strong and well-limbed people." (Dampier in Pinkerton 1886: 162) Like Schouten, Dampier was also fascinated by the hair-do and facial decoration of New Ireland men. He noted that,

> …Their hair naturally curled and short, which they shave into several forms, and dye it also of divers colours-viz. red, white and yellow. They have broad, round faces with great bottle-noses, yet agreeable enough till they disfigure by painting and wearing great things through their noses…. They have also great holes in their ears, wherein they wear such stuff as in their noses. They are very dexterous, active fellows in their proas, which are very ingeniously built. They are narrow and long, with outriggers on one side, The head and stern higher than the rest and carved with many devices- viz. some fowl, fish or a man's head painted or carved; … but with what instruments they make their proas or carved work, I know not, for they seem to be utterly ignorant of iron….. Their weapons are chiefly lances, swords and slings, and some bows and arrows. They also have wooden spears for striking fish…. Their speech is clear and distinct. The words they use most when near us were *vacousee, allamais* and

they pointed to the shore. Their signs of friendship are either a great truncheon or a bough of a tree full of leaves put on their heads, often striking their heads with their hands." (Dampier, in Pinkerton 1886: 162-163)

Traveling south, Dampier next encountered what he referred to as Anthony Cave's Island (called Tanga today). Many canoes came out to the ships, signaling to Dampier to come on shore. Dampier wrote,

> ... Though we had steered to keep under the high island [Malendok] yet we were driven to the flat one [Boang]. At this time 3 of the natives came on board. I gave each of them a knife, a looking glass and a string of beads. I showed them pumpkins and cocoa nut shells and made signs to them to bring some aboard and presently had 3 cocoa nuts out of one of the canoes. I showed them nutmegs and by their signs I guessed they had some on the island. I also showed them some gold dust, which they seemed to know and called out "Manneel, Manneel" and pointed towards the land. (Dampier 1770, in Pinkerton 1886: 164-166)

The words "maneel, maneel" are the formal words of greeting extended to strangers coming from other islands. (Robert Foster, personal communication) This was an invitation to Dampier to come ashore. Dampier further noted, "Awhile after these men were gone, two or three canoes came from the flat island at which the others seemed displeased and used very menacing gestures and I believe speeches to each other...." (Dampier 1770 in Pinkerton 1886:166) Once again, Dampier endeavored to initiate exchange by giving gifts and showing people what he wanted, though he received little in return. He deduced from their behavior that the Tangan Islanders understood what he desired in exchange. There seems to have been competition between the men of the two islands, who may, in fact, have been traditional enemies to one another, over access to Dampier's ship.

Dampier continued to sail south, southeast. As he rounded the headland, which he named Cape St. George, he noted, "... A huge black Man came off to us in a Canoa, but would not come aboard. He made the same signs of Friendship to us, as the rest we had met with; yet seem'd to differ in his Language, not using any of those words which the others did. We saw neither Smaoks nor Plantations near this Headland." (Dampier 1981: 213) Dampier was the first European to recognize that the Bismarck Archipelago was separate from the mainland of New Guinea. He gave the name "Nova-Britannia" to both New Ireland and New Britain, since he considered them to be a single island.

Dampier used the same phrases in describing the various groups of men he encountered in the New Ireland area, implying that he saw this area as having a common culture. Dampier's description of the New Irelanders, in contrast to that of Tasman, indicates that he found their appearance "well limbed" and "agreeable enough," though dying the hair, painting the face, and wearing a bone through the nasal septum, he felt, were disfiguring. Their signs of friendship seem to have been the same. He described the difference between proas and canoes and admired the "ingenious fancy" of their art and their skill at carving and in making their canoes in the absence of iron implements. He also noted that the islands were densely populated and thick with garden sites. In characterizing the New Irelanders, Dampier tended more towards detailed objective description and was less inclined than earlier explorers to use the European cultural stereotypes of "Noble Savage" or "Wild Man."

Phillip Carteret

The New Ireland area was visited by Phillip Carteret, in 1767. Carteret was commander of the sloop "Swallow," part of an expedition under Captain Wallis, chartered by the Earl of Egmont, First Lord of the Admiralty, to search for lands thought to lie between Cape Horn and New Zealand in the Southern Seas. After the expedition negotiated the Straits of Magellan, Captain Wallis sailed off in the faster vessel "Dolphin," leaving the smaller "Swallow" behind. Carteret, undaunted, decided to strike out on his own across the Pacific. Reaching New Ireland, he spent seven days near Cape St. George replenishing supplies but not encountering any people. While in this location, Carteret's men gathered coconuts, and the tops of coconut palms, which they called "cabbages," from an area containing "…between three & foure hundred of those Trees, well loaded with Nuts; … many of them were differently marked, and that there were some few Huts about them but no Inhabitants; [Carteret notes] This was a plain proof to me that they could not be far off." (Carteret 1965, Vol.1: 182-183)

Though Carteret remained in the general area for seven days, no one came out to his ship or appeared on the shore. He was afraid that, as he had cut down some of their marked trees, the New Irelanders would take their revenge on him and his men. Fear might have kept the inhabitants out of sight, or they may have been temporarily in bush settlements inland. The marked trees, loaded with nuts, may well have been tabooed to allow accumulation for a feast. Carteret was well aware that his men had cut down someone else's coconut trees and taken their coconuts, to which they had no right and for which no recompense was paid. Further up the coast, he entered another harbor where his men collected another 1,000 coconuts from marked trees, without seeing any people.

The strong northwest current he encountered after he left the harbor suggested to him that he was not in a bay at all. He found himself in a large strait separating two islands. He named the northern one "Nova Hibernia," that is, New Ireland, while the southern one retained the name given it by Dampier, "Nova Britannia," or New Britain.

Off the northwest coast of New Ireland, opposite Djaul Island, Carteret's ship was becalmed, and

> ...A little way to the Westward of it 9 or 10 Canoes come off to us from Nova Hibernia In which there might be about 150 men they come close alongside so as to hand things from one another on a long stick but they would non of them come onboard, we got a few tryfling things from them in lieu of others, they seemed to be very fond of all Kinds of iron and other Such things as mentioned before [beads, ribbons, mirrors and cloth], Some of their Canoes are very Nicely built very long and narrow with one out Rigger, One of these canoes was almost as long as our ship & it must have been between 80 and 90 foot long, made out of one Tree [it had] hadsom carved ornaments about it, there was 33 men in her all their Canoes was road with paddles,... their fishing Nets, and rope are good and well made the Armes they had with them were the spears and long sticks... they did not seem to have any metals... they are the black wooly headed Negroes... and go quite naked not a bit of covering over Any part of the body except a few ornaments of their own making [shell ornaments according to Hawksworth 1773] about their Arms & legs, but seem to take great pride in their beard which some of them had very large ones powdered with white powder as well as their wooly heads I know not if these People have any knowledge of

fire Arms, ... they keep a constant look out after our guns as if they had apprehended danger from them." (Carteret 1965, Vol.1: 191-192)

Caution seems to have characterized the one encounter that Carteret had with the people of Djaul Island, off the coast of New Ireland. He wanted to trade with them but had only a few things to give, and got only "tryfling things" in return. The New Irelanders communicated to Carteret that they desired anything made of iron, with which they had become familiar by this time, as well as the other things he offered. Carter*et al.*so commented on the appearance of the New Ireland men. The absence of clothing, the powdering of hair and beard with white lime, and the use of shell ornaments and feathers for decoration made the New Irelanders appear strikingly different to him. He was impressed with their canoes and the fact that they had a canoe made from a single tree which carried thirty-three men and which was almost as long as his ship. Though they carried weapons with them, they made no attempt to attack the ship, but they were not willing to board it. Carteret concluded that they were knowledgeable about Europeans and guns, since they kept looking at the ship's cannons. Though both sides were wary, no hostile action took place.

Louis Antoine de Bougainville

Less than a year later, Louis Antoine de Bougainville was to pass through the area. Bougainville was born in Paris in 1729. He was a well-educated man who had published a treatise on calculus in 1755; and as a soldier, had served as Aide-de-Camp to Montcalm in Canada, where he had direct experience with the Huron. He then switched to the naval service and soon became a captain. Later, Bougainville embarked on a voyage around the world under the auspices of the king of France, whose purpose "…was to search for new lands suitable for colonization, to open up a new route to China, and to seek spice-plants to be taken to Ile de France." (Spate 1986:95) The need to regain prestige lost in the defeat in Canada also served as a spur for France and for Bougainville himself.

Bougainville left France in November 1766, going westward around the Horn of South America and out into the Pacific. He visited Tahiti, where, as we noted earlier, he was taken with the nobility of the Tahitians. After going as far west as the Great Barrier Reef of Australia, he turned east, going as far as Bougainville, and headed west again to the southern tip of New Ireland. His ships were in need of repairs, his men were ill with scurvy, and food supplies were low. So Bougainville anchored in a harbor which he named Port Praslin (named Gower Harbour by Carteret). There he found a sign which Carteret had left nailed to a tree, as well as the remains of the latter's camp, a native canoe and indications of native habitation. (Bougainville 1967 [1769]: 326) Bougainville spent eight days in this harbor repairing the ship but was unable to find food to replenish his supplies.

He then proceeded around the southern tip of New Ireland and up the east coast. The ships were probably near Namatanai four days later, when they were visited by seven canoes [periaguas]. Bougainville's description of the events of that day notes the men's nudity and their body decorations in ways these had been described by previous European explorers. The Europeans sought to exchange trinkets for supplies and tried to entice the New Irelanders to board the ship, while the New Irelanders wanted the Europeans to land on shore. Bougainville then wrote that,

> The next day there came a much greater number of them, who made no difficulty of coming along-side the ship. One of their conductors, who seemed to be the chief, carried a staff about two or

three feet long, painted red, with a knob at each end, which, in approaching us, he raised with both hands over his head, and continued some time in that attitude. All these negroes seem to be dressed in their best....We were desirous of forming an intercourse in order to engage them to bring us some refreshments, but their treachery soon convinced us that we could not succeed in that attempt....They strove to seize what was offered them, and would give nothing in exchange. We could scarce get a few roots of yams from them; therefore we left off giving them, and they retired....

Upon the whole it seemed that the visits they made us these two last days had been with no other view than to reconnoitre us and to concert a plan of attack. [On the following day, the New Irelanders launched a concerted attack with stones and arrows on the smaller of Bougainville's vessels] ....The action was short for one platoon disconcerted their scheme, many threw themselves into the sea and some periaguas were abandoned. (Bougainville 1967 [1769]: 342-345)

This encounter is what we know about Bougainville's interaction with the New Irelanders. At this point we know that he is desperately in need of supplies, and he himself says that he is eager to exchange some of the goods that he carries for food and water. The New Irelanders' invitation for Bougainville to come ashore was in line with their rules of exchange. Outsiders coming by ship to visit and exchange would have always landed on shore, where they were received and then the exchange would take place on shore. From Bougainville's description it would appear that the New Irelanders came out to the ships dressed as for war. This was probably in order only to show strength, since such a show of strength in the form of a mock show of aggression is known to typically occur in connection with welcoming outsiders who come to exchange. And applying the decoration and adornment used for warfare is a frequent accompaniment of exchange elsewhere in Melanesia.

Exchanges often are carried out with groups who are in the category of traditional enemies. Even though hostilities of a minor sort occurred on the first day, when the New Irelanders tried to entice Bougainville to come onshore, when the New Irelanders returned on the second day in larger numbers, there still was a possibility of carrying out exchange. The lack of success in exchange on the second day led to the attack at daybreak on the third. This attack could be interpreted as an attempt either to overwhelm the ships or just to drive them away.

During his stay in North America, Bougainville had observed the Huron, who served as the model of the Noble Savage for Voltaire and Rousseau. To Bougainville, a sophisticated intellectual who had read Rousseau, Tahiti represented a Paradise. In fact, the Tahitian Ahutoru was on his way to France at the time Bougainville visited New Ireland. From his description of them and his interaction with them, we can see that the naked, "wooly haired black men" of New Ireland who attacked him appeared to Bougainville as Wild Men in comparison to the "Noble" Tahitians.

Evidence of New Irelanders' Views

Between 1615 and 1800, five European expeditions which visited New Ireland left records of their experiences with the inhabitants. What was the impact on the New Irelanders of the visits of Europeans to their shores during these two centuries? The encounters, though sometimes of a violent nature, were short-lived. For almost two hundred years, the New Irelanders seem to have responded to Europeans in much the same way throughout this time. The Europeans tried to entice them to bring supplies by offering them trinkets, but they were not interested in exchanging until the Europeans began to offer them iron². The New Irelanders had a form of greeting which was uniformly used and recognized throughout the region. This gesture of greeting, which transcended linguistic differences, was used with strangers of all kinds. This was the gesture of greeting made towards the Europeans. Schouten, Dampier and Bougainville reported that people came out in canoes and held clubs over their heads or touched their heads. In two of the three cases this was followed by New Ireland behavior indicating that they wanted the Europeans to come ashore, since this would have been appropriate behavior for New Irelanders interested in exchange. None of the Europeans accepted the invitations to come ashore. The New Irelanders would have interpreted this refusal as an unfriendly gesture. They then, in some cases, attacked.

What was the New Irelanders' view, in general, of this succession of events? Had they provided us with their view on the arrival of the Europeans, they might have said the following: "Strange looking men came to our shores. We welcomed them with the greeting that all men understand, and we invited them to land. They did not seem to acknowledge our greeting and did not accept our invitation to come ashore. Their strangeness made our usual kind of reception and interaction with them impossible. They seemed menacing to us and we wanted them to leave, and so we attacked them."

New Irelanders did become aware of the power of guns, the massiveness of European ships compared to their own, and the usefulness of iron. Europeans had now to be included in the category of humans. Their very different appearance and their clothing, ships, guns, and other material objects had to be incorporated within expanded New Ireland cultural categories or placed within newly created sub-categories.

Discussion

The Europeans brought their own ways of viewing Others, depicted in the previous chapter, to their experiences with New Irelanders. The explorers were always on their guard and expected that they might be attacked at any moment by those they saw as fierce groups of armed "savages." To the fully clothed Europeans, the nakedness of the New Irelanders provided a dramatic contrast. If, to the Europeans, the Tahitians and Tongans represented Noble Savages, then the people of the Solomon Islands and New Ireland represented Wild Men and the "brutish" Other. The Tongans at first welcomed the Europeans and gave them food, and as a consequence they called the place the Friendly Islands. The Tahitians not only boarded the ships of the Europeans, but some trusted Europeans sufficiently to allow themselves to be taken to Europe. While the Polynesians seem to have welcomed the Europeans, the New Irelanders, perhaps sensing the Europeans' fear of them, were distrustful; and after initially curious encounters, they were frequently attacked. The view of Polynesians as Noble and Melanesians as Wild Men presaged a later classification developed by Dumont d'Urville as a result of his own voyages in the Pacific, which we will discuss in the following chapter. In his classification, the Polynesians were seen as civilized, "more like us," while the dark-skinned Melanesians were seen as uncouth, disagreeable and barbaric.

NOTES

1. It is labeled, "Thus appears the Vessel of Noua guinea and People Dwelling therein," since Tasman thought that the island of New Ireland was part of New Guinea. [Editor's note: According to the Metropolitan Museum of Art, the drawing was done in 1643. (https://www.metmuseum.org/toah/ht/09/ocm.html)]

2. Schouten and Tasman seem only to have had successful exchanges in places in the Pacific where there were chiefs, as in Tonga (the Friendly Islands) and Fiji. One might advance the hypothesis that successful extensive exchanges took place only where there were chiefs who facilitated the process. Where there were no chiefs, but only independent villages with Big Men, as was the case in New Ireland, exchange was much more difficult.

5. BETWEEN BEACH AND SHIP: THE DEVELOPMENT OF EXCHANGE WITHIN THE LIMINAL AREA

During the first part of the nineteenth century, many different types of voyagers traveled along the coast of New Ireland, and encounters between New Irelanders and Europeans, became much more common. A regular pattern of exchange between Europeans and New Irelanders was developing, but European exploitation of the commercial possibilities of the New Ireland region had not yet begun.

Mrs. William Kent accompanied her husband, the Captain of the H.M.S. Buffalo, in the year 1803 on a trip from Sydney to Calcutta. In letters she wrote to her mother while near Feni and Tanga, she described the New Irelanders through her female eyes. She noted on July 3, 1803, that "Four canoes came off with six Natives in two of them and four in each of the others.... A silk handkerchief being thrown they ventured near enough to pick it up. Staid a few minutes and then returned as fast as possible to the shore."

They had come merely to gratify their curiosity without bringing even a Coca Nut. They were large athletic people of a dark copper colour and entirely naked.... Altho I am not without suspicion of their being cannibals from the circumstances of there being among the curiositys I collected two human bones. One of these, a large arm bone is fixed as a handle to a Spear with six rows of human teeth round it. I am afraid to tell you my cabin is ornamented with this relic, least you should think I am turned cannibal too.... Well! but these said Giants that deal in human bones favored us with their company almost the whole of yesterday and I could not help observing that every part of their pretty person - were totally neglected but their precious heads on which they bestow a world of pains. (Kent 1803 Vol. 4: 30-31)

This is the first example of artifact collection, which became of increasing importance later in the nineteenth century.

Mrs. Kent assumed that the New Irelanders were cannibals from the human arm bone attached as a handle to the spear she collected. This is the same kind of spear which Schouten included in his word list almost two hundred years earlier. Mrs. Kent portrayed the New Irelanders, for the first time, as Noble Savages. These "copper-colored, athletic giants" were perhaps to her reminiscent of the classic age. But this idea was coupled with the menacing notion of them as cannibals and Wild Men.

The Duperrey Expedition

The Duperrey Expedition, the first scientific expedition to visit New Ireland, arrived at Port Praslin, in the south of New Ireland, on August 11, 1823. The expedition had crossed the Pacific from east to west, intending to explore Easter Island, the Society Islands, Micronesia, and New Guinea. Extensive publications resulted from this expedition, including the first detailed "ethnographic" account of the inhabitants of New Ireland by the expedition's naturalist, Lesson[1]. He had joined the French Navy as an Assistant Surgeon, but his official role in the expedition was as pharmacist and botanist. Lesson's observations are clearly framed within the natural history approach. In contrast to earlier visitors, Lesson spent time exploring on shore. As he presented his observations of New Ireland, he also recorded its profound effects upon him, a mixture of pleasure, sadness and unease. Lesson observed:

> ... We had scarcely arrived when the Corvette Coquille called us to assemble because the islanders had blockaded the entrance of the bay with a small pirogue containing seven naked black men; these blacks slowly came up to us, speaking loudly, and placed their hands on their heads; we imitated this gesture; they appeared to express friendship and immediately came alongside our vessel and did not hesitate to come on board. Everything about them proclaimed that they had already associated with Europeans because they knew the practice of firearms and evidenced a lively fear of their power; moreover, they continued to admire iron and appreciated its usefulness and this metal was the most precious prize which one could be in a position to give them by way of exchange. These blacks, as a token of their good intentions, had come without arms, all they carry with them are some articles of exchange of little value such as roots, a small number of "caribbean cabbages" and several bunches of bananas, but they appear enchanting in their person and noble in the arrangement of their appearance. If our pale and colorless faces seemed strange to them, it must be recognized that their black and oily skin, their head hair, disheveled and covered with a very red ochre dissolved in fish oil, forming a thick cement on their heads, gave their complete nudity a very singular aspect; adding to this ensemble, a stick placed through the nasal septum and white bars on the face enhanced by a red powder covering the cheek bones. The iron utensils and small mirrors that were given to them completely

satisfied them .... We asked coconuts of them, but they responded that they had some only at their village. (Lesson 1839, Vol.2: 11-15)[2]

Later, Lesson wrote,

> Two new pirogues had arrived, one of them a large war craft carrying about fifty men... and did not appear to contain arms unless the natives concealed them with great care.... They were sufficiently honest in their trading and asked of us as the price of their commodities [coconuts, bananas, yams, poultry and pigs] a piece of iron; the rings of wine casks, broken into pieces and sharpened to a point, formed the money which we paid for the fruits destined for the crew. Our new friends were nevertheless skillful as thieves, for they took possession with dexterity of all that offered itself to their convenience; but it is necessary to add, that they made restitution as soon as one imposed on them the necessity of the object they had taken away, and this restitution created no sense of shame in them.... On the day of the 14th... the islanders came [with]... young dogs which they offered to us for our table. They also sold us living phalangers [marsupials] which they had painstakingly muzzled, ... taking the precaution of breaking their feet. The meat of this particular quadraped, giving off a strong sort of aroma, is considered very tasty by our friends the Papouas. The market had been established in the "porte-haubans" as a neutral territory, and some natives who had recently come through the mountains, provided the first idea of their village to us and we exchanged chickens and pigs, for which they demanded an exorbitant price. This proves that these animals must be rare to them. (Lesson 1839, Vol.2: 15-23)

BETWEEN BEACH AND SHIP: THE DEVELOPMENT OF EXCHANGE

By the time of the Duperrey expedition in 1823, exchanges between Europeans and New Irelanders were usually transacted from canoes alongside the ship. New Irelanders had given up attempts to have Europeans come on shore to exchange. They knew what the Europeans desired in order to replenish their supplies. They had grasped that Europeans wanted only live animals, not butchered and cooked meat. The New Irelanders were also aware of what the French had, which they strongly desired to receive in exchange: iron. They were delighted with the sharpened pieces of wine-cask rings, the iron utensils, and the small mirrors which the French gave them. A scale of exchange values was in the process of being established, since Lesson commented that "exorbitant prices" were demanded by the New Irelanders for some things. They had begun to perceive the Europeans as a new kind of exchange partner, towards whom one behaved differently than towards those from other islands in the region who came to exchange. The Europeans were also the source of new kinds of goods which they readily incorporated into their category of exchange goods, and which they eagerly sought. Lesson sees the New Irelanders as honest traders, but they took things and showed no shame when forced to return them.

The New Irelanders were aware of firearms, were frightened of them, and fully accepted the superiority of European weaponry. They no longer brought arms with them, that is, sling stones and clubs, but, instead, expressed friendly intentions by their usual gesture of friendship, which Lesson correctly interpreted and imitated. The villagers were at this point more receptive to interaction with Europeans who appeared friendly and accepting of them. People were willing to escort Blosseville to their village, Likiliki. They allowed him to witness ritual activity including the dance of a *dukduk* figure and permitted him to enter their "Idol House," which contained large carved figures. Lesson described the New Irelanders as "enchanting" and "noble in appearance," echoing Mrs. Kent's description in contrast to the description of many of the earlier explorers, who seemed to perceive the New Irelanders only as savage brutes and Wild Men.

M.J. Dumont d'Urville

Dumont d'Urville had been Executive Officer of the expedition led by his friend Duperrey. Born in 1790, the son of an aristocratic judge, he was well educated. Inspired by voyages of discovery, he joined the French Navy at age seventeen. On his return to France with Duperrey, he planned his own voyage of exploration to the southern Pacific. He was sponsored by the Naval Ministry and was given the ship "Astrolabe." On July 6, 1827, he anchored in Carteret Harbor in the south of New Ireland and fired his cannon to announce his presence. Several men came out and exchanged a fish and a phalanger for iron. (d'Urville 1832, vol.4: 500) The next day, two men came aboard the ship, and d'Urville observed,

> ...One is a man about forty to forty-five years old and the other a young man of eighteen years. Both are completely nude, black, and of an unpleasant exterior. Their hair is frizzy, the nasal septum pierced with a bone. These two savages show neither intelligence nor liveliness, nor are they capable of curiousity about new objects which are shown to them. They appear greedy for iron, but not at all disposed to make the least advance to us in order to obtain it. We tried in vain to explain to them in all possible ways that if they would bring us pigs, fish, cocos, yams, and bananas, they would receive iron in abundance. (d'Urville 1832, vol.4: 505)

BETWEEN BEACH AND SHIP: THE DEVELOPMENT OF EXCHANGE

d'Urville found that his men could not obtain supplies themselves from the area around Carteret Harbor, so they increased their efforts to gain foodstuffs from the New Irelanders. When men came on board on the following day, d'Urville attempted to explain to them that he was prepared to pay dearly for supplies, and they promised to bring pigs and fruit the next day.

d'Urville was skeptical about this, writing that, "...Their ways are hardly tolerable; I think them very miserable. Their stupidity, their indolence, and their apathy proclaim neither a people who are cultivators, nor even one disposed to hunting and fishing." (d'Urville 1832, vol.4: 507-508) However, d'Urville was proven wrong, for on the following day several men arrived in two canoes to exchange green bananas, taro, yams, and a single small pig for an ax. According to d'Urville, "These islanders wish to receive only iron axes and material (fabric) in their exchanges; yet they prove to be very difficult and very demanding in their transactions." (d'Urville 1832, vol.4: 510)

In his description of the people, d'Urville noted that they seemed to be very poor, since they did not have the large canoes that he had seen earlier at Port Praslin. Nor did they wear the beautiful tridacna bracelets which he had seen before. "These men, despite their hideous aspect and their dirtiness, show themselves to be gentle and submissive, and without doubt timid. On the other hand their inclination to steal is very great and their mistrust excessive. They did not want to show us where to find their houses; and Ms. Gaimard [the natural historian and philologist of the voyage] had vainly exhausted all the means of charm necessary to try to get them to take him to their village." (d'Urville 1832, vol.4: 511) Nonetheless, Dr. Gaimard was able to collect a word list in Carteret Harbor of the Siar language. (Beaumont 1972: 30)

By this time, 1827, the people of New Ireland were accustomed to having European ships desirous of reprovisioning with fresh supplies anchored in their harbors. They would bring coconuts, yams and pigs in their canoes out to the ship only if they got in return the things they desired, mainly iron. d'Urville saw them as niggardly in their exchanging, but from their point of view they surely were acting as sharp traders. They would rather hold on to their provisions than let them go for less than they considered them to be worth, or for things that they did not desire, a pattern of haggling different from their own way of exchange.

Two Frenchmen, Lesson and d'Urville, came to New Ireland on the Duperrey expedition (d'Urville also came a second time), and claimed to be objective observers describing its inhabitants. Lesson saw them as "noble in the arrangement of their appearance" and "enchanting in their person," while d'Urville saw them as very miserable, stupid and indolent. Clearly their differing points of view overrode their seeming scientific objectivity and produced contradictory pictures. d'Urville's depiction of the New Irelanders as the lowest form of humanity, without the capacity to cultivate, hunt, or fish, reflects his disdainful attitude. His character was described by Lesson as based on "... a deep contempt for the human species." (Lesson, cited in d'Urville 1988:xlvii)

As an educated man, d'Urville was likely to have been familiar with the evolutionary thinking of Turgot and Condorcet. d'Urville classified the peoples of the Pacific into Polynesians, Micronesians, Malaysians and Melanesians, in a way that reflected this evolutionary point of view. A two-fold racial division was presented in the first volume prepared by the zoologists Quoy and Gaimard, and edited by d'Urville. (Quoy and Gaimard 1830: 17-35) Adopted from Johann Forster, it identified first the "yellow" race (which Forster had labeled "white") as found in Polynesia and Micronesia, on the islands of New Zealand, the Friendly Islands (Tonga), other Polynesian

BETWEEN BEACH AND SHIP: THE DEVELOPMENT OF EXCHANGE

islands and the Carolines. Its members were characterized by handsome body build and great moral strength.

The second racial category was the "black" race, which was said to be distinct from the "negro" race of Africa. This included the population of New Holland (Australia), New Guinea (who were referred to as "Papouas"), and islands east of New Guinea including New Ireland. They were seen as being in a simple state. The New Irelanders were presented as typical of this race and described as entirely nude, not very industrious, distrustful and wretched. This racial classification of peoples of the Pacific, with "Noble" Polynesians at the top and the "Wild" Melanesians at the bottom was in keeping with the natural history approach of the time, classifying different populations into "biological" types along with mammals and other life forms. d'Urville's racist thinking, in the guise of a scientific approach, represented the expansion of the idea of the Wild Man and an eclipse of the Noble Savage. The prejudice which placed "civilized" Europeans at the top of the hierarchy, Polynesians beneath them, and the black-skinned Others at the bottom, thus was given pseudo-scientific support.

Increased Frequency of Contact: Whalers and Traders

By 1830, frequency of contact between New Irelanders and outsiders had increased, as various countries sponsored nautical surveys and scientific expeditions in the Pacific Ocean. Captain Benjamin Morrell appears to have been the first American to visit New Ireland. Morrell arrived at St. George Channel between New Britain and New Ireland on November 4, 1830. The presence of resources which he thought to have market value was primary in his mind as he sailed up the channel. The trade in sandalwood had developed in the Pacific by this time, due to the enormous demand from the Chinese for this commodity, and Morrell was looking for it. He saw and remarked upon hard woods (but not sandalwood), bêche-de-mer, pearl oysters, the hawkesbill tortoise, red coral, and ambergris.

By this time, the New Irelanders were eager to trade, and Morrell needed to replenish supplies. He noted that, "In the course of the day, we hove-to several times to permit the canoes from New Ireland to come alongside with their coconuts, plantains, bananas, yams and fowls which we purchased for small pieces of iron hoop, and a few China beads." (Morrell 1832: 454) Exchange between New Irelanders and visitors had become so common that Morrell observed, "Wood, water and fruit of the best quality may be obtained with ease at any of the harbours on the west side of the island; and in some of the ports you may purchase hogs and poultry at your own price." (Morrell 1832: 455)

Morrell described the New Irelanders admiringly, and observed that, "Their countenances are generally intelligent and expressive of considerable mental capacity." (1832: 454) His wife, Abby Jane, accompanied him on his voyage around the world, and she published her own account, which was identical to her husband's. However, she saw the New Irelanders as Mrs. Kent did, remarking that, "Few people that I have seen are better formed than these islanders...." (Morrell 1833: 73-74)

Morrell's account was the first to view New Ireland's natural resources in terms of their potential for economic exploitation. This market orientation would become dominant later in the nineteenth century. After the massacre of some of his men in the Solomons, Capt. Morrell was wary, and he remained content to do his exploration from his ship.

BETWEEN BEACH AND SHIP: THE DEVELOPMENT OF EXCHANGE

At the end of the eighteenth century, English and American whalers moved into the South Pacific and by the first decades of the nineteenth century, whaling had become an important activity in this area. American sailors looked down on whalers as "stinkpots." A whaler under American registry might include a crew of Portuguese, African-Americans, other Americans, Dutchmen, Frenchmen, Britishers, Spaniards and Pacific Islanders, including Maoris, Marquesans, Tahitians, and especially Hawaiians. (Chatterton 1925:103; Dodge 1965:33, 47) The captains commanding such crews were described as "...well-to-do, retired Quaker skippers of the most strict narrow-mindedness,... Puritanical personality... strong, independent, fanatically conservative, [and]... of an enclosed kind of piety." (Chatterton 1925:100-101) The search for whales took both British and American whaling vessels into the waters around New Ireland, a major feeding area for whales. The whalers sought supplies from the islanders[3].

Thomas Beale, who was a surgeon on two English vessels hunting sperm whales from 1830 to 1832, provided an account of contact with New Irelanders[4]. On January 29, 1832, his ship was off of St. John's Island (Feni). By this time a regular pattern of trade between islanders and sailors had developed.

> ...Two boats were sent on shore on the south side of Saint John's Island to endeavour to procure some yams from its inhabitants, - and we had no sooner got within a half a ship's length of the shore than we saw one of the natives wading towards us with a small basket containing ten or a dozen bulbous roots, somewhat resembling a potato, and which we afterwards found was not much inferior in taste. When he arrived near the boat, we gave him a piece of old iron hoop about four inches long for them, with which he appeared delighted,

and scampering off to the shore, he soon spread wide his great success among his fellow countrymen, who immediately followed his example, and in about two hours we had half filled our boat with these roots, and having consumed our stock of old iron, were obliged to return to the ship for a further supply.... When we again drew near to the shore, we perceived that a very great number of people had congregated upon it, most of whom were waiting with their baskets of potatoes ready for exchange: ...They soon made a rush towards our boats, and the commodities were exchanged on both sides with great celerity." (Beale 1839: 319-320)

Beale noted that, "...they traded with great good-will and fairness." (Beale 1839: 322) On the following day, the New Irelanders reappeared to "barter" again, but this time they came freshly decorated and carrying their weapons. Beale sees the people of Feni as "bold" and "warlike," "easily excited to quarrel" and "dextrous in handling weapons." He notes, "Several tall and warlike-looking fellows, armed with enormous clubs and long spears, took possession of the beach from the first of the morning, and watched all of our proceedings with a rather jealous eye, not seeming to wish us to land." (Beale 1839: 322-323)

The Beale account contains the first recorded observations of New Ireland women. They were sighted behind some trees, and the sailors were not sure at first whether they were men or women. When the sailors moved their boat closer, the men on the beach made the women leave. When the boat was about to leave, the women reappeared. Beale held out a necklace of large glass beads. One young woman rushed through the water to the boat and Beale put it around her neck. Beale noted, "She wore no clothes whatever, but she appeared exceedingly coy, and much aggitated, no doubt from the novelty of her situation. She was young, and her features, though not beautiful, were exceedingly interesting; and, altogether, she was said by all of us to be a pretty girl." (Beale 1839: 326)

New Irelanders were now aware of the commodities which the Europeans sought; and the Europeans understood that, more than anything, the New Irelanders desired hoop iron. The amounts of food being exchanged were much larger now, and many more New Irelanders were involved. Both sides seemed satisfied with what they received in exchange. There was an atmosphere of good will, and Beale noted that the New Irelanders traded with fairness. While the Europeans remained "on their guard," the New Irelanders were not particularly cautious, though Beale observes that there were several tall, heavily armed men guarding the beach. These men were probably clan warriors, and the message they communicated was: don't land.

In earlier encounters, the New Irelanders seemed to be trying to frame exchanges with Europeans within their conceptualization of ceremonial exchange. By this time, however, a new pattern of exchange with European outsiders had developed: barter, transacted in a neutral area -- neither onshore nor on the ship, but in the liminal area in between. The presence of warriors on the beach restricted the exchange to this border area.

Though the New Irelanders were no longer trying to fit Europeans into the category of inter-island exchangers, some of the behavior which was part of that pattern, namely elaborate body decoration, continued. The weaponry they carried was probably less for protection, but worn because it was a part of the traditional attire worn during exchange ceremonies. From Schouten's description to Beale's, no foreign items seem to have been added to the attire of the New Irelanders. Though iron was being traded with great frequency, it does not seem to have been used in weaponry.

Castaways

Whalers could be away from their home ports for as long as three or even four years. Sailors frequently jumped ship. As a consequence, castaways were to be found in the New Ireland area. Dispatches to the Governor of New South Wales in 1840 noted that, "...There are European and American seamen at present domiciled on the Admiralty Islands, on New Ireland, New Georgia.... [p.825]...The majority of Europeans scattered about the islands is undoubtedly composed of seamen who have deserted from or been wrecked in whalers." (Dispatches to the Secretary of State 1840:825-827) The motives of castaways who remained on Pacific islands varied. They frequently had a great impact on events and the culture of the people they lived with.

John Coulter's experiences on New Ireland were greatly enriched by his encounter with a castaway from an English whaler. Coulter was a physician on the vessel Hound on its voyage around the world in 1834-1836. In 1835, after sailing along the east coast of New Ireland, the ship entered a deep harbor. A canoe came out carrying two men, one of them, described by Coulter as "of most commanding appearance," who he assumed was "the king or the chief." The other was an English-speaking white man, draped in a native mat cloak, but otherwise naked. This man, Thomas Manners, a native of London, had been a sailor on a whaler until he tired of the sea-going life and had been landed at his own request on New Ireland ten years earlier. He had been given four wives by Boolooma, the local leader ("king"), one of them being Boolooma's daughter. (Coulter 1847, vol.1: 244-246) Using Manners as an interpreter, the Hound's captain made arrangements to trade for supplies. On Manners' advice, he and the crew remained aboard ship, while Coulter came ashore "under the protection of the king's son." Boolooma placed a taboo on Coulter and his gun by tying sinnet around the gun and around Coulter's neck[5].

BETWEEN BEACH AND SHIP: THE DEVELOPMENT OF EXCHANGE

At the time of Coulter's visit, the people were in the midst of warfare with enemies in another district. Coulter participated in a raid to retrieve three captured prisoners. Their party attacked, recaptured the prisoners, and was then, in turn, attacked by the more numerous enemy group. Recognizing that his group was outnumbered, Coulter fired both barrels of his gun into the crowd. "This new instrument of warfare, both in effect and sound, at once staggered them." (Coulter 1847, vol.1: 287) Coulter's intervention enabled the group to safely extricate themselves. The next day, instead of returning home by the original route, they moved on into a "very wild looking district that was inhabited by a friendly tribe." The village of these allies was at the head of a valley which opened out to the sea. The party returned home by sea, going past the bay belonging to a hostile group. There they were attacked by a much larger force of canoes, and Coulter again fired his gun, killing several people. The checkerboard pattern of enemies and allies discussed in Chapter 2 is what Coulter was describing.

As a result of accusations of "thievery" by the captain, Manners suggested that they depart to avoid the possibility of unpleasant hostilities. The ship then left the bay and moved up the east coast of New Ireland. Several other attempts were made to trade with people further up the coast, "…but not having the advantage of an interpreter, our visits were sometimes misconstrued, and every indication of hostility shown to us.." (Coulter 1847, vol.2: 30-31) Clearly, the new pattern of exchange had developed in some places and not in others[6].

Manners was used by the captain as an intermediary to carry out trade, making this enterprise much easier than in previous cases. Maude points out that "beachcombers," or castaways, frequently served as intermediaries, facilitating trade with Europeans who visited, and that in other areas of the

Pacific beachcombers had taught islanders the function of money. (Maude 1964:268,270)[7]. Manners shared many characteristics of those Europeans who ended up on Pacific Islands as castaways or beachcombers. Maude notes,

> This peculiar position of the beachcomber, in and out of the indigenous society made him an excellent mediator... the interpreter of one culture to another....The beachcomber narratives make it clear that above all they were expected to expound at gatherings large and small on the nature of the white man's country, his customs, religion, economic system, and technology. Crude though many of these explanations may have been they were at least given by someone fluent in the local language who, in contrast to his successors, had no particular ax to grind and no vested interest in change himself. (Maude 1964:276)

It is likely that Manners played this role in the New Ireland village where he lived.

Manners' presence in this village undoubtedly enabled Boolooma to become more powerful than other political leaders in the area. In his discussion of the political system, Coulter described it as a "true despotism." The chief was said to have the right to "levy troops," and men responded willingly to his request. This portrayal of the power of the chief probably represents a combination of the effect of Manner's presence on Boolooma's position plus Coulter's typical European expectation of finding chiefs. When Coulter visited an allied village in a different district, he remarked on the absence of chiefs or leaders, since no one separated himself out from the rest of the population to greet him.

BETWEEN BEACH AND SHIP: THE DEVELOPMENT OF EXCHANGE

Maude points out that in other parts of the Pacific where there were chieftainships -- places such as Hawaii, Tonga, and Fiji, some chiefs used the military knowledge of castaways to their great advantage in helping them to develop proto-states. (Maude 1964) This was clearly not the case in New Ireland, which was characterized by a different form of political organization. Nevertheless, it is clear that Boolooma used his castaway, Manners, to gain political advantage over other leaders of the district. This presages what would happen later, when New Ireland leaders attempted to use European traders, missionaries, and government officials to increase their own political power.

Whalers' Reports

Though there were many whalers in the waters off New Ireland during the period from 1820 to1850, most only recorded sighting New Ireland in their ships' logs, and did not mention interaction with the New Irelanders. An exception was Eldred Fyshe, surgeon on the barque "Coronet," out of Nantucket, who kept the ship's log. (P.M.B.375) During the month of February 1838 the "Coronet" killed three whales in the sea between Gardener's Island (Tabar) and New Ireland. Fyshe's log described the following incident:

> While cruising here, every day that we stood in towards land several canoes came off to us and the natives brought with them cocoa Nuts, yams, taro, sugar cane, arrow root, spears, clubs, shells, tortoise shell, nets, calabashes, and various other articles, which they gave for small pieces of [iron] hoop, balls of cotton. stripes of red shirt, and such like things.... They seem to be of a friendly disposition and not at all suspicious. and are certainly one of the finest race of beings I ever beheld.... We sold the natives whale's flesh for cocoa-

nuts and they seemed to like it very well. On the 10th, I went on shore at Gardener's Island [Tabar] ... and began trading with the natives.... I certainly had a very narrow escape here .... One of the crew lit a pipe and began smoking. No sooner did the natives see this than those who were unarmed made off and those who had Spears levelled them at us. I soon saw the cause and told the man to leave off smoking. He did so, and threw the pipe overboard, which pleased the poor fellows very much." (Fyshe, February, 1838, P.M.B.375)[8].

The New Irelanders seem to have been happy to exchange for whale meat, as well as for iron and cloth. Though there were whales in this area, the New Irelanders never hunted them, in contrast to the Fijians[9]. Though the people at this time were unfamiliar with tobacco and frightened at the sight of pipe smoking, in thirty years tobacco would be an important item of exchange.

Captain Sir Edward Belcher, entering Gower's Harbor (Port Praslin) on July 5, 1840, related,

> ...We fell in with a party of 5 natives, one of whom spoke a little English [Belcher called him "Tom Starling"]. From him we learned that the visits of British vessels from Sydney were frequent; the natives who communicated with them resided on the eastern side of the island; and that their supplies consisted chiefly of wild hogs, fruits and vegetables. He was anxious to sleep on board the schooner, to which we consented, and his allies, youths from 16 to 18, were dispatched home, with directions to return the following morning with stock, etc. (Belcher 1843: 72)

Like Captain Morrell earlier, Capt. Belcher was interested in the commercial possibilities to be exploited in the islands that he visited.

BETWEEN BEACH AND SHIP: THE DEVELOPMENT OF EXCHANGE

Concerning New Ireland, he observed, "In a mercantile point of view I cannot at present perceive how these islands can prove interesting beyond the fancy woods and tortoise shell, of which the latter substance every canoe appeared to possess several plates. It is of good quality, better than I have before noticed in the Pacific, and from the manner in which it was offered no doubt vessels come here to trade for it; indeed we have learnt as much from Tom Starling." (Belcher 1843: 77) Belcher learned that traders had been coming to the island specifically to exchange goods for tortoise shell. His was the first record of ships coming to New Ireland to exchange goods for a commodity which they could later resell elsewhere, rather than merely bartering for food supplies for their ships. At Gower's Harbor, Belcher found few people and carried out little exchange. He learned from the English-speaking New Irelander there that most of the contacts with foreigners had occurred on the east coast. The contact between some New Irelanders and English speakers, probably tortoise-shell traders from Australia, had been of sufficient intensity and duration to enable "Tom Starling" to learn some English. "Tom Starling" became a middleman like Manners, the castaway, and was eager for further contact.

When the British warship "Maeander," under Captain Henry Keppel, passed along the west coast of New Ireland in 1850, it was besieged by canoes. Keppel noted that, "One and all were clamorous for barter: empty bottles, buttons, and bits of iron hoop, were most in demand. Clothes, or the materials for making them, were treated with great contempt." (Keppel 1853: 205) Though they came alongside the ship to trade, they could not be induced to come on board. The Maeander then anchored in Carteret Harbor, which Keppel observed, "…is a place occasionally visited by English and American whalers, - as was proved by a salutation which met our ears, while we were standing in for shore. `What ship that?' shouted a black savage, one of a party in a canoe; 'Tobac got!'- 'God damn!'- 'Rum got!'- 'Give rope!'- while delivering himself of these lessons in English and American, without wishing for an invitation, he sprang into the main chains, and thence on the quarterdeck." (Keppel 1853: 207)

After bartering for fruit, yams, and pigs and taking on water, Keppel visited a village, "...under the guidance of a savage who spoke and understood a little English...."

> Our party roamed about in twos and threes, while the savages were in tens and twenties; this however was scarcely prudent, as they might, had they been in the humor, have easily disposed of the white men. All accounts describe the natives about Carteret Harbour as not only grasping and avaricious, but treacherous and cunning cannibals. One man, who spoke a little English, denied to me that they ever ate men: he, however, admitted that, when they killed an enemy, they occasionally eat the palm of his hand, or some such dainty bit. (Keppel 1853: 208-210)

While he described the local people as dreadful, his own encounters with them suggest the opposite, since they took him to their village and showed him, with great courtesy, whatever he wanted to see. Keppel reported that the New Irelanders were interested in exchange and knew what they wanted. They were not interested in cloth or clothing, but only in buttons, bottles, and iron. In return they gave him an abundant supply of food. In contrast to Fyshe's earlier account, tobacco was known and desired around Carteret Harbor.

Intense whaling activity continued to occur in the area of New Ireland. Whaling ships were able to remain in these waters for lengthy stretches because they could depend on getting fresh supplies from the New Irelanders.

BETWEEN BEACH AND SHIP: THE DEVELOPMENT OF EXCHANGE

The log of the "Java II," out of New Bedford, kept by Capt. N. S. Smith, contains many examples of such exchanges and shows the equivalences of food for goods which had emerged:

> Nov.9 [1869]- New Ire. 6 mi. dist. several canoes off got 5 fowl, 1 small pig, 1 small bl. yams, 1 1/2 bl. tarra, 100 coconuts, old and young, 25 bun. bananas, 7 masks, 5 water melons, and nuts. for all of which paid old iron hoop cut in 2 and 3 in. pieces.

> Jan.1, 1870- After dinner went in on the L. side of Day's I. [Lihir] At sunset came off with 15 bbl. yams, 2 Hogs, 4 small pigs, and some breadfruit. Did not land but found the natives quiet and peaceable and if there had been any cause for landing, should not have hesitated a moment. Traded off 2 fath. red cloth cut in 1/2 inch strips. ...iron hoop cut in 2 in. pieces. An iron knife for a small pig. A hatchet for a large one. (Java II Log)

Pieces of hoop iron, and objects of iron such as knives and hatchets, were in great demand. In addition to food supplies, masks are mentioned for the first time as objects to be purchased for iron. Though the Duke of York Islands are not within our area of concern, they are located adjacent to New Ireland, and the Java II had an exchange showing that tobacco had become an important medium of exchange:

> Feb. 12, 1870- Left Duke of York I. Got 27 Hogs. Paid on the average 3/4 lb. of Tobacco each. 140 fowl. 1 small plug each. Fish quite plenty. 25 bun. Bananas. 10 doz. eggs, 4 for 1 pipe, 1 bl. yams. 17 bbl. tarra plenty of broom stuff. 1500 cocoa nuts. 30 for one small plug. 2 bbls. nuts. 1-27" grind stone. 2 lbs tobacco." (Java II Log 1869-1870)

During the second period of its stay in New Ireland waters, the "Java II" rounded Cape St. George. The log notes: "Feb. 7th... Took a boat and went in to King Tom's place which is just to N. of the Small Is. Nothing to be got but tarrow. plenty of that- & good. Red cloth appeared to be the best trade." (Java II Log 1869-1870)

Since institutionalized chiefs are not recorded for New Ireland, who is "King Tom"? Is this Tom Starling from the Belcher account? We can only speculate that Tom Starling's command of English had helped him gain control over trade with Europeans and enabled him to rise in power and prestige above other men of his village to the point where the Americans referred to him as a "king."

Discussion

The first 70 years of the nineteenth century were marked by a great increase in the frequency of visits by European ships to New Ireland. The responses of Western visitors to New Irelanders were quite varied. Dumont d'Urville saw them as so apathetic and indolent, that they could not possible be cultivators, or even hunters and fishermen. Fyshe, on the other hand, was tremendously impressed with the New Irelanders' abilities as carvers and boat builders, particularly since they did not seem to possess iron tools at the time of his visit. Voyagers brought different, contradictory cultural attitudes with them -- ideas which determined how they saw the New Irelanders and how they interacted with them. d'Urville's picture of New Irelanders portrayed them as closer to Wild Men, while Fyshe's view of them was more in line with that of the Noble Savage.

Some of the visitors to New Ireland during this period were members of scientific expeditions, like those of Duperrey and d'Urville, while others like

BETWEEN BEACH AND SHIP: THE DEVELOPMENT OF EXCHANGE

Beale, Coulter and Fyshe were surgeons on whalers, men with scientific backgrounds. The records of these expeditions included volumes on cartography, physics, zoology, botany and philology. Word lists were collected in various locations. Though these volumes attested to the use of a scientific approach, when it came to describing cultural differences and recording observations of New Irelanders and other people encountered, personal biases, which often echoed ethnocentric thinking, determined the outcome.

In Hawaii and Fiji, European deserters and castaways acted as mercenaries and sometimes advisors. Melanesia, on the other hand, on the basis of accounts from Malaita and Rossel Island, had a well-publicized reputation as a land of cannibals, extremely inhospitable to castaways. (Maude 1964:263) However, the stories of men like Manners and several others (such as Lifu in the Loyalties and San Cristobal) who had remained several years under favorable conditions on New Ireland received little publicity and did not change the reputation of Melanesians among Westerners.

The artifacts of the New Irelanders, began to be collected as "artificial curiosities" at the beginning of the nineteenth century. Collecting also reflect the varying views of New Irelanders held by Europeans. Most of the objects collected in the Pacific and sent back to Europe and America fell into two broad categories: weaponry (clubs and spears) and sculpture, masks, or other objects used in religious ritual. The Western interest in weaponry appears to have reflected a view of non-European Others engaged in warfare and killing, characteristics which, as we have noted earlier, typified savagery, barbarism and the conceptualization of the Wild Man. Sculpture and masks, which Westerners frequently referred to as "idols" and associated with religious ritual, represented two contradictory ideas. On the one hand, these idols represented pagan worship associated with the Wild Man, while, on the other hand they conveyed an aesthetic sensibility on the part of their makers associated with views of Noble Savages. The weaponry of the New Irelanders collected by Coulter and Mrs. Kent were transformed into curios, taken as part of the exchange and brought home to be admired as "artificial curiosities," souvenirs of the "savages" and Wild Men encountered. The masks taken by the "Java II" probably represented to the New England captains the numinous power captured in grotesque, yet aesthetically riveting, carved objects which to them signified the mixed message of exotic New Ireland which they wished to convey to those who awaited their return. The masks conveyed power and danger, but also a certain nobility.

Captains Morrell and Belcher both recognized the various natural resources in New Ireland which could be exploited for their commercial possibilities. Fine woods, bêche-de-mer, tortoise shell and pearl oysters were the kinds of materials desired for European markets. However, unlike other Pacific islands such as Hawaii, New Ireland did not have sandalwood, which was the basis for a lively international trade. Tortoise-shell, obtained by traders in New Ireland after 1840, and bêche-de-mer, however, were becoming important in trade with China.

The differences in political organization between Polynesia and Melanesia, played a role in the contrasting ways that the people of these two areas organized their contacts with Europeans and affected ensuing developments. It was much easier for Europeans to deal with a single individual, such as a Polynesian chief, who, speaking for his entire group, could provide provisions and invite them on shore. In New Ireland, on the other hand, there were fewer powerful individuals with whom the Europeans could deal.

BETWEEN BEACH AND SHIP: THE DEVELOPMENT OF EXCHANGE

During the nineteenth century, Europeans were no longer attacked by New Irelanders, in contrast to the treatment given earlier visitors[9]. The New Irelanders were impressed by the power of European guns, were not belligerent and freely boarded European ships.

The frequency and volume of exchange increased greatly. Food production may have been expanded in order to ensure a continuing supply to exchange with Europeans. However, since their gardens were very productive, they probably easily covered increased demands. Hoop iron had become the most desired item for New Irelanders. It was used to make adze blades for tools which were substituted for stone tools in making canoes and carvings. Whalers had much old hoop iron on hand which they could easily use in trade. Buttons, bottles, and strips of cloth which could be used in decoration were also accepted by the New Irelanders, but not clothing. Later, fathoms of red cloth were the best trade item, at least around Cape St. George. By the time of the voyage of the "Java II," tobacco had become a most important medium of exchange in some places. Though the whalers were interested primarily in getting supplies, they did accept locally made artifacts offered to them by New Irelanders.

New Ireland- European barter exchange occurred either from canoes located alongside the European ships (the more frequent pattern), or from European long boats which came close to the shore. Exchanges did not take place in villages, which very few foreigners visited; nor did they take place on the ships. The zone in which this activity was carried out, between the ship and the shore, was understood by both parties as the appropriate one for this new type of exchange. Though this barter was different from their traditional inter-island exchange at the beginning, for the most part, the New Irelanders comported themselves in the ways similar to those used in inter-island exchange. The New Irelanders used beauty magic, painting and decorating themselves , and sometimes carried weapons, before participating in inter-island exchange, to dazzle their inter-island exchange partners, so that they would give more[10]. The New Irelanders also may have beautified themselves so the Europeans would give them the European "valuables" they desired.

New Irelanders recognized the Europeans as bringers of iron, especially iron axes. These iron axes made it easier to clear land for cultivation, fell trees for use as canoes, build men's houses and decorate them, and manufacture ritual objects and weaponry. Though the basic features of New Ireland life seem to have remained much the same, iron certainly made men's economic tasks less arduous. The New Irelanders continued to control European access to their beaches and villages.

The New Irelanders also tried to keep Europeans away from their women, probably because they wanted to prevent the women, who had a reputation for assertiveness, from having sexual relations with European men[11]. This attempt to maintain a separation between Europeans and New Ireland women contrasts with what occurred on Polynesian islands like Tahiti, Hawaii and the Marquesas, where women freely boarded the European ships and often engaged in sexual intercourse with Europeans, sometimes with wide ranging repercussions. (See Sahlins 1981.)

After 250 years of contact, Europeans were still stopping at New Ireland only to trade for fresh supplies and rarely ventured off their boats. The New Irelanders controlled the situation and continued to restrict European access to their villages, trading only in the liminal areas which had been established. In contrast, in the Polynesian islands of Hawaii, Fiji, the Marquesas and Tahiti during the same period, trading posts and missions had been established, and

BETWEEN BEACH AND SHIP: THE DEVELOPMENT OF EXCHANGE

Europeans' conflicts over colonial zones of influence already were bringing great changes.

NOTES

1. Lesson first published a two-part article, "Memoir on New Ireland and its Inhabitants," which included an account of a village by Blosseville, another member of the expedition, in the *Journal of Voyages, Discoveries and Modern Navigation (Geographic Archives of the Nineteenth Century*, 1829) Some of this material and a short article by Dr. Garnot was summarized in the account of the *Voyages*. (1839) We have used these descriptions in our reconstruction of New Ireland culture in Chapter 1.

2. This is our translation from the French.

3. Descriptions of these encounters are to be found in both published works and unpublished ships' logs.

4. Beale's "natural history" of whales and description of whaling were the main sources used by Melville for *Moby Dick* and the observations of New Irelanders by Beale, the physician, can be considered as objective as his work on the whales.

5. Coulter's descriptions of New Ireland life have been incorporated into our reconstruction of the pre-contact culture in Chapter 2.

6. At the end of his journey Coulter notes, "All the artificial curiosities I had, such as spears, clubs, carved paddles &c., had to be stored until they were valued for duty." (Coulter 1847, vol.2: 277)

7. Capt. Edward Tregurtha (cited in Villiers 1931: 221), master of the whaler "Caroline," out of Hobart, Tasmania, in his log mentions picking up a

castaway on New Ireland named Black, meaning there was more than one castaway on New Ireland.

8. New Irelanders did not use red cloth for clothing, but instead put it on *tatanua* masks.

9. In our discussions with New Irelanders, they were not familiar with hunting whales; nor was there any remembrance that they had hunted whales in the past. (Rubel and Rosman, 1987 Field Notes)

10. The Trobriand Islanders, before embarking on a kula expedition, also attempted to make themselves so attractive their *kula* partners would "throw the *vaygu'a* [*kula* valuables] at us." (Malinowski 1922: 336) [Editor's Note: The Trobriand Islands are located in the Solomon Sea, approximately 300 miles southwest of New Ireland.]

11. Captain Tregurtha's log (cited in Villiers 1931: 222) describes how, when going in to St. Mary's Bay to barter with the New Irelanders, "a gang of naked women came to the beach and by lascivious actions invited us on shore." Captain Tregurtha thought that this was a ruse employed to entice them to come closer in order to capture the whale boat.

6. NEW IRELANDERS ENCOUNTER CAPITALISM

New Irelanders began to lose control over their own destiny during the latter part of the nineteenth century. In the early 1880s, the location of trade shifted away from the liminal zone between beach and knee-high waters to trading stations set up by alien European traders in or near villages. The commodities involved changed as well. Traders already had been coming to the island since the 1840s for tortoise shell. (Belcher 1840) bêche-de-mer (trepang, or sea cucumber) fishermen were in the area as well. (Hernsheim 1983: 29) European exchanges with indigenous people were no longer to replenish supplies. The Europeans now sought commodities to be sold on the world market, especially tortoise shell, bêche-de-mer, green snail shells, and, what was soon to become the overwhelmingly important commodity, copra (dried coconut).

At this time, the German trading company Godeffroy & Son, from Hamburg, dominated the Pacific economically. Most of their trade was in copra, but they also bought tortoise-shell and bêche-de-mer. Godeffroy had traders on many islands in Micronesia successfully trading for copra. While trading they also were accumulating ethnographic objects and natural history specimens for the Godeffroy Museum. Some, like the trader Kubary, also were writing ethnographies, which were published in a by the Museum.

On the Micronesian island of Yap, a curious encounter took place between Godeffroy's agent, Alfred Tetens, and an American castaway, David

O'Keefe. The story of David O'Keefe presents an interesting allegory about the interaction of indigenous peoples of the Pacific and capitalism. O'Keefe (later referred to as His Majesty O'Keefe) was successful in gathering copra because he came to understand important aspects of Yapese culture. The Yapese spent more time making circular stone money than collecting coconuts. This group of native people did not understand capitalism. They preferred to work to create stone money, a valuable in their ceremonies, rather than to pick coconuts for traders. O'Keefe came to understand the importance of the stone money (*fei*) to the Yapese, with whom he was living. He began to manufacture stone money in order to induce the people to pick and exchange copra for it. O'Keefe used Western technology, such as dynamite and grinding tools, to manufacture stone money.

Having established itself in Samoa in 1857, the Godeffroy Company set up two trading stations on the Gazelle Peninsula in New Britain with resident European traders in 1873. Within four weeks of their construction, the stations were besieged by the local people and set afire[1]. To the people of the Gazelle Peninsula, the Europeans were alien invaders of their land. Not all of the local people participated in the attack. The survivors, John Nash and William Wawn, fled to Port Hunter in the Duke of York Islands. In his own account of this incident, Capt. Wawn noted that, "The principal 'fighting chief' of the tribe that attacked us… was friendly…. But for him we must have been killed." (Wawn 1893: 287) Wawn returned a decade later as captain of a vessel engaged in blackbirding and again met this man, who was now "the head chief of the whole tribe." John Knowles, a half-Tongan trader working for Godeffroy, had manned a trading station on New Ireland at Kuras (near Kuramut) on the west coast in 1878. (Deane 1933: 53-54) However, this station was abandoned in 1879 after Knowles killed Captain Levison in a dispute. (Powell 1883: 267-269)

Trading Stations

The first successful trading station on New Ireland seems to have been the one established on Nusa, just north of New Ireland, by Eduard Hernsheim in 1880. Hernsheim had been born in 1847 in Mainz, the son of a middle-class lawyer. His parents, born Jewish, had converted to Lutheranism. At the age of twenty-five, Hernsheim, with his Master's license and his own ship, came to the Pacific. By 1874 he had bought land on Palau, in Micronesia, and set up his first trading station there. He left behind two European traders to exchange European goods for trepang and tortoise shell. In Micronesia, Hernsheim was primarily in competition with Godeffroy & Sons, who were already well established in the area. After a time in the trepang trade in Yap (where O'Keefe had preceeded him) and the Palau Islands, where he was not making much money, he decided to shift to copra. According to Hernsheim, "…It was plain to me that in order to do business on a larger scale I would have to shift to buying copra, the only product which was available in large quantities in the South Seas." (Hernsheim 1983: 27)

He then decided to move to the Bismarck Archipelago. In 1875, Hernsheim and Blohm, a disaffected trader for Godeffroy on Yap, traveled to the Duke of York Islands. They learned that a Methodist minister, the Reverend George Brown, had already set up a settlement at Port Hunter. Brown had brought with him missionaries from Samoa, Tonga, and Fiji; and Blohm's Samoan wife felt at home with them. Blohm established a trading station for Hernsheim in 1875 at Port Hunter and moved to Makada, on the Duke of York Islands, in 1876. This station did not flourish because, "…the savage natives had little produce to sell and scarcely any needs.... They were much too lazy and timid to bring us the coconuts growing wild in the bush." (Hernsheim 1983: 31) Hernsheim made several reconnoitering trips to New Ireland and found the same situation there. Hernsheim accused the New Irelanders of being "lazy," just as Tentens and O'Keefe had accused the Yap Islanders who refused to pick coconuts for them. The Yapese preferred to devote their energies to making stone money for ritual purposes, while the New Irelanders devoted themselves to production for *malanggan* ceremonies. At this point, there were few incentives for local New Ireland populations to engage in copra trade on a regular basis.

In 1878, the price of copra on the world market rose sharply, making copra trade a more profitable enterprise. In Hernsheim's view, "The rise in the prices for copra had also stimulated strong competition among the old firms and led to the establishment of new businesses. The only virgin territory was in the west [the Bismarcks], and it was only there that produce could be obtained by barter from the completely uncivilized and untouched natives at nominal prices." (Hernsheim 1983: 43) Hernsheim decided to shift the base of his operations from Jaluit, in the Marshall Islands, to Makada, on the Duke of York Islands. He continued to maintain and operate his Micronesian trading network while personally managing the Makada station.

In contrast to Micronesia, where there were chiefs with whom the traders could do business, in the Bismarck Archipelago, Hernsheim noted that, "...It was impossible to make long-term agreements with these savages: there were no chiefs and no large villages. Every family lived on its own, mostly in a state of feud with its neighbors. We were obliged to buy in coconuts all over the place and to bring these nuts to Makada where we had them opened, cut into copra and dried so that it took a full schooner load to make 1000 pounds of copra. "In general, it soon became plain that it would take years for any really profitable trade to develop here. Business was confined to the most primitive type of barter. The people had no needs and although the goods in demand here -- beads, hoop-iron, and empty bottles -- cost practically nothing, on the other hand, it was quite impossible to buy any substantial quantity of any of the export commodities available." (Hernsheim 1983: 47-48) New Irelanders at this point had not yet bought into the capitalist system.

At his home in Matupi, New Britain, to which Hernsheim moved in 1879, he succeeded in creating a cocoon of his own culture. Hugh Romilly, a British government official, reported that Hernsheim had a French chef, a billiard table, and a bowling alley, and that dinner at his house excelled any dinner one could obtain in Australia. (Romilly 1886: 195) Hernsheim and the traders and ship captains who worked for him were socially worlds apart[2].

Hernsheim decided to expand his operations into relatively untouched New Ireland. Up to that point, the only trading station, which had been established on New Ireland, had been manned by John Knowles, the half-Tongan trader working for Godeffroy. He had abandoned the station in 1879 after killing Captain Levison, who also worked for Godeffroy, in a dispute over copra. (See a lengthy account of this incident in Powell 1883: 267-269.)

Hernsheim related: "Off northern New Ireland near the Steffen Strait, we had discovered an extensive archipelago of islands covered with coconut groves for miles on end. However, the numerous native population appeared to be too savage for anyone to settle among them. When a ship appeared they usually rushed into the water in hundreds and swam out to it with great bundles of coconuts which they bartered for small pieces of hoop. In this way small ships like the "Alice" could be filled to the gunwale with coconuts within a few hours, but as these coconuts were still encased in their outer husks, they took up so much room that the whole cargo was worth very little." (Hernsheim 1983: 55) This parallels earlier exchanges which took place when ships put in for supplies which were exchanged for hoop iron in the liminal area. The local people had become aware that the traders wanted only coconuts. Hernsheim first had to create new demands among the New Irelanders. To improve his business, Hernsheim realized that,

> It was essential to establish our own station on the spot where natives could be systematically taught to make copra or at least to bring in the coconut kernals cut out of the shell ready for drying. I therefore sailed for Steffen Strait with two steamers and anchored near an island called Nusa, which, together with the north cape of New Ireland, seemed to form a good harbor. The people there appeared to be trusting and friendly and I decided simply to go ashore in a boat....

> At the beach we were welcomed by more natives in large numbers, who, with deafening shouts of joy, lifted the boat with me and the rest of the boat's crew high into the air and deposited us on dry land. They took me by the hand and led me a half an hour's walk into the interior, till we came to a house on an open clearing.... The natives brought along great bundles of bananas, coconuts, spears and oars, which were all piled up behind me. As I had unfortunately not brought any presents with me, the only gift I could present...was a box of matches and a newspaper I happened to have in my pocket." (Hernsheim 1983: 56)

Hernsheim's diary indicates that he walked inland on the north cape of New Ireland, not on Nusa Island.

Hernsheim explored the coast of New Ireland by ship, sailing around the north cape to the east coast, trading for coconuts along the way. He visited another village also inland from the coast. Though the pattern of exchange of coconuts for hoop iron was a continuation of the earlier pattern of exchange, the reception Hernsheim received was quite different. People seemed eager to take him to their villages. They showered him with gifts, though he gave little in return. In the second village he visited, people gave him foodstuffs, spears, oars, and "carved and painted ornaments" in which he showed an interest. From his description these seem to have been *malanggan*-like carvings. (Hernsheim 1983: 56-57, 122-123) The New Irelanders of this North Cape area seem to have been familiar with Europeans and their products. Some of the men of this village were prepared to go with him to Matupi, indicating that they saw an advantage to contact with Europeans and learning about them. Hernsheim did not mention encountering anyone who represented himself as a leader or "chief" in these villages.

Hernsheim decided to establish his station on Nusa Island (near present-day Kavieng), where coconuts were abundant. In February 1880 he selected John Nash, who had manned the unsuccessful Godeffroy station established on New Britain in 1873, to be in charge of the station in Nusa. Hernsheim described how he acquired land for his station: "The procedure adopted in purchasing land in those days was to point out a piece of land, or at most to pale out [stake out] the boundaries and then to give the natives a few trade goods and to make a few crosses with a pen held in the fingers of the natives, on a piece of paper establishing the purchase. These marks were witnessed by the signatures of the white men present. It was of course not possible to prove that the natives who signed were the owners of the land, or understood the contents of the documents, and only actual occupation could guarantee possession." (Hernsheim 1983: 57) (See Chapter 10 for examples of such deeds.)

Hernsheim was concerned about keeping out his competitors, though he recognized that keeping the location of his station secret was not possible, since the traders, like Nash, who already were established on the stations were "unreliable types often addicted to drink." Nash himself, in fact, turned out not to be dependable. He left Hernsheim's employ within several months in order to work on New Ireland for one of Hernsheim's competitors, Captain Beaver from Sydney. Under the new manager Schulle, the station at Nusa became much more productive. In describing the first few months of trade, Hernsheim observed, "After a few initial misunderstandings, relations with the natives there remained good for a very long time."

Within a few months these people who had in the beginning brought us human flesh for sale and in many other ways shown that they were complete savages, had become sufficiently familiar with our ways and requirements for us to be able to open additional stations and put in traders everywhere. They soon learned to bring not only coconuts but ready-cut coconut kernals to the stations, so that the trader only had to carry out the drying process." (Hernsheim 1983: 60)

Hernsheim noted that, "The most highly-prized trade goods were beads and ironware. The tobacco habit first had to be artificially inculcated in the natives in order to create a constant demand for a quickly consumed commodity, in place of goods made of iron which remain serviceable over a long period. The natives who had been in Matupi brought back pipes and tobacco, and soon schools for smoking were set up with traders as instructors, in which the new pastime was propagated, so that in a few years' time tobacco was the most coveted and indispensable commodity among the natives."

(Hernsheim 1983: 60) Though tobacco had already been introduced in 1870 by whalers as a medium of exchange in the south. this was not yet the case in the North Cape area until Hernsheim introduced it. It was better to trade a consumable good like tobacco, which had constantly to be replenished, in exchange for coconuts, rather than iron, which did not. This insured a steady supply of coconuts

Schulle, who replaced Nash, made a success of the Nusa trading station and then expanded the operation to establish new stations down the coast at Navangai (Lavongai- Tigak-speaking), Butbut (Putput- Tigak-speaking), Kablamann (Kablaman-Tigak-speaking), Kapsu (Tigak-Kara border), Lagunbunje (?), and Lamorotte (Lemakot? Kara-speaking).

In early 1880, Hernsheim also explored business prospects in the northern Solomons, and he decided not to compete with the Australian firms already established there. While there, he recruited Solomon Islanders to help man his stations on New Ireland. Hernsheim's small steamers continued to gather coconuts with varying degrees of success from places like Lihir, where no stations had been established. Hernsheim reported that 58,000 pounds of copra were collected at the Nusa station over a 16-day period in June 1880. (Hernsheim 1883: 131)[3]. Though the data Hernsheim gave were not systematically recorded, they nevertheless revealed the extent of the trade and how it increased, despite Hernsheim's problems with his traders and difficulties with the local people. The yams collected were probably used to feed Hernshcim's labor force at his "factory" at Matupi, where the copra was processed for shipment to Europe. The bêche-de-mer trade continued to follow the earlier pattern. Capt. Thomas Farrell, an Australian, was a trader and labor recruiter in the Duke of York Islands. While in Samoa, he took up with Emma Forsayth, later known as Queen Emma. "They left Samoa late in 1878 as Mrs.

Emma Forsayth and Captain Tom Farrell. By mid-1879, they were established in Mioko, Duke of York Islands,...as Mr. and Mrs. Farrell." (Robson 1965: 95) Farrell set up his trading station opposite the already existing Godeffroy station at Mioko. He continued his labor recruiting, and subsequently established other trading stations on New Britain.

Using the capital Farrell acquired, he and Emma expanded their own trading network and contemplated setting up a plantation. Early in 1882, they were joined in Mioko by Richard Parkinson, who had married Emma's sister Phebe. Parkinson had learned about the plantation business in Samoa. He established the first plantations in the Bismarcks in the Blanche Bay area of New Britain for Emma Forsayth and Thomas Farrell. By 1884 they also had trading stations on New Ireland at Nusa and Biroa.

Though Hernsheim had a monopoly in northern New Ireland in 1880, he soon had competition from Godeffroy & Sons and from traders like Captains Brodie, Ferguson, and Beaver, who operated out of Sydney. They had been trading directly from one or more ships since the 1870s, covering a territory including the Bismarcks and the Solomon Islands. Brodie's ship, the "Lavinia," had been captured and burned, with several men killed, at Port Praslin in New Ireland in 1875. (Brown 1908: 99) This direct type of trade from ships continued after Hernsheim had established his station on the island itself. Traders would sometimes, in advance, leave trade goods and return later to collect copra. (Hernsheim 1983: 119)

Though Hernsheim's network of trading stations in northern New Ireland expanded from 1880 on, serious problems soon developed. Hernsheim noted:

> The blasted Sandbergen [Hernsheim's trader at Lavongai] put on such a stupid act again that he nearly ruined the whole business.

The day after my departure he went to Nusa in the canoe, to fetch the carpenter to Navangai [Lavongai], as the boat had sprung a leak that same night. The next day Gasser [the trader at Nusa] also went there from Nusa to see what had happened to the boat. While he was there a native sprang over his fence and Sandbergen shot him in the leg. The native threw his spear at him, and when a few more natives hurried to the scene, Sandbergen, the Chinese carpenter and Gasser ran away. This naturally made the natives bolder and they pursued and wounded them. Fortunately, Ancou's [the Nusa chief's] kanakas were nearby and chased the Navangai men back and brought the fugitives to Nusa where they have been living ever since in fear and trembling.

Of course, all the trade was stolen and what is even more annoying, the boat was chopped up into little bits. Schulle calmed the people down somewhat and went to Navangai where he shot four natives dead, who were then eaten up by the Nusa people. Some buildings were also set on fire. At all events we must try to make peace with these natives as soon as possible, or if this should prove impossible we will have to call up the friendly inhabitants of Nusa and Butbut to help us clean up those Navangai people and show them that we are not afraid. (August 8, 1880, Hernsheim 1983: 135)

On May 24, 1881, Hernsheim recorded the killing of Sztudinka, his trader at Butbut. Sztudinka was shot by one of the Solomon Islanders, the "Kanakas" (a derogatory term), working on the station, and the station was then looted and burned, with a loss to Hernsheim of $1000 in goods, products and outstanding debts. The murderer fled to the bush. (1983: 141)

New Irelanders' Responses to Trading Stations

Local populations responded differently to the establishment of trading stations. At Nusa, where Hernsheim established his first station, the people were his allies, to the point of aiding Hernsheim's trader when he sought to "punish" the people of Navongai after they disrupted the trading station there. This was because the villagers of Nusa were the enemies of those of Navongai. Contrary to what one might expect, the local people were not united against the Europeans. New Ireland villages were fitting the Europeans into their checkerboard pattern of alternation of allies and enemies, in which neighboring villages were enemies, while more distant villages were allies. Hernsheim established his line of trading stations down the northeast coast of New Ireland unaware of this. When he set up his first station at Nusa, he was thenceforth identified with the Nusa people. The difficulties Hernsheim had with the people at Navongai might have been because of his identification with Nusa. This would explain why, when Schulle killed four Navongai men, their bodies were eaten by the Nusa people, since one ate only the bodies of one's enemies. Cannibalism, the eating of one's enemy, had not changed despite the setting up of trading stations on the island. In New Ireland, there was no indigenous political authority which extended over large areas, but only politically autonomous villages where leadership was of the Big Man type.

Traders like Schulle could take things into their own hands and become the law. When a white man was attacked or killed, or when a station was looted and burned, Westerners retaliated by killing local people. Sometimes, the wrong person was shot, as when Schulle mistakenly shot a Butbut man. The Butbut people were recompensed for Schulle's "mistake," but Schulle went unpunished because there was no authority, European or otherwise, on the island. (Hernsheim 1983: 138)

Traders' Behavior

Traders were sent by Hernsheim to various stations, but they moved frequently from place to place. Stations were isolated, lonely places. Earlier, Christophen had asked Hernsheim to bring him a woman from Jaluit, Hernsheim's former headquarters in the Marshalls. (1983: 133) However, there is no indication that the traders at that time had long term sexual relationships with any New Ireland women. Stations seemed to open and close with great frequency. For example, the station at Kabotheron located on an island along Nusa channel, was opened in the spring of 1880, closed in September of that year and then reopened and closed again in 1881. Schulle, who left Hernsheim's employment, in signed a contract with him in 1884 to manage all the stations on the north coast, with all copra to be sold to Hernsheim. By 1885, "Unfortunately complaints were continually coming in about Schulle's behavior to both whites and natives. Apparently, the man was a bout drinker and brutally cruel to subordinates and natives when intoxicated... so that I thought it advisable to sever my connection with him as soon as possible." (Hernsheim 1983: 97) Hernsheim valued Schulle, who, as we have seen, was tough and brought in the copra. He did not criticize Schulle's behavior when he killed four villagers in a punitive raid, but would not put up with Schulle's drunkenness and complaints about his brutality. Like the traders, the captains of Hernsheim's inter-island trading vessels were also subject to bouts of drunkenness. These captains and traders, in lonely isolated locations were the models for characters in the novels by Maugham and Conrad.

Most of Hernsheim's stations also seemed to employ men brought from the Solomon Islands. (Hernsheim 1983: 133) By 1879 Hernsheim had also brought in Chinese carpenters to cut ship-building timber in New Britain for export to Hong Kong, and some of them also worked for him in New Ireland. (1983: 51)[4]

Punitive Expeditions

Once the Europeans began to establish themselves in the Bismarck Archipelago, their relations with the native population became a matter of control. When murder and cannibalism were committed against white men or their agents, retaliatory punitive expeditions were launched. When a Fijian minister and three Fijian teachers were killed on the Gazelle Peninsula of New Britain in 1878, Rev. George Brown organized a retaliatory expedition. Nine of the ten Europeans then living on the peninsula, led by Rev. Brown, carried out the raid, in which at least a dozen villagers were shot, houses were burned, and gardens and canoes were destroyed.

Another punitive expedition was conducted in 1881 to punish the Utuan people of the Duke of York Islands for the murder of Kleinschmidt, a naturalist who was collecting specimens and artifacts for the Godeffroy Museum. Hugh Romilly, the British Deputy Commissioner of the Western Pacific, observed, "He [Kleinschmidt] had bought a small island near the Duke of York, and paid one chief a certain amount of trade for it. As a matter of course, the island did not belong to the chief, but to a tribe, and the tribe did not consider that they had sold it, whatever the chief did. Accordingly, they not only continued picking cocoa-nuts there, but objected to Kleinschmidt doing so too. On this Kleinschmidt sent them a message that he would shoot anyone picking cocoa-nuts there, and went over there with two of his men. While there they were all three killed." (Romilly 1893: 160)

These killings were a consequence of conflicting legal systems. Kleinschmidt's concept of ownership of land was different from that held by the people of the Duke of York Islands. Rev. Danks, the Methodist missionary on the Duke of York Islands, presented a somewhat different picture. Danks said, "…He [Kleinschmidt] was very intolerant of some of their customs, and especially of their land laws -- one of which is that while the land itself may belong to one man, the trees growing on it may belong to another. He claimed that the white man's law (that when land is bought all growing thereon should go with it) ought to be the black man's law." (Deane 1933: 152)

Captain Farrell, together with Captain Rabardy of the "Genil," who had come to the area with the Marquis de Rays expedition (see below), headed an attack after the local people had refused to surrender Kleinschmidt's murderers. After being repulsed by Utuan gunfire, many Utuans were shot, and the murderers were captured and executed. Hernsheim noted: "It was later maintained that by this means a general uprising by the blacks against the whites had been nipped in the bud, and that they had also saved the lives of those of us living on Matupi. I myself had reason to believe that we were perfectly safe and that, in this land where there was neither law nor Government, we had less to fear from the savages than from filibustering white men." (1983: 69) However, Blohm, Hernsheim's trader at Mioko on the Duke of York Islands, and Rev. Danks both did feel that a plot was being hatched to kill all the whites at Mioko at the first opportunity, and that the punitive raid led by Farrell had been justified. (Deane 1933: 155) The intrusive presence of the Europeans and the punitive expeditions they conducted produced a strong response on the part of the indigenous people. They looted and burned trading stations and killed the people they saw as invaders. A rising war of terror was developing.

Competition Among Aspiring Colonial Powers

At the same time that traders and missionaries were conducting punitive expeditions, they tried to enlist their European governments to act to protect them. European governments -- particularly the British, German, and French -- were interested in extending their spheres of influence in order to ultimately establish colonies. They viewed each other with mutual suspicion and shortly would be competing to set up colonies in the areas that they had not yet divided up. It was the traders who forced the European powers to increase their political involvement in this area. Theodor Weber, the manager of Godeffroy & Son, had been appointed German Consul in Apia, Samoa, and travelled through the Bismarck Archipelago, visiting Makada in the Duke of York Islands, Hernsheim's base in 1878. According to Hernsheim, "…It was his intention simply to make sure, by concluding agreements with native chiefs, that no other nation could anticipate us." (1983: 49) In 1879, Hernsheim's brother Franz was appointed German Consul in Jaluit, the Marshall Islands. "This was of great importance to us, as Herr Weber's position as Consul in Apia had undoubtedly given him and the business interest he represented, a decided advantage." (Hernsheim 1983: 50)

"Showing the flag" had more to do with the competition between imperialist powers than relations with the indigenous population. The British also considered the Bismarck Archipelago to be within their imperial sphere of influence, since a number of Australian traders operated there. Romilly, representing the High Commissioner in in Fiji, visited the Bismarcks with three British naval schooners after Captain Farrell's punitive expedition of 1881, in order to bring about a peaceful settlement between Europeans and natives. In July 1881 the gunboat "Habicht" came from Apia to the Bismarcks with German Consul-General Zembsch, as part of a cruise of the Western Pacific. Hernsheim, who accompanied the party to New Ireland, noted,

> ...[I] took part as guide in all the expeditions undertaken for the purpose of investigating and punishing the various murders committed there....
>
> Most of these expeditions were fruitless mainly because we had to rely on allegations made by a number of traders of very low moral calibre and were unable to communicate with the natives. The punishment carried out in some places on the orders of the Counsul-General was confined to destruction of property by burning down a few huts and knocking down plantations of no great intrinsic value, the loss of which would not inflict any lasting injury on the natives. It was nevertheless important to demonstrate to these savages, once and for all, that whites were capable of taking action in appreciable numbers and with powerful weapons. (Hernsheim 1983: 70)

Terror was being used here to subordinate the local population, which responded violently to European intrusion into their lives. As the colonial operation is set in place, terror would become an increasingly important weapon used by the Europeans to gain hegemonic control. On returning to Europe in 1882, Hernsheim received his commission as Imperial Consul for the Marshall Islands and the whole of the north-western Pacific region, from the Carolines to the New Britain Archipelago, furthering Germany's move toward establishing a colony in the Pacific.

Pacification of Rebellious Natives by Violence and Other Means

The new Consul General, Dr. Stubel, arrived in the Bismarcks in February 1884 and set out with Hernsheim on the gunboat "Hyane" to tour the stations. At Nusa they found that Hernsheim's agent, Brandt, had had a dispute with the local people, had tried to make them pay a fine, and had been attacked and the station torched. After Brandt killed a local villager, he and Boolsen, the other trader there, fled by boat to Kapsu, thirty miles down the coast. The "Hyane" was fired on, though no one was hurt, and responded with cannon fire aimed to frighten rather than hit anyone. Rifle fire was returned from the shore. (Hernsheim 1983: 83-88, 160-162)

On the way to Kapsu, Hernsheim speculated that, ..".The natives had obviously revolted and if this uprising had extended along the whole coast it must be assumed that Kapsu and the other places had also been taken, that all our men had been murdered and that all the work we had put in here over the past few years had been completely wasted." (1983: 84) At Kapsu, they found Boolsen and Brandt safe. (Hernsheim 1983: 84-85) The Hyane returned to Nusa and fired twenty shells at the island. A landing party then went ashore, found no one, and burned down all the houses in the village and demolished everything else. The next day, the party landed on the mainland opposite Nusa and was greeted with gunfire. The surgeon received a spear through the thigh. They then retreated to the ship. To retaliate for the loss of the station, the "Hyane" had fallen back upon the institution of terror, destroying the entire village.

Hernsheim, however, wanted to restore peaceful relations with the local people in order to continue trading, and the latter also wanted peace. He noted,

Send boat with Solomons boys to Nauwan [on the mainland opposite Nusa Island] to communicate with the natives. After a short time they come back bringing a bundle of spears, some shell money ... as peace offerings and announce that the kanakas wanted to stop fighting. We go ashore ourselves and conclude peace.... Spear broken in half in the middle as a sign for Matupi ships. Brandt shot a kanaka dead without cause.... Spears are to be sent by the Admiralty to the War Museum as permanent trophy of battle and victory. News of the glorious action is cabled home from Sydney- doctor wounded-decoration assured. (1983: 161-162)

Hernsheim recognized that peace could not be imposed on the New Irelanders. He could only make peace with them in the New Ireland way, which proved to be more effective than launching punitive raids.

Punishment in the Bismarcks was often meted out indiscriminately by the Europeans. It is difficult to ascertain from European accounts the causes of the disputes between the local people and the Europeans. These disputes resulted in murders, which were followed by punitive expeditions. As Hernsheim observed, traders making allegations were untrustworthy witnesses and the New Irelanders' version of the event was not told, because Europeans were unable to communicate with the natives. Groups like the Utuan people were collectively held responsible and punished, in contrast to justice in European societies, where only guilty persons were punished. The purposes of punitive expeditions were, as Hernsheim observed, to show the power of the Europeans and intimidate the indigenous population, frightening them into submission to European power.

Efforts to Conclude "Treaties"

When the European governments first sent political representatives like Weber and Romilly into the area, the latter tried to conclude treaties with "native chiefs," as they had done in Polynesia and other parts of the world. However, as we noted earlier, the political system in the Bismarck Archipelago, for the most part, was of the Big Men type rather than chiefdomships. Treaties did not bind anyone, since the leaders signing them did not represent large numbers of people. Hernsheim's "peace" treaty with the people of Nusa, done in the New Ireland fashion, with the giving of shell valuables and the breaking of the spear as a symbol of peace (see Chapter 2), had as much validity as peace-making between two New Ireland groups, which is to say that it terminated present hostilities but did not guarantee that they would not occur again in the future.

In 1881, attacks by New Irelanders on trading stations still involved the use of spears, though Solomon Islanders working on the trading stations had access to firearms. By 1883, the Queensland labor vessels were said to be supplying the people of New Britain with firearms, and Hernsheim was exchanging copra for Snider rifle cartridges. (Wawn 1973: 289; see also Mouton 1974: 68.) Some people on New Ireland had guns by 1884. They were being used in conjunction with spears, as in the skirmish with the "Hyane." The change in weaponry had ramifications: the unequal distribution of guns upset what had earlier been a balance of power. Solomon Islanders, who worked on all of the Hernsheim stations, seem to have played an important role in the interaction between the Europeans and the New Irelanders, though the details of that role are unknown. The Solomon Islanders were the cause of friction and disputes with the local people on a number of occasions. They had been involved in trading for copra and in labor recruiting somewhat earlier than the New Irelanders, and their greater experience with Europeans was probably why traders like Capt. Farrell and Hernsheim employed them in the Bismarcks. (Bennett 1987)

French Traders in Southern New Ireland

While an expanding network of trading stations was being established at the northern end of New Ireland, a totally different type of European intrusion was occurring in the south. In January 1880, a colony was founded at Port Praslin, near the southern tip of New Ireland, under the sponsorship of a French aristocrat, the Marquis de Rays. The idea was to establish a French colony in the Pacific. The Marquis selected this spot because Duperrey's account of this area had captured his imagination, though he himself had never visited New Ireland or been any place in the Pacific. (Michener and Day 1957:45-46) Four ships brought settlers from France to New Ireland. The first group of settlers, who landed from the "Chandernagore," immediately saw the unsuitability of the area for agriculture; and they crossed the Cape to the east coast, to Likiliki (or Metlik), the village Blosseville had visited. Fifty acres were purchased from the local people in exchange for a string of beads. Streets and a central square were pegged out. And the area was provided with a steam boiler, a fireplace, a large quantity of bricks for a cathedral foundation, sugar refining equipment, a steam crane, a saw mill, and agricultural implements. (Brown 1908: 363) But the settlers lacked a sufficient supply of axes and spades, and they were short of food -- evidence of poor planning. The settlers obtained yams, taro and pigs by trading axes, butcher knives, and beads with the local people. (Mouton 1974: 56) The colonists, however, never succeeded in establishing a viable economic base for this colony and were dependent on provisioning from abroad and from local villages.

The impact of the Marquis de Rays' colony on the surrounding population was intense, though of short duration. By this time, local people were familiar with Europeans. (Mouton 1974, Niau 1936)[5] The people on Lambom Island were helpful and accompanied the settlers up the east coast by canoe to Mimias to trade for provisions. "King Maragano" of Lambom Island was one of the local leaders with whom Captain Rabardy of the "Genil" had established friendly relations. These local Big Men, to whom other villagers deferred, were referred to as "kings" by the Europeans. (See Baudouin 1885.)

Maragano had no compunction in selling the southern part of New Ireland to Captain Rabardy, as Niau sarcastically described:

> At 10 a.m. Maragano, King of Lamboum, attended by his court of five savages came on board in full dress, this time consisting of a straw through his nose. The royal throne was a crate of fowls; between the governor (Rabardy) and the king a table on which was the price of the kingdom; namely, a red coat, a plug of tobacco, some clay pipes, a bag of beads, and several red handkerchiefs....'Is it true', Rabardy asked Maragano, `that your ancestors reigned formerly over southern New Ireland?' `Quite true,' answered the king. ...He made a grab at the table, clutched the price of his former kingdom, and made as if to run off to his canoe when Lawyer Chambaud firmly took him by the arm, and made him place a large X, on specially stamped paper, in order to validate the sale.... Thus were the million acres of New Ireland bought from a native king, who did not possess them. (Niau 1936: 121-122)

Friendly relations were established with the people on the coast, but the settlers had little contact with those of the interior, whom they referred to as "Men-Busch." Mouton encountered the Golon (Gololon or Kulolon) from the interior, when a party of thirty men armed with sticks, spears, and clubs came down to the beach, where cargo lay awaiting transshipment after the colony had failed. Mouton, aged sixteen, afraid of attack and looting by the Golon men, gave the Lambom men with him firearms to use. The Lambom people were trusted to the point where Mouton was not afraid to give them guns. If Mouton was attacked, the Lambom people were willing to defend him by attacking the `bushmen'. Mouton had been fitted into the pre-contact pattern of friendly and enemy groups described earlier.

There is no information about how the European colonists were communicating with the New Irelanders. Mouton had learned Pidgin English in his stopover in Singapore on the way to New Ireland, noting, "…It was not very long before I could quite use the Pidgin English, and this became very useful later." (1973: 42) Biskup, the editor of Mouton's memoirs, concludes that, "What he (Mouton) seems to be saying is that there was little difference between Singapore Pidgin and that used in the Bismarck Archipelago." (1974: 42, fn 11)

Capt. Farrell helped to evacuate the surviving colonists from Port Breton in February 1882 in exchange for all the abandoned machinery, a small steamer, and goods. He also paid them 500 pounds plus coal and provisions, to enable their ship "Genil" to reach Sydney. Some of the men who had come as colonists on the expedition (including Mouton's father, Tetzlaff, Semerida, Lemesle, Benninger, Coulfuty, Brandt, Coenen and Dupre) remained in the Bismarck Archipelago area as traders, many of them working for Hernsheim. (Mouton 1974: 48-49, fn 18)

Under the leadership of Marquis de Rays, a charlatan who had never set foot in the Pacific, naive Frenchmen had sailed out to establish an outpost of

French culture and expand the imperial realm. The attempt to set up a French colony on New Ireland was a caricature of colonialism, doomed to failure.

The description of the purchase of land by the colonists from Maragano reveals several things. The Europeans were so intent on buying land, that they engaged with him in what was a mockery of honestly constituted land purchase. Because of Maragano's assertion that he was the local leader with whom the Europeans must deal, and his cozying-up to the European leaders, the latter called him "King of Lambom." In reality, he was no more than another New Ireland Big Man.

The New Irelanders probably could not understand why the French, who possessed superior equipment, were not able to make a success of farming, while they themselves were economically successful in the same place. The failure of the French must have been perceived by the surrounding New Irelanders as representing the fallibility of Europeans.

In contrast to farming, the trading stations established by Hernsheim and others represented a less intrusive presence for the New Irelanders and benefited them in terms of what they obtained. For the New Irelanders, little remained from this intense period of contact, except the stuff that myths are made of. (See, for example, the Lak myth, in Albert n.d.)

Discussion

The sustained contact between Europeans and New Irelanders during the period from 1870 to 1884 resulted in a number of important changes in the lives of New Irelanders. For the first time, Europeans lived in close proximity with some of the people of the island. For the Europeans, the trading stations represented outposts of loneliness and isolation. A curious reversal took place for some of the traders. They became "savages," Wild Men isolated from their own cultures, drunken brutes who killed people without cause, a theme central to Joseph Conrad's writing. This reversion to savagery is the story of Kurtz in *Heart of Darkness*.

The Europeans had differing attitudes towards Melanesians and Polynesians. Several traders, including Blohm, Christophen and Capt. Farrell, had Polynesian or Micronesian wives or women living with them, but none seemed to have formed relationships with or married women from New Ireland. In contrast to them, Hernsheim remained an urbane, cultivated man who tried to recreate his own cultural setting. He felt himself superior to, and looked down upon most of the other European traders as drunken brutes. Though he was not aloof from contact with New Irelanders, he also saw them as "savages," much lower on the evolutionary scale than himself with "primitive" forms of political organization and "the most primitive type of barter."

Still another European adaptation was that of Mouton. He came to the islands as an adolescent boy with the Marquis de Rays expedition, lived with a Tolai woman, and learned the Tolai language. He later married an Australian woman and divided his time between Sydney and Rabaul, where his business interests included ownership of the *Rabaul Times* and the first cinema in Rabaul.

During the time that Europeans were engaged in trading for supplies, with their ships as the base of operations, New Irelanders had controlled the exchange process. They determined where it would occur, and they could also, if they wished, turn their canoes around and not exchange at all. Exchange in the liminal area appears to have been satisfactory to both sides. The Europeans got their supplies in abundance and the New Irelanders got their iron and the other items they desired. Trading stations, however, brought strangers with their foreign cultures right into their villages.

The establishment of trading stations created a volatile and unbalanced situation. The New Irelanders outnumbered the Europeans, but the Europeans had guns. The first trading stations in the Bismarcks, set up on New Britain, constituted intrusions, and were met with violent responses. The people of New Britain, like the New Irelanders shortly later, saw the Europeans as enemies in their midst. The Europeans had contempt for them and did not propose to live like New Irelanders, as had castaways such as Manners, who lived a village and was given wives.

The New Irelanders did not want Europeans living in their villages, even though trading stations brought goods they desired. Their initial response to the setting up of stations was to torch them and drive the traders out, the latter fearing for their lives. The New Irelanders, however, did eventually permit Europeans to establish trading stations in their villages. But this act allowed an intrusion into their lives and began a period when control over their destiny would be lost.

There is no information about the day-to-day interaction between the Europeans on trading stations and local people, except when hostilities between them broke out. When traders like Brandt or Sandbergen would "shoot a kanaka dead without cause," local villagers would drive the trader out and burn the station. When incidents occurred, the European reaction was to shoot people. Their response to the burning of stations was to bring in gunboats and burn down entire villages, attempting to force people collectively into submission.

NEW IRELANDERS ENCOUNTER CAPITALISM

When the locus of exchange moved from the liminal area between the beach and the boat to the trading station on village land, the nature of exchange also changed. Capitalist forms of exchange, based on supply and demand, introduced by the traders at their trading stations, involved different rules of exchange. Hernsheim tried to teach the New Irelanders that they would have to bring him a steady supply of copra, bêche-de-mer, and tortoise shell, in order to get the goods they desired. At first, many were uncertain what to bring for exchange. Recognizing that items New Irelanders desired had a long life, Hernsheim taught them to smoke tobacco, so as to create a felt need which could only be satisfied by their trading copra for tobacco on a regular basis.

Hernsheim's capitalist operation was but dimly understood by the New Irelanders, until other traders appeared and began to compete with Hernsheim and one another. The New Irelanders then began to understand that the price of copra could vary and that they could sell to the trader who gave them more beads and of different colors, better axes, and even guns. They had little notion of the price which a trader received when he sold the copra on the world market, or what the beads and other trade goods cost him there. Up to this point, New Irelanders had viewed their own indigenous exchanges in terms of fixed values - a certain amount of shell money for a canoe, a fishing net, a spear, and the recitation of a magic spell. This was clearly contrary to capitalist principles. To the New Irelanders, coconuts and yams were not items to be exchanged, yet these were the items that traders wanted to buy. New Irelanders' ideas about values in exchange, at this point, began to change in significant ways. The price which the traders were willing to give them for copra or yams varied in ways that they could not control, in contrast to their earlier fixed system of exchange. That was how the capitalist system ultimately tied the New Irelanders to Germany and the world market.

The setting up of trading stations did not preclude the continuation of trading for copra from ships, as long as it remained profitable, since it was less of an intrusion. However, as the trading station business thrived, Europeans established more trading stations. The production of coconuts must have been expanded in order for hundreds of thousands of pounds of copra to have been collected per month. The New Irelanders had obviously learned what Hernsheim had taught them. They probably increased their copra production because they wanted what the European traders offered, especially tobacco.

Political leaders in areas where trading stations had been established became more powerful and wealthy in trade goods than those in areas where trading stations were absent, upsetting the New Irelanders' regional balance of power. The Big Man with whom the castaway Manners lived became more powerful because of Manners' knowledge. At a later time, Big Men in villages where trading stations were set up became more powerful because of greater access to trade goods. Big Men who made the first contacts with Europeans probably were very assertive individuals. Maragano, the Big Man of Lambom Island, had to flee from his home on the mainland because of a charge of adultery. Despite his marginal status on Lambom Island, his assertiveness enabled him to achieve Big Man status there; and he was the individual whom the Europeans dealt with and referred to as "King." The establishment of trading stations in particular places made the groups that lived there important as nodes in the exchange network. This was the case with Nusa, and to a lesser extent with Kapsu as well. A similar effect was brought about in the area around Port Breton for a time as a result of the abortive Marquis de Rays colony. Europeans sought to make long term agreements or contracts with the indigenous population, to guarantee a continuing supply of copra, or to purchase land for trading stations; and thus they looked for "chiefs" who could speak for and had authority over "tribes." There was no referent in European languages for the type of leadership position which the Big Man represented. As explorers had done before them, they referred to all leaders as "chiefs" or "kings."

The Europeans also introduced the notion of alienation of land. Land was clan owned and did not often pass from one clan to another[6]. Despite this, some Big Men like Maragano began to "sell" land to Europeans when they had no personal rights over that land. Europeans assumed that Big Men did have the right to "sell" clan land, and that they now "owned" it. The alienation of clan-owned land created friction because the New Irelanders had one set of ideas about the relationship to land that conflicted with that of the Europeans.

A pattern of trading stations was superimposed upon the pre-contact checkerboard pattern of alternation of enemies and allies. When trading stations were established at two locations where the people were traditional enemies to one another, the intersection of the enemies and allies pattern with that of the trading station produced interesting results. For example, Hernsheim called on the Nusa people to help him put down the "uprising" of the Lavongai. Europeans simply became other allies in the pattern. At Port Breton, the people of Lambom Island were in close contact with and benefitted from their interaction with the Europeans, while their traditional enemies, the interior Golon, did not. When foreigners were incorporated within the category of allies, they automatically were put into the category of enemies by others. Hernsheim realized that simply ending a conflict by force would not work; and he reestablished peace with the people at Butbut and at Nusa in the traditional New Ireland manner. Just as the Europeans were fitted into the New Irelanders' pattern of enemies and allies, so also Hernsheim was fitted into the indigenous pattern of peacemaking.

Since warfare was endemic in this area, the introduction of guns through trade or as a result of labor recruiting, to be discussed in the next chapter, also resulted in significant changes in the balance of power. Groups that had acquired one or two guns had advantages over their enemies who had none. Leaders who acquired guns became much more important since the power they had over others was thereby increased. Acquisition of guns also made New Irelanders more formidable in hostilities against Europeans.

The time immediately preceding the colonial period must have been perceived by New Irelanders as a very unstable one, since their earlier way of life was being threatened. New Irelanders were no longer able to completely control who came to live on the island. The trading stations being established brought disputes and conflicts into villages, and villagers were provoked into attacking them.

A war between New Irelanders and all Europeans had been initiated on New Britain with the burning of the first trading stations, the killing of Fijians, and Rev. Brown's retaliatory raid. Overpowering the Europeans and forcing them off the islands must have appeared as a hopeless proposition when the first gunboat, the "Habicht," appeared. Gunboats blowing up villages, and punitive expeditions were repeated many times during the colonial period.

NOTES

1. This event is still remembered, and was told to Klaus Neumann by John Vuia, a Tolai political leader from Matupi. (Neumann 1992:85)

2. Years later, Phebe Parkinson, wife of Richard Parkinson, who had established the first plantation in New Britain, wrote to the wife of Rev. Rickard, the Methodist missionary, and reminded her of a dinner party at

NEW IRELANDERS ENCOUNTER CAPITALISM

Hernsheim's and the "enjoyable hours we had with him reading Shakespear." (Phoebe Parkinson Correspondence

3. Plantation Produce

Dates	Crops	Plantations			
		Nusa	Lihir	Kapsu	Kablaman
May 26, 1880	Copra	30,000 lbs.			
June 16, 1880		58,000 lbs.			
June 26, 1880	Yams		18,000 lbs.		
August 8, 1880	Yams	(Nusa?) 90,000 lbs.			
September 17, 1880	Yams		1,000 lbs.		25,000 lbs.
[No figures for 1881 or 1882]					
April 23, 1883		91,000 lbs. 60,000 lbs. (waiting)		160,000 lbs.	
June 5, 1883		70,000 lbs.			
July 10, 1883				90,000 lbs.	
July 10, 1883	Bêche-de-mer	10,000 lbs.		32 bags	
July 10, 1883	[Yams?]			120,000 lbs. (waiting)	

Dates	Crops	Plantations			
		Nusa	Lihir	Kapsu	Kablaman
Sept. 30, 1883	[Yams?]			94,000 lbs. (waiting) 23,000 lbs.	
Sept. 30, 1883	Bêche-de-mer			800 lbs.	
Source: Hernsheim 1983					

4. The descendants of these Chinese immigrants, who took New Ireland

5. While Niau is an important source on the Marquis de Rays expedition, his book was based primarily on his parents' recollections of their experiences as members of the expedition. His descriptions reveal his biased attitudes and his contempt for New Irelanders. For example, he states, "The natives devour each other quite impartially when nothing else is to be had." (Niau 1936)

6. New Ireland clans were based on matrilineal descent, as we discussed in Chapter 2. Since Europeans understood neither the organizational features of matrilineal descent nor the nature of membership in matrilineal clans, they could not know who was and who was not a member of a clan. All the members of a matrilineal clan must agree to sell their clan land; but Europeans had no idea who made up that membership.

7. BLACKBIRDING: SHANGHAIING NEW IRELAND WORKERS FOR THE PLANTATIONS

The plantations which had been established in Queensland, Fiji, and Samoa required extensive labor. When local labor was found to be insufficient for the plantations, recruitment from elsewhere, or "blackbirding," was instituted. Sometimes the same individuals, like Captains Wawn and Farrell, recruited laborers in the Bismarck Archipelago for the German plantations in Samoa while trading for copra. Labor recruitment was another aspect of capitalism which the indigenous population did not clearly understand. At first attracted by the gifts offered by the labor recruiters, they did not comprehend that they were committing themselves to indentured service for several years. Nor did they understand that the commitment involved going on European ships to a strange country. And they did not know what life on the plantation would be like.

Between 1870 and 1880, British and Australian labor recruiters for Queensland sugar plantations had focused their attention on the Solomon Islands and New Hebrides. When they began to have difficulty in recruiting men from those areas, they turned to the Bismarck Archipelago as a new source of labor. For the first time, in November 1882, the "Lord of the Isles" visited the northern part of New Ireland near Nusa and successfully recruited 178 men for Fijian sugar plantations. Its success prompted ships recruiting for Queensland plantations to turn their attention to the Bismarcks in search of men. The "Hopeful," from Townsville, Queensland, tried unsuccessfully to recruit men from the southwestern part of New Ireland in 1883 but eventually returned to Queensland with some whom they had kidnapped. Fijian and Samoan catechists from Rev. Benjamin Danks's Methodist mission on the Duke of York Islands may have actively dissuaded potential recruits from going on the "Hopeful." (Docker 1970:176-177; see also Chapter 8.)

First-hand Accounts of Labor Recruiters

The process of recruiting for Queensland plantations is vividly described by Capt. Wawn. In April 1883 he went to Port Hunter on the Duke of York Islands, picked up interpreters, and then sailed to the west coast of New Ireland, where he recruited along the coast between Cape Givry and Cape Strauch -- in both Barok and Patpatar language areas. Wawn reported:

> On the third day, April 28, I engaged seventy-one men by 3 p.m., being even obliged to send back several who came off in the recruiting boats, as my licensed quota was made up. I had now 143 men and one woman on board; and, had I been able to carry them, I might have doubled that number in the course of the next twenty-four hours.

> The excitement all along this part of the coast was intense. The boats were sometimes fairly rushed by men eager to get away, who tumbled in without waiting to be asked, and fought and struggled with such of their friends as strove to detain them. Many, who were afraid they might miss the opportunity, paddled off to the ship in small canoes or on bamboo catamarans.... or with the aid of dry logs.... Some of the older men, who disapproved of this wholesale exodus, also took to their canoes and chased the runaways. All round the ship

at least fifty canoes carrying over a hundred men, were paddling about, chasing or being chased.... There was no waiting for 'pay', nor yet for any agreement with regard to the term of service in Queensland, or the remuneration at the end of it. All they wanted was to get away.... Next [day], we took stock of the crowd we had on board, taking down their names and explaining the terms of agreement for service in Queensland. Lastly, we served out blankets, pipes, and tobacco to them. Many had never used tobacco as yet, but they all seemed eager enough to learn how to do so. (Wawn 1893: 295-297)

While Wawn was in the channel between the Duke of York Islands and New Ireland, about a half-mile from the New Ireland coast, fourteen men "slipped overboard and made for shore." The early recruits clambered aboard Wawn's ship, desiring a new experience, though clearly, they did not comprehend what was involved. However, by the time the ship reached the Duke of York Islands, fourteen men experienced a change of heart. A conflict was being played out here between older men, probably community leaders, who did not want productive younger laborers to leave, and the latter, who saw labor recruitment as an adventure.

The "Fanny," the "Jessie Kelly," the "Stanley," and the "Lord of the Isles," together with the "Hopeful," had recruited 528 laborers from New Ireland in one month. (Docker 1970:179) After the initial recruiting in 1883, the attention of the labor recruiters shifted to the small islands off New Ireland: Tanga, Lihir, and Tabar. Recruiting was successful, although two men from the "Forest King" were tried in Brisbane, Australia and found guilty of kidnapping six men from Tabar in June 1884. (Wawn 1893:333)

A.J. Duffield was a British Government Agent who came to the Pacific to see for himself "the mysteries of the slave trade." He was aboard the "Heath" when it arrived off New Ireland on January 21, 1884, and proceeded to recruit laborers from the off-islands. Duffield provides a description of "the way of kidnapping of these people":

> ... There are two lifeboats attached to each slaver. Early in the morning these are manned with a mixed crew of 'old boys' who had been kidnapped at Fiji or the New Hebrides. Each carries a rifle and five rounds of cartridges. The recruiter goes in one boat- the Government Agent in the other. There is a box of 'trade' in each boat. As the boats reach the shore the natives swarm down to the beach, and many swim off to the boats, men and women, hoping to have a chance of stealing something. The recruiter soon finds out if the natives are friendly or not. He opens his shop, so to speak, begins playing on a Jew's-harp or talking in broken English, hoping the natives will understand him. After a tedious while it becomes known that the recruiter will give two knives, a thimbleful of beads, two tobacco pipes, some figs of tobacco, three fish hooks, a Jew's-harp, a looking glass, and a gawdy pocket-handkerchief, for one man. This is too little, or it is sufficient, according to the plenty or scarcity of men.... The property is divided among the man's friends, whom he leaves behind, a portion of it goes to the 'King' or head man.... It is the recruiter's duty to tell all the people who are thus bought that they are going to work on a sugar plantation in Queensland for three years; that they will be well fed, and clothed, and lodged, and at the end of three years they will all come back again with the sum of L 18 in their pockets, or as many beads and pipes as this money will buy.

BLACKBIRDING: SHANGHAIING NEW IRELAND WORKERS

> Great numbers of men and women were thus obtained in these islands -- minus the information which it was the duty of the recruiter to give the islander.... I will venture to say that no islander ever came to Queensland from those islands who knew what he was coming for -- the work he was expected to do, the hours he was to work, or the years he was to stay. The native language is not known by anyone out of the islands.... The language in which the recruiter generally talks to the people whom he is going to enlist, or kidnap, or beguile, is the limited language of sign or pantomime. (Duffield 1889: 104-106)

Once the New Irelanders were on board, the women among them were given gowns to wear. However, they chose to tear them into strips to adorn their heads rather than to wear them, since traditionally they wore no clothing. The men and women were given foods like rice and became very fond of tea. During the voyage, they occupied their time making "minute beads" of shell, presumably creating shell money.

The process of recruiting also is described by Douglas Rannie, who became a government agent operating out of Queensland in 1884. His task was to see to it that labor recruiting regulations were observed. At Tanga, his ship, the "Heron," picked up an interpreter named Mungish, who had been to Queensland. A "chief" named Ambulull, many of whose men had previously gone to Queensland, informed the mate that he himself wanted to go there. The "chief" and twelve of his men were recruited, since the mate felt that the presence of the "chief" on board would help to induce others to come.

After recruiting forty men from different villages on Tanga, the "Heron" proceeded to Lihir. "Here we were confronted by a crowd of men on the beach with their faces all whitewashed, their ribs all painted white, and with white stripes drawn down their legs." (1912: 53) Rannie's rowers warned him against going any closer, and, in fact, they were attacked with slingstones from the shore. It seems likely that Ambulull, the "chief," was their enemy, so they felt it necessary to attack.

They immediately went on to "Mallymean" (Mali Island, off Lihir), where the reception was much friendlier. "They were much impressed, and could hardly credit the news when Mungish, our interpreter, told them that Ambulull, the chief of the Caen group [Tanga], was on board, and going to Queensland.... Ambulull, I learned, was a chief of great note among all these small islands, and had earned wide renown in bygone years as a wise man as well as a warrior." (Rannie 1912:55-56)

Although Ambulull, the so-called "chief," accompanied the recruiters throughout Lihir, they only got nine recruits, six men and three women. Mungish was given "a wealth of stuff" for his services as interpreter, so much that he was dissuaded from going himself to Queensland, and returned to his home on Tanga, where the ship took on a large amount of food. On August 31, 1884, it returned to Rockhampton, in Queensland.

The "Heron" had its greatest success recruiting on Tanga because Ambulull was from Tanga. If he was willing to go to Queensland, many other Tangan men were eager to join him, though labor recruitment appealed primarily to boys and young men. Although the recruiters were duty bound to explain exactly what the conditions of employment were to be, Duffield and Rannie were convinced that these were not really understood. (See also Alexander MacDonald, in Saunders 1982: 131.) Interpreters were taken aboard to assist in explaining what was involved. Basically, the appeal of the recruiters played upon the New Irelanders' sense of adventure. The goods, some of which were given in advance and distributed to friends and relatives, acted as an additional inducement.

BLACKBIRDING: SHANGHAIING NEW IRELAND WORKERS

There is little information about the life of the New Irelanders on Queensland plantations and no indication of their feelings about it or reaction to it. There was no existing legislation about maximum hours of work for indentured laborers from Melanesia. Saunders has noted that, "...Violence and coercion were central elements in the operation of the plantation...." (1982:76) Laborers lived either in housing constructed by their masters or in huts modeled after their own houses, but of inferior material. They preferred these because people from the same area could stay together. (Saunders 1982) The incidence of illness and death on the plantations was very high. It is not surprising that some New Irelanders tried to flee. Corris notes that, "...Some New Irelanders absconded from a plantation in the Mackay district and went wild in the bush, raiding plantations and especially the chicken coops. Another group fled a plantation and attempted to sail for home in an open boat, but lacking oars, they drifted back to shore and were captured." (Corris 1968:95) This desperate attempt to flee represents a response to the terrible conditions of life on the plantations.

Though many labor recruits died in Queensland, others lived to return to their homes in New Ireland. Rannie describes the return of recruits in 1887 and the great welcome they received. His ship, the "Para," went up the east coast. "...At these villages we kept landing our return islanders in twos and threes." (Rannie 1912: 260)

Two recruits were landed close to Cape Santa Maria, at a "passage" where people from the interior came down to exchange goods with coastal people.

> Suddenly, a native walked out with spear and club, and looking at us for a second or two was about to spring back in the scrub whence he had emerged. But our two returns in the boats recognized

him and called him by name.... Then he shouted some words in his own dialect which started such a demoniac yelling.... these wild bushmen were only shouting for joy and to welcome back their more adventurous comrades, whom they had long given up hopes of seeing again.... They crowded round the boats eager and anxious to see the wealth of goods brought back by their countrymen.... They beheld the accumulation of tomahawks, knives, axes, beads, mirrors, mouth-organs, jews' harps, fish-hooks and fancy prints.... Many desired here and [there] to engage themselves for Queensland, but as they were now German subjects, we had to refuse them." (Rannie 1912: 262-263)

At Lihir, Rannie was presented with an interesting problem. One of the men recruited from there, in Queensland, had married a woman from Nusa, where they had a child.

The husband and wife had to separate at once and forever. The woman dared not go ashore at her husband's place as she would be certain to be killed and eaten there. For the same reason the husband would not accompany his wife to her native place.... I naturally decided that the mother should retain possession of her child." (Rannie 1912: 271)

The father was very angry, and when the ship was about to leave came on board with ten other men, dressed for war, and tried to kidnap the boy. The mother knifed him in the chest and retrieved her child. Rannie seemed to have made his decision without knowing that descent in New Ireland is matrilineal.

From Lihir, the "Para" went on to Tabar, where "One of the men whom we had to land was a man of distinction amongst them. Those ashore paid him every deference, and he ordered them about in the most autocratic manner. He made them load my boat with food and vegetables of many kinds, for which he allowed no pay to be taken.... I managed to obtain with some little difficulty two of their demon-gods." (Rannie 1912: 272-73)[1].

The "Para" went through the "Staffen Straits," stopping at Nusa, and then sailing down the west coast.

> We had a few men to land on this side, but found their friends very shy and unwilling to come near the boats.... As we proceeded further along the coast the natives began to show more signs of civilisation. Still further along... most of the men wore a narrow strip of calico or print about them. I attributed this approach to decency and also the absence of offensive weapons, to the influence of native Fiji missionary teachers, who had been placed at different spots along the coast.... Although these natives had made a start to embrace the Christian faith, they had not yet given up their cannibalistic practices. (Rannie 1912: 275)

The "Para" then stopped at Matupi, and Rannie met Emma Forsayth at a dinner given for him by Eduard Hernsheim. He attended the celebration on July 4, 1887, at Ralum, Mrs. Forsayth's residence, where the American Consul also had his house.

Europeans' Differing Official Positions on Labor Recruitment

Europeans publicly took different positions on labor recruitment. The missionaries opposed labor recruitment on moral grounds and also because it interfered with their own business of missionizing. Still others equated it with kidnapping and protested on humane grounds because of its effects on the people being recruited. It also was seen as having disruptive effects on the life of the indigenous population. It interfered with trading station activity, which people like Hernsheim wanted to foster. Hernsheim expressed his opinion in a Queensland newspaper:

> Firstly, this [recruiting] resulted in the removal of a large number of the young men and women of working age; secondly, the chiefs obtained in this way all the goods and arms they needed without having to work for them; and thirdly, this recruiting led to a great deal of trouble and shooting between the natives and ships' crews in which it was difficult to decide which side had been the aggressor. (Hernsheim 1983: 78)

Though Hernsheim opposed labor recruiters, his own traders sometimes became involved with them. The traders not only provided them with interpreters, but sometimes even recruited men for them. Hernsheim recorded, on June 5, 1883, that,"Stanley [a labor trader] went to Nusa by boat and with the help of Lemesle [a trader who had come with the Marquis de Rays expedition] or of his Solomons boys got 6 or 7 boys there, of course they were stolen." (1983: 150) On September 3, 1883, he noted, "Brandt [also from the Marquis de Rays expedition] has far too many dealings with the labor ships...is reported to have accepted gifts of trade goods.... The labor ships give the traders absolutely anything they want so as to get interpreters. "Mary" ["Ninfoo"] lost 72 men again in Nusa. Bad treatment, fight on Nusa point. Ten labor ships been there." (Hernsheim 1983: 155)

By 1883, only three years after Hernsheim had opened the first trading station there, the small island of Nusa appears to have become the hub of an enormous amount of activity. Not only did recruiting take place there, but Nusa appears to have become an indispensable source of interpreters for recruiters going to other areas. Presumably, the Nusa people spoke some English or Pidgin English, which the labor recruiters understood. In order to operate beyond their own Tigak-speaking district, the Nusa people who became interpreters had to speak other New Ireland languages. When men jumped ship at Nusa, as in the case of the "Mary Ninfoo," this brought men from other parts of New Ireland into the Nusa community, with a possibly disruptive effect. Nusa was becoming a center of commercial activity involving the Europeans and the local people there were benefiting from being central nodes in this newly emerging economic network.

A complaint made by Togalo, who served in the crew of a labor recruiting vessel, presents a New Ireland point of view on labor recruiting. Dated January 3, 1884, it was included in Rev. Rickard's papers. Togalo said,

> Four of us -- Topulut, Tomarakau, Kupu and myself left Waira about a month ago in the Queensland Labour vessel "Fanny" as boat's crew. We went first to Kalil where we bought 4 natives at Kabanut we bought 1 at another place, where there is a white trader living.... And at another place we bought two. I do not know of any others which were bought, though there were about 40 on board when we left. I do think most of the others were stolen for I am sure that no trade was given for them, but they were enticed near to the boat by trade being offered and taken into the boat. I do not think that the Captain and the Government Agent knew that the natives were stolen for neither of them went in the boats and we were charged not to tell them. A black man named `Dick' had charge of one boat, and a white man, perhaps the mate called something like `Prank or Frank' had charge of the officers. At one place, the natives fired upon us from a cliff above the boat; we fired upon them and killed three.

We saw a great deal of immorality on the part of the sailors to the women both on shore and on board. The sailors called it 'niknik' [Rickard notes on the margin in parenthesis, 'word used by Australian blacks for adultery']. We never heard that word before. They were angry with us because we did not persuade the natives to come aboard but we did not know the language of the people in those places, as they sent me and Topulut ashore on the far end of New Ireland. Then left us saying that the ship was going to Queensland and they would send Kupu and Tomarakou [sic] ashore after which they never did. We believe that they have stolen these two also. for we know that they were never very willing to go to Queensland and they expected to be landed with us. We had great difficulty in getting home from that distant place on New Ireland. (Rickard 1882-1893: 96)

These New Ireland men saw fellow New Irelanders being kidnapped and stolen; and, in fact, some of the New Ireland boat crew members themselves had been kidnapped to Queensland. Though this is the first mention of concourse between sailors and New Ireland women, it is likely that it was more widespread[2].

The arms which New Irelanders were getting from labor recruiters gave Europeans great concern. Capt. Wawn claimed that, though the thousands of Snider rifles in the hands of the Solomon Islands people had the mark of British manufacture, they had been sold to the Solomon Islanders by German traders. He also stated that Hernsheim himself, despite his protestations, was exchanging Snider cartridges for copra in New Britain. In 1877, a Liberal government in Australia had passed regulations which prohibited the export of firearms to the Pacific Islands. Docker notes that if such a law had been enforced, labor recruiting would have become impossible, but the government looked the other way. (Docker 1970: 145)

The effect of recently introduced arms was reported by Romilly as he travelled along the coast of New Ireland. He saw "...another party of cannibals...eating three men in a small island about two hundred yards from the ship. They received muskets from labour ships about a week ago, and are like children with new toys. They at once went to war with their neighbours, and three men were bagged." (Romilly 1893:187)

There also were reports of incidents of recruiters shooting natives. Hernsheim, in 1883, described in his diary the episode of the "Ninfoo," a German owned schooner involved in inter-island trade. Hernsheim observed: "27 August (1883): I hear from the New Ireland boys that "Ninfoo "has been creating disgraceful havoc up there.... "Ninfoo" mate shot dead two men on Enuk and burnt down all the houses. Temple ornaments stolen. Witnesses: Midir and Lemus. Perhaps I should report to Consulate General in Samoa." (Hernsheim 1983: 150, 153)

Another account of the same incident, from D. Nisbet, Government Agent of the "Falcon," is presented by Corris: "The men in the boats [of the "Niafu" or "Ninfoo"] were standing up shooting at the natives on the shore who were slinging stones at them. The German second mate of the "Niafu" told the "Falcon's" government agent that he was shooting at the natives because four of his recruits had deserted at that place. The natives, on the other hand, claimed that the recruiters were shooting at them because they had provided them with no recruits." (Corris 1968:90, from Extract of Diary of D. Nisbet, Government Agent, "Falcon," enclosed in Agent General of Immigration to Colonial Secretary, 15 Feb. 1884, F.C.S.O., 380-1884)

Hugh Romilly, a British Deputy Commissioner, was sent to assess the effects of labor recruiting. He chartered Hernsheim's schooner "Montiara" in 1883 to go to New Ireland to "...follow the tracks of the labour ships, and explain personally to the natives what they would have to expect should they ship to Queensland." (Romilly 1893:178) He concluded that,

> The labor vessels have taken away some two thousand of the best men- a loss which, out of a population of at the outside of fifty thousand, is felt severely.... Of the goods left behind by the labour ships in exchange for labourers, the muskets become useless with rust and neglect; glass trade beads and trade calico soon lose their charm and the merits of tobacco are only beginning to be appreciated just as the supply is becoming exhausted. Then the New Irelanders find themselves in a bad way indeed; the deadly weapons on which they relied, useless; their tribe weakened by the loss of their best men; and their neighbors threatening on account of this loss. (Romilly 1886: 39-40)

He commented later on, "I believe they all kidnap more or less, and there have been some very bad cases. The result is that wretched traders, living by themselves in spots visited by these ships, get murdered out of revenge by the natives." (Romilly 1893:182)

A series of new regulations regarding labor recruitment were then put into effect by the Australian government in March 1884. The March act prohibited recruiters from retaking men who had deserted. On the other hand, in Wawn's view, "An islander might now engage to come to Queensland, get 'trade' to the value of a pound or two, give it to his friends, cadge all he could on board, and then cooly walk or swim ashore." (1893: 332)

The period of blackbirding on New Ireland was an extremely brief one. It began in November 1882, and, "In May 1884 the Premier announced that because of the high death rate he had given orders to all government agents that no more recruits were to be taken from New Ireland and New Britain, 'as the natives were totally unfit for the work, and only came to the colony to die'." (Corris 1968:95) In August 1884, New Ireland became a German colony, and all labor recruiting for Australia ended.

Discussion

Labor recruiting represented a new type of contact between New Irelanders and Westerners. Trading stations had placed Europeans on New Ireland itself, but the recruiters brought New Irelanders into the midst of Western culture. Young men often went willingly in search of adventure. Sometimes they went at the behest of their clan leader, who desired the trade goods labor recruiters offered. At other times, they were "stolen" from their villages, the unwilling victims of kidnappings. Women who had been left behind heard the exciting tales of returnees and expressed a desire to be recruited. The horizons of those who went were greatly expanded, as they learned something of another language and saw a different culture operating.

However, life on the Queensland plantations was lonely, hard and very cruel. Plantation conditions were so horrible, that some resorted to desperate measures and tried to escape in canoes without paddles. Many died there.

New Irelanders met people from other South Pacific islands, and sometimes even married them. Those returning received a 'box' filled with all kinds of trade goods, which guaranteed them an immediate improvement in their social and political status, since they used the goods to their great advantage in the New Ireland exchange system.

Men of mountainous interior villages, who for the most part had been isolated from Europeans, came to the "passages" where trade took place and were recruited there. Corris notes, "Markets between bush and salt-water people also offered opportunities to recruiters.... Recruiting ships often anchored at places where markets were held and waited for market-day when they might hope to recruit some volunteers from the bush through the intermediacy of the coastal people." (1973: 56)

Labor recruiters found themselves caught up in local networks of enemies and allies as the traders had been. Just as trade had affected the nature of political leadership, labor recruiting also had an effect. The nature of warfare and the balance of power between enemies was significantly altered when guns were distributed by some blackbirders to help them get recruits.

Returning laborers often used their language ability acquired abroad, serving as interpreters for traders and recruiters and further enhancing their political positions. Men who had served as laborers in Queensland often learned English. Rannie's use of Mungish exemplifies this. Those New Irelanders who became labor recruits, and were fortunate enough to return home had a more intensive exposure to Euro-Australian culture, eating European foods and wearing European clothing. However, the first thing recruits did on returning home was to cast off their European clothes. Recruits no doubt brought back stories from Australia, which were a mix of wonder at the marvels of Euro-Australian culture on the one hand, and tales of hardship, death and degradation on the other. The fortunate ones who returned found their positions enhanced by having gone.

Though German and British officialdom in the Pacific tried to control the chaotic blackbirding situation and prevent kidnapping, it was clear that the increasing labor demands of the colonial economic juggernaut had to be fed.

The islanders recruited (or stolen) from New Ireland and other parts of Melanesia were primarily on the losing end. Though they received goods and a view of "civilization," this was no recompense for the disruption caused on a broader scale, in terms of the reduction of the local labor force, disease, depopulation, effects on the indigenous political structure, and the introduction of new weaponry.

NOTES

1. The ethnographic objects given to Rannie are, at present, in the Museum at the University of Glasgow. Even at this time, Europeans coming to New Ireland were attracted by the ceremonial objects of the New Irelanders, which today are in the category of Tribal Art and are in great demand.

2. Sahlins points out the important role that women played in the interaction between English sailors and Hawaiians. Hawaii. (Sahlins 1985, see also Hezel 1983 for a discussion of similar occurrences in Ponape and Kosrae.)

8. CHRISTIANITY COMES TO NEW IRELAND: ESTABLISHMENT OF MISSIONARY STATIONS

Though missionary activity began in the Pacific at the end of the eighteenth century, when the London Missionary Society (LMS) sent parties to set up missions in Tahiti and the Marquesas, it did not begin in New Ireland until 1875. Before 1860, missionary activity in the Pacific was primarily in the hands of Protestants representing the extension of the Evangelical Revival in England. Their mission was "...to convince all men (in whatever state, all equally condemned) of their innate depravity, of their need for a saviour or mediation with God, and finally of belief in the atonement and the consequent salvation of believers." (Gunson 1978:27) In Polynesia and in the Bismarck Archipelago, missionaries typically arrived first, and then a colonial administration was established.

The motives of those drawn to missionary work in the distant and dangerous Pacific were two-fold: Firstly, they desired to serve God by converting the "savages," enabling the latter to redeem their souls and not descend into hell. This combined with a second feeling that by doing this, they themselves were growing spiritually and saving their own souls. Missionaries saw themselves as men of destiny determined to overthrow idolatry and heathenism and establish the true church, although the preconceptions of some missionaries regarding the "ignoble heathen" were modified by their experience and their intellectual curiosity to learn more about the way of life of the people whose lives they had come to change. (Langmore 1989:110)

The notion of rebirth through revival and conversion was central to Wesleyan belief[1]. Gunson observes, "We find repeatedly in Wesleyan journals the renewal of the original experience of conversion. Soul-searching was much more exacting and there would appear to have been more recognized stages of faith and holiness." (Gunson 1978:47)

The missionaries coming to the Pacific in the first days came from the lowest classes, characterized in the early nineteenth century as the "mechanics" class. As Gunson points out, they were the opposite of the South Sea Islander who, as we have noted earlier was regarded as "…the epitome of the natural man, a 'noble savage' and fit companion for a king." (1978:31) Though of humble origins, they were men with a "calling," men who wished to better themselves. (Gunson 1978)

As time passed, however, LMS missionaries belonging to the "greater middle class" began to come to the Pacific. From the beginning of the nineteenth century, the missionary rose in status, and the "noble savage" of the Enlightenment became the "ignoble savage," leading what the missionaries saw as a life of degradation. (Langmore 1989:108)

Wesleyan Methodist missionaries who missionized in the Bismarck Archipelago tended to come from rural areas and had close connections with the Wesleyans in Australia and New Zealand. After the Australasian Wesleyan Methodist Missionary Society separated from the Wesleyan Methodist Missionary Society, educational qualifications and attainment became less important than they had been for the London Missionary Society.

CHRISTIANITY COMES TO NEW IRELAND

The paternalistic, authoritarian attitude of the missionaries who came to New Ireland is conveyed in their journals and writings. The first generation of missionaries in many places, like Papua, were charismatic leaders, "men set apart from other men," "extraordinary men," in contrast to later generations who consolidated and routinized missionary activity. (Langmore 1989:206)

Though indigenization of the church and its leadership was a long-term goal, it was not achieved in New Ireland until long after this period, as we shall see. Despite the fact that the missionaries had "...nowhere raised up a nation of believers," the whole of Melanesia was looked upon as a promising area for pioneer missionary works. (Gunson 1978:334-5)

Missionaries, the first Europeans to arrive on New Ireland shores with the intention of setting up permanent establishments, came with the goal of changing other aspects of New Irelanders' life as well as the belief system. The cultural traits which they considered to be "savage" and "barbaric," such as nudity, ceremonial sexual license, warfare and cannibalism, had to be eradicated. To the missionaries, Christianity and the ways of civilization were to be adopted by the New Irelanders, along with the Protestant ethic and capitalist ideas such as working hard to raise more coconuts to produce more copra.

The Methodist, Reverend George Brown

The Methodist Reverend George Brown was the first missionary in the Bismarcks. He arrived there in 1875, just two months prior to Hernsheim's establishment of his trading station in the Duke of York Islands. Rev. Brown was born 1835 in Barnard Castle, near Durham. Though George Brown's father had started as an office boy, he later became a lawyer and the editor of a newspaper, so Brown himself was born into the bourgeoisie. At the age of twenty, he shipped out to sea. Later, he decided to go to New Zealand, where he underwent a spiritual conversion as a result of the influence of his minister uncle. He became a preacher in the Auckland circuit of the Young Men's Christian Association, and within a short time decided to devote his life to missionary work. After he married the daughter of a Methodist missionary, Rev. Brown and his new wife were sent in 1860 to their first mission station -- in Samoa. There he learned the Samoan language and developed his interest in natural history and Samoan customs.

Being an adventurous man, Rev. Brown wanted to missionize in an area where no white man had lived before. In 1874, while in Samoa, he obtained permission from the Executive Committee of the Board of Missions in Sydney to "send the missionary ship 'John Wesley' to New Britain and New Ireland to commence missionary operations." (Brown 1908: 69) Rev. Brown argued that such a mission would be inexpensive to maintain if one employed South Sea Island missionaries, with or without supervisors present. (Crocombe 1982: 3) Brown was drawn to this area because, "practically nothing was known of those islands or the people living there." (Brown 1910: v)

In addition to bringing the Gospel to indigenous people, there was something of an explorer in Rev. Brown which attracted him to unknown places and people with different ways of life. However, his view of the Bismarck Archipelago as *terra incognita* was something of an exaggeration. By 1875, Hernsheim had observed, "The natives were therefore already used to white men and some of them understood some pidgin English." (1983: 29)

Before beginning his work in the Bismarcks, Reverend Brown first went to Fiji to enlist several Fijian Methodist lay teachers to come with him. In his talks to them, Rev. Brown emphasized the difficulties they faced -- the "ferocity of the natives," as well as the unhealthiness of the climate. (Garrett

1982: 221) Two months later, on August 15, 1875, with his Fijian assistants, he set up a missionary station at Port Hunter, in the Duke of York Islands. Rev. Brown's rationale for his policy was "...that they would be able to speak sympathetically and effectively about their own conversion experiences, that they would be able to relate easily to Melanesian cultures, and that they would make few demands on the mission's meager resources because of their ability to live like their hosts." (Boutelier et.al 1978: 84)

Rev. Brown made his first visit to the coast of New Ireland on October 5, 1875. He took with him three Fijian teachers and two "influential chiefs" from Port Hunter, who were well known in that part of New Ireland, in order to use their connections to make contact with leaders there. Presumably he hoped to follow the pattern of conversion used in Fiji, in which chiefs were convinced to convert, and their people followed suit. However, as he was soon to learn, leaders in the Bismarcks did not have the power that Fijian chiefs had.

On landing at Batigoro, on the west coast, where his Port Hunter chiefs were indeed well known, Brown was welcomed in a friendly manner, indicating that he was not the first white man that they had encountered. At the village, Brown noted, "They were very quiet and unobtrusive, and all the women and girls wore a leaf or small piece of cloth, which, small as it was, showed that they had some sense of modesty, a virtue of which our Duke of York ladies appeared to be totally deficient." (1908: 110) The next day, as the ship traveled along the coast, the Port Hunter chiefs wanted to stop at villages. Rev. Brown observed, "I well knew that the chiefs only wished me to call for some little peddling transactions of their own." (1908: 110) Rev. Brown was looking for "the chief Tomum," whom another "chief," Topulu from Port Hunter, had told him to seek out. Tomum was encountered accidentally at

Dilout, and at his insistence, Brown and his party went on to stay at his village, Kail (or Kait). That evening, surrounded by a crowd, Rev. Brown evangelized,

> ...[Telling] them a little about the One God, and Father of all, the heaven which He has prepared for those who love Him, and the hell which they may shun by the acceptance of that Gospel which we declared unto them. I spoke... of the great and glorious privileges of the religion of Jesus, and also tried to show them the temporal advantages which would accrue from the civilizing and enlightening effects of Christianity. Waruwarum and Liblib [the two Port Hunter "chiefs"] acted as interpreters, and, as far as I could judge, they succeeded very well.... Tomum promised to visit me and to receive a teacher." (Brown 1908: 111)

In the evening, Brown had given Tomum a few presents while Tomum was aboard Brown's launch, including some yards of gaudy print for the women and girls. The following morning, Tomum returned with some "yams etc." for Brown.

Rev. Brown and his party then walked north along the coast and stopped at a large village called Waatpi (Watpi) where he witnessed "the inevitable Dukduk or dancing mask affair. I noticed here that all people outside kept clear of the masked figures, as they have the privilege of beating or stoning any who came in their way." (Brown 1908: 111) The Duke of York men told Rev. Brown that the Waatpi people had threatened them. He observed, "In receiving native tales I found that I must always guard against the danger of utterly discrediting every tale they tell against the people with whom they do not wish us to form any alliance." (1908: 112) On his return to Port Hunter, Rev. Brown felt that his first visit to New Ireland had been very successful.

Rev. Brown recognized that the two Port Hunter Big Men were trying to use him. The story told by the Duke of York people to Rev. Brown at Waatpi indicates that the Waatpi people were their enemies and they wanted to turn Rev. Brown against them as well. In these encounters, the Duke of York people were trying to fit Rev. Brown into the existing pattern of enemies and allies. The Duke of York men were able to serve as Rev. Brown's interpreters, communicating in Pidgin English with him, and with the New Ireland people because their two languages were closely related, belonging to the same Patpatar-Tolai subgroup.

One may wonder what the New Irelanders thought about the religious ideas that Rev. Brown was presenting to them. They might have understood the concept of God, the metaphoric Father of us all, but what could a matrilineal people make of the divine position of Jesus, the Son of God, who derived his divinity from His Father? The ideas of heaven and hell, which constituted the cosmology of Christianity, surely had no meaning for them. The temporal advantages of conversion to Christianity, however, were exemplified by the Fijian catechists and their lifestyle.

Rev. Brown made several subsequent trips to New Ireland to select a site for his first mission station. On October 5th, he went to Kalil, where he obtained a number of spears which had human arm or leg bones at one end. He was told that the owner of the spear had killed an enemy, eaten him, and placed the long bone at the end of his spear. Missionaries brought home such tokens of cannibalism, the archetypal symbols of savagery, to demonstrate the enormous problems they faced in gaining converts in the wilds of the Pacific.

There were some contradictions in Rev. Brown's view of the New Irelanders. On the one hand, he viewed them as humans who could be saved from hell if they converted to Christianity. On the other hand, his collection of such spears would indicate that he also characterized them as ferocious wild cannibals.

During November 1875, a house was built, and the first station was established at Kalil with two Fijian teachers. On returning to New Ireland, Rev. Brown employed La Bera, the Kalil "chief," to make contact with leaders of other nearby villages along the coast, ensuring that he would meet only the latter's allies, not his enemies. La Bera sought to make Rev. Brown into an ally, and to use him to further his own ends.

Rev. Brown needed to develop a written alphabet in order to translate the Holy Gospels and prayer service into the vernacular. At Kalil, Brown began to address the language problem, observing, "…after prayer, I got a lot of the men into the house to give me some words and sentences from which to form an alphabet for the use of the teachers." (1908:134)

On the following day, Brown conducted the first Christian service to be held on New Ireland at Kalil. Armed men from Kabanut joined the people of Kalil. La Bera was dressed in a shirt and waistcloth, and his wives and daughters wore handkerchiefs or small pieces of cloth. Rev. Brown conducted the service in Fijian and Pidgin English, which his assistant translated into the Duke of York language; and La Bera retranslated into Kandas, the language of the audience. Reverend Brown explained what the *Lotu*, or church service, meant, the position of the teachers, and the responsibilities of the villagers towards the teachers. Greatly encouraged by this, Brown wrote in his diary that night:

CHRISTIANITY COMES TO NEW IRELAND

> No mission could have had a more promising beginning than ours has had in all these islands. I believe that our principle difficulties in the future will arise from the great differences between the dialects, the constant feuds between the villages, and the want of authority amongst the chiefs.... the reception of the religion of Jesus will soon produce peace and order where now all is discord and confusion. (1908: 136)

When the first church in New Ireland opened at Kalil on March 18, 1876, Rev. Brown took the opportunity to inculcate capitalist behavior in his listeners. Brown stated,

> I ...gave the people a little talk about social matters in my sermon. They were anxious to get clothes, but scarcely knew how to do so. I advised them to plant nuts on a large scale, and they promised to do this. I also impressed upon them very definitely the necessity for building better houses. (1908: 156)

In order to seek possible locations for missions, Rev. Brown crossed New Ireland from the west coast to the east coast, beginning on May 30, 1876. Brown's party included Hicks (a trader for Godeffroy), Holmes, four men from Kalil including one of the Fijian teachers, and two boat crews from the Duke of York Islands. They arrived at Rataman, a village seven miles inland containing about two hundred people, where they were greeted by a ceremonial mock attack. (Brown 1908: 161-162)

After spending the night on Dolomakas Bay, a leader, Sagina, led the party further on to his own village, Kudukudu, five miles down the coast. As he was leaving the village,

...He [Sangina, the chief] put his arm around my neck and I tried to pay him the same courtesy, but as he was a fine tall man over six feet in height, I could only manage comfortably to reach his waist; and we walked along thus most lovingly, surrounded by a noisy mob all talking and shouting in great excitement.... when I looked back, and saw how far I was from the rest of my party, I had rather an uncomfortable feeling when thinking how easy it would be for that big fellow to tighten his grasp of my throat a little more, and how powerless I should be in such a case, surrounded as we were by so many of his people. (Brown 1908: 165-166)

Rev. Brown became even more aware of the multiplicity of languages on New Ireland. Thirty miles north of Kalil, Labera (La Bera), the "chief" of Kalil, who accompanied him, "...could not understand these people at first, though he afterwards understood a little when they talked in another dialect." (Brown 1908: 175) Rev. Brown must have moved from the Patpatar-speaking area into the Barok-speaking area. As a consequence, Brown arranged for the Fijian teachers to prepare vocabularies of several local languages.

After a year's residence in the Bismarck Archipelago, Brown returned to Sydney in late August, 1876. He was reappointed to the New Britain mission, and arrived back at Port Hunter in August 21, 1877, to find that only three Fijian missionaries were actually at missions in the field. The rest were at Port Hunter. One of the first teachers stationed at Kalil, Pauliasi Bunoa, documents the difficulties. "Those were hard and trying days; we were much afflicted. The people looked at us in wonder and did not understand our speech and work. They were suspicious too and at times would neither sell nor give us food. Many days have my family and I been hungry and could get nothing to eat; and no one would assist me to build my house or plant my food without being heavily paid." (Brown, quoted in Williams 1972: 108) Brown's assumption that New Irelanders would be receptive to other Pacific Islanders coming as missionaries proved to be incorrect.

Returning to New Ireland to reestablish teachers there, on October 31st, he wrote, "We held our usual prayer-meeting this morning and I returned from it with a very thankful heart, for this was the first time that any of these people had taken any public part in our service. I called upon... [Petero] Topilike of New Ireland…. Topilike's prayer was in the New Ireland language, of which I only understood a little, but it was very appropriate. We prayed in Fijian, in Samoan, in English, in Duke of York, and New Ireland languages...." (Brown 1908: 231) Petero Topilike and Apisa Turane, both from Kalil, were the first New Irelanders to be baptized after they had received religious instruction.

In early December 1877, Brown returned to New Ireland again, bringing over the teachers' wives and goods. He was encouraged to find that Le Bera, the Big Man at Kalil, was observing the Sabbath and had renounced cannibalism. "Some weeks ago the bushmen were fighting, and one man was killed. They brought the body a long distance to Le Bera, fully expecting that he would buy it as he used to do; but he positively refused to do so, telling them that he was 'lotu' now, and that he had given up cannibalism." (1908: 233)[2].

Rev. Brown was forced to return to Australia in early 1878 to defend himself against the charges resulting from the punitive expedition to avenge the killing on New Britain of Fijian catechists. He was eventually exonerated. He returned to the Bismarcks, where the Port Hunter mission was being manned by Rev. Benjamin Danks and his wife. Rev. Brown's Duke of York allies were dressing like Fijian teachers in order to entrap their enemies. While at Kabanut, to the north, he learned that,

> ...Topulu (King Dick), our Duke of York chief, had been engaged by some people further down the coast to help them with his musket in their fight with the Eretubu people. We were told that he had trapped the Eretubu natives down to the beach by dressing himself and party as teachers, who wished to buy food, and so had been able to shoot three of the unfortunate people. As this conduct would most certainly imperil the lives of our teachers, I determined to go on and investigate the matter. On our way down we met Topulu and party returning, and I had a somewhat stormy interview with the old man. He of course denied the accusation, but I told him that if I found that he had really committed the murders I would pay for the men, and he would have to refund the amount to me. (1908: 382)

The missionary activity of Rev. Brown's Fijians in New Ireland became imperiled by Topulu's fraudulent act. Allies of the Eretubu people categorized Brown as an ally of Topulu's, and therefore their enemy. In order to resolve the difficulties, Brown paid compensation to the Eretubu people. The outcome was ambiguous. As the New Irelanders saw it, Brown's payment of compensation allied him even more with Topulu. Brown's reasons for making the payment were to ensure that his Fijian catechists would not be attacked in the future.

The connection between Rev. Brown and Topulu reveals how indigenous leaders and missionaries used one another to further their own ends. As Rev. Brown utilized a connection of Topulu's on his first visit to the island, Topulu used his tie to Rev. Brown for his own purposes. Topulu was reputedly the biggest of the local political leaders because of the dealings of his clan with European traders. Topulu's "father" was particularly successful. He managed to monopolize this [Sydney based] trade to such an extent that he could supply large enough quantities of tortoise shell to make it worthwhile for John Stevens to maintain a station in Port Hunter in the early 1870s." (Sack 1973: 64) A monopoly over trade with Europeans greatly enhanced a Big Man's political influence and power beyond what it otherwise would have been.

Since Topulu had a house on the land where the first mission house was built, it is very likely that he had sold or given the mission the land for their first station. They were so afraid to offend him that they never removed his house. (Deane 1933: 196) Rev. Danks describes what Topulu was like as a young man, noting that, "...[He] seems to have had great influence, the young warriors following him gladly in all he undertook to do. He introduced new customs from other parts, new songs, dances, and new articles of faith. He was wild, restless and ambitious.... He invented many new ornaments wherewith to adorn himself." (Deane 1933: 196) Though Topulu sang the praises of traditional weapons, he was inclined to rely on the musket, which he probably got from the traders at Port Hunter.

Rev. Brown probably established his first mission station at Port Hunter because Topulu and his clan were the most powerful in the area. Their prior contacts with European traders, in addition to enhancing their power, made them familiar with European ways; and Topulu probably knew Pidgin English. By using Topulu's relationship to the New Ireland chief Tomum, Rev. Brown placed himself in Topulu's debt. Topulu's enemies might have feared him, not only because he was a fierce warrior with a gun, but also because they identified him with Brown.

In 1880 Rev. Brown, still seeking a shorter route to the east coast, crossed the mountains, accompanied by his wife and son, and spent the night at a village on the east coast opposite Lihir. A man in Rev. Brown's party overheard villagers saying that Rev. Brown and his party were from the Duke of York Islands. The people of this village were allies of the Eretubu people from the interior. They wanted to avenge the three Eretubu people who had been killed by Topulu, by killing Brown and his party. Rev. Brown and Topulu were perceived as allies. What Topulu did, Rev. Brown thus was responsible for. In addition, Brown's assistant from the Duke of York Islands, Kaplen, was recognized as "the son [really nephew] of Topulu."[3] Rev. Brown noted, "…By all their ideas of justice it was quite right for them to kill him [Kaplen], and all who were with him, as payment for the injury done them." (1908: 384) With the Fijian preacher translating into Patpatar, Brown tried to convince the villagers that he had come in peace by citing the fact that he had brought along his wife and son.

When the party came to the village of Eretubu on their return trip over the mountains, Brown paid the people their compensation for the three men shot by "King Dick," because, as he stated, "Our teachers go there to buy food, and I wished to show that we have no sympathy at all with Dick in his wicked doings." (1908: 386) This action probably had the opposite effect, confirming in the minds of the Eretubu people that Rev. Brown was Topulu's ally.

Latukefu has noted that although marriages between Fijian missionaries and local Melanesian women were common, marriage between local people and Samoans was extremely rare. One of the Fijian catechists who came in 1875 wished to marry a New Ireland girl from Kabanut. The missionaries decided that she would have to be brought to Port Hunter to be instructed in "spiritual and temporal affairs." (1978: 98) The marriage took place sometime later.

Christianity and Gender Roles

In some villages it was felt that Christianity belonged solely to the men. (Threlfall 1975: 50) In New Ireland culture ritual activities associated with death and mourning and cults like the *dukduk* and *Sokopana* were exclusively controlled by men. Since the presence of women at the ceremonies diluted the ritual power of men, they were excluded. The Christian message which Rev. George Brown preached -- emphasizing death, resurrection, and the saving of one's soul -- seemed to place it squarely within the male province of mortuary rites and religious cults. It is no wonder that Christianity at first was seen as "belonging solely to the men."

Using Power to "Civilize" New Irelanders

Rev. Brown himself was seen as a powerful figure controlling the supernatural, as manifested in his oratory at services. Such oratory was an important aspect of the Big Man's role. Rev. Brown sometimes carried and used a gun, further enhancing his power.

Why would a New Ireland political leader befriend Rev. Brown, allowing him to build a mission station in his village and enlisting him as an ally? Though Brown gave out Western goods, he seems to have been ungenerous. Therefore, no great economic advantages were to be had from him. However, with his gun, he could be an important political ally, and he seemed to have an important message about the supernatural. These factors were enough to incline a political leader to exchange visits with Brown and encourage him to send a teacher to establish a mission. Since then, the image of Rev. Brown has assumed mythic qualities for New Irelanders, who still recall his first visit. (Rubel and Rosman, 1987 Field Notes)

What was Rev. Brown trying to accomplish during his five year stay in the Bismarcks? Brown was intent on saving souls and "civilizing" savages at the same time, since they were two sides of the same coin. Modesty and the wearing of clothes, building better houses, and giving up cannibalism were all part of Rev. Brown's vision of the civilized man. He tried to convey the Protestant ethic to them, to convince them that they should work harder and plant coconuts on a large scale. To the New Irelanders, the acceptance of Christianity meant a Western way of life as exemplified by the Fijian teachers. If they desired the things of civilization, acceptance of Christianity was the price. Reverend Brown envisioned the conversion of New Irelanders to Christianity as bringing peace to a land riven by warfare. However, Brown's own imperialistic Christian world saw justification for nations warring with one another, and missionaries going on retaliatory raids.

For the most part, however, the actual conveyers of the message of God were the Fijian catechists whom Rev. Brown established at a few mission stations on the west coast. The Fijian teachers used the alphabet devised by Rev. Brown to collect Patpatar vocabulary, to learn the language so that they could work with the people, translate for Rev. Brown, and translate the Gospel and prayers.

Like some other missionaries of his time, Rev. Brown's interests went beyond missionary work. He was influenced by the developing discipline of anthropology. Though he fancied himself a natural scientist, in reality he represented a curious bridge between earlier voyagers and travelers and the ethnographers of a later time. In his various ethnographic accounts of both Melanesians and Polynesians, he presented detailed descriptions of culture traits. But until they became Christians, he treated the New Irelanders in much the same way that he treated natural history specimens, such as the insects and birds he also studied. Regarding Brown's artifact collecting, Kleinschmidt is reputed to have told Rev. Danks that, "...Among the people of Sydney, Cooktown and other places our mission has a very bad name; it is generally believed that we trade and use our teachers for the purpose of securing the best curios. He assured us that Mr. Brown cared more about his name being given to a new snake, bird, or insect than he did for all the souls of the New Britain people put together." (Deane 1933: 76) The great size of Brown's ethnographic collection indicates the zeal with which he pursued this activity[4].

Reverend Benjamin Danks

Rev. Brown's successor, Rev. Benjamin Danks, and his wife arrived at Port Hunter in December 1878. During his early trips to expand missionary activity on New Ireland, Danks opened a new church at Kapatakoro, and purchased land for still another church at King, on the west coast. He had to visit the Fijian teachers periodically to deal with problems that arose. At Kapatakoro, Juliasi, the Fijian teacher, was having problems with a villager who "...had built his house right up against the church, and who deliberately disturbed the congregations during service time." (Deane 1933: 71) The "headmen" agreed to remove the house, but Danks found that nothing had been done when he returned. The house was forcibly removed by his boat crew since "the land was ours by purchase, and the man was a trespasser." (Deane 1933: 73) In order to prevent ill feeling, Danks requested that the owner of the house exchange goods with him.

In line with his crusade to get people to wear clothing, Danks describes at a later point how, "I urged that all who wished to come about the house should come dressed if only in an apron of leaves. For some days they kept it up, then leaves began to accumulate at my gateway. I found that the people dropped their leaves at the gate as they left the premises. When the stock accumulated there, they ceased to bring fresh ones, but simply turned over the old leaves...." (Deane 1933: 94-95)

Although the missionaries were making a strong effort to end nudity, people still resisted wearing clothing. In the eyes of the missionaries, nakedness was equated with paganism and unclothed people could not really be Christians, so they tried to get people to clothe themselves. In the eyes of the New Irelanders, going unclothed and decorating the hair and body in particular ways were important to their cultural identity.

The parallels between Christianity and indigenous cults are illustrated by Rev. Danks's difficulties at Kabanut. Danks noted, "...I found that the church had been built on *dukduk* ground and so the women would not come to the services. As the building was somewhat out of repair we arranged that it should be taken down and re-erected on a place to which the women could come." (Deane 1933: 81) Earlier on, in New Britain, after Danks had built a church on a piece of land sold to him, he discovered that women could not enter the church because they would not walk on the ground, presumably because it had formerly been a site for *dukduk* ceremonies. Neumann notes, for the Tolai, "The retired pastor Ainui ToVuvu of Ialakua stressed to me that in Rauluana the lotu was first allocated a taraiu, a place belonging to the tubuan, which was taboo for women and uninitiated men." (Neumann 1992: 90) The incident in New Ireland suggests that the taboo could never be lifted, and that was why the church had to be moved.

This would seem to indicate that the New Irelanders did see Christianity as a cult or secret society like the *dukduk*. Just as the women were not allowed to see or know about the secrets of the *dukduk*, New Irelanders probably reasoned that the same held for the "secrets" of Christianity, especially if the church was located on *dukduk* ground. The men of the village sold this site to the mission assuming that Christianity was, like *dukduk*, a sect for men only. The presence of only male Methodist missionaries reinforced this point.

Rev. Danks, as we noted earlier, was strongly opposed to labor recruitment because it pulled people out of their villages, disrupted the course of missionary work, and made the local population fear and distrust all white people. Rev. Danks's position drew him into conflict with Europeans. Danks prepared a list of points for his Fijian teachers to convey to the local people.

1. The white man's year is equal to two of yours (With them each monsoon meant a kilala, or a year.)

2. You cannot return home until your term of service has expired, the term being equal to six of your years.

3. The Samoan climate may not agree with you, and you may die and be buried in a strange land.

4. You will be expected to give the whole of your time to plantation work.

5. If you are placed under a good man you will be well cared for; but if otherwise, you will be miserable.

6. You will receive food and clothing while there and the payment promised you.

7. You will be brought back home at the expiration of your terms of engagement.... My record reads: The trouble is deepening and the breach between ourselves and these men widening. (Deane 1933:80-81)

Rev. Rickard, who joined the Methodist mission in 1882, when labor recruiting was intense, observed, "The great raid which the labour vessels have lately made upon our population has left us a little sore; and, to present appearances, a little worse for their visit.... These ships trade on our work, in which they really pay a high compliment to it. They are afraid to go to any place where the mission has not worked, until they get a few of the young men on board who have been under the influence of the lotu to support them in case of an attack, or lead the way; therefore, they come to the mission centers first, though so far, very little of their recruiting has been done beyond the circuit of mission operations." (Deane 1933: 244-245)

Fijian Teachers

The Fijian teachers physically placed themselves between the recruiters and the local villagers, and people appear to have been ashamed to oppose their wishes. (Wawn 1893: 292) The recitation of Danks' seven points alone might not have had this effect. From Rev. Rickard's point of view, the labor recruiters "traded on our work." Rickard saw them using young men influenced by the missions, since the recruiters were afraid to go into areas where the missionaries were not active without having these men with them. However, Rickard's claim that the recruiters restricted their activities primarily to the area of mission operations was not the case, since they were most successful when they recruited on the east coast of New Ireland and the offshore islands, beyond the area of missionary influence. There, they used interpreters from Nusa or elsewhere, as we have noted earlier, who were probably not mission-trained.

In September 1880, a Synod was convened on the Duke of York Islands to deal with the problem of Fijian teachers from the mission who were also working for traders. Danks noted, "The traders wanted the help of our teachers. I had refused to consent to their being so engaged. A few of the teachers had been tempted overmuch and had disobeyed orders in this regard.... At this Synod it was agreed that assistance should only be given by the teachers to traders who assisted us by abstaining from trading on the Sunday and who treated the natives well; and the assistance to be rendered should be only in connection with house-building." (Deane 1933: 123-124) The traders probably assumed that, because of the Fijians' connection to the mission, the local people would relate better to them than to white men in charge of the stations.

By January 1881, missionary activity had become quite extensive. There were twenty-six stations, covering the whole of the Duke of York Islands, a hundred miles of New Ireland coast, and 70 or 80 miles of the Gazelle Peninsula in New Britain. However, though stations opened, they often closed again due to the death or departure of Fijian teachers.

Though some Fijian teachers left, others made a successful adjustment to life in New Ireland villages. The Fijian teacher, Kolinio, had married a New Ireland woman and, "He lived next door to his revered father-in-law, a chief of some note named Hodo." (Deane 1933:249) With matrilineal descent and uxorilocal post-marital residence, it was relatively easy to incorporate male outsiders into the existing kinship system. However, Fijians were viewed in different ways. Pauliasi, the Fijian teacher stationed at Kalil, said that the villagers initially considered him to be a "white man," since he was light-skinned. Pauliasi then told Danks, "To-day I heard the women saying to each other: this is now the true white man; the others are like ourselves." (Deane 1933: 252)

The assignments of Revs. Rooney (1882) and Rickard to the New Britain mission did not solve the problem of the shortage of "South Sea Islands" teachers who manned the stations in New Ireland. By 1884, however, six "local preachers" had been trained on New Britain, and two local men had been appointed school masters on the Duke of York Islands. "Rev. Danks continued Rev. Brown's work on local languages. He points out that, From the commencement of the mission a strong attempt was made by the missionaries to provide books in the vernacular.... During the three years' actual residence on Duke of York I had translated: The Gospel according to St Mathew; a small life of Christ containing one hundred lessons... revised the catechism; and, conjointly with Mr Brown, prepared a dictionary in the Duke of York language, containing about four thousand words." (Deane 1933: 219) For Danks, books in the vernacular were essential for use in schools set up for the training of local people as teachers. He also indicates he had "a considerable knowledge of the New Ireland dialect [Patpatar, spoken at Kalil]." (Deane 1933: 288)

In Rev. Danks's opinion, by 1883 considerable progress had been made in the work of the mission on the west coast. On a visit to Kalil, where Pauliasi, one of the first Fijian teachers to come with Rev. Brown, was in charge, 100 people attended the service held there. Labera, one of Rev. Brown's earliest converts, attended the Sunday school organized for villagers, along with eight other men, twelve women and six children. (Deane 1933: 249)

Though Revs. Brown and Danks both had visited east coast villages, the leaders of villages there had not yet accepted the church on its terms when Rev. Danks visited Kudukudu and met the headman Sangina (Sagina), whom Rev. Brown had met earlier. Kudukudu was later to become a pivotal point in the expansion of the Methodist mission along the east coast. Rev. Danks described being ushered into the presence of an elderly Sangina, who does not deign to talk to him. When Rev. Danks told Sangina that he intended to spend the night in another village, Sangina became insulted and forbade him from leaving the village. According to Rev. Danks, "…We were on ticklish ground for jealousy had evidently prompted him to send for me…. The teachers then told me that this very man had sworn fearful oaths to the effect that he would kill and eat the next teacher who dared to cross over to his side, because they never visited him or slept in his village; and that, in consequence of this, none of them had crossed over for many months." (Deane 1933: 255) Sangina was attempting to bring about closer relations with the Methodists in order to enhance his position, but he would accept them only on his terms. He was envious of other chiefs whose power and prestige were increased by the establishment of a church in their villages. He wanted the church in Kudukudu, providing that the Methodists gave him the recognition to which he thought he was entitled.

Reverend Rickard

Several years later, Rev. Rickard explored the possibilities of expanding the scope of missionary activity in the northern part of the island on the advice of traders, who told him that, "…On the other side the population is enormously greater and a better class of natives, situated far more conveniently for mission work in large centers instead of being scattered as in most parts of this district." (Rickard Letter to Rev. Kelynack, Jan. 13, 1886; Rickard Letters 1886: 290)

Rickard's own attitude towards the New Irelanders is revealed in his statement about "masses of human beings with the same physical peculiarities as the Nusa people and who like them in moral and character resemble more the wild beasts than men...." "Yet any Christian could weep in pity over them as our Saviour did over Jerusalem and feel that it were worth the lives and experiences of 100 missionaries to bring these uncared for little ones beneath the expanded wings of Divine protection and redeeming love.... All the people we have spoken of are notorious cannibals." (Rickard Letters 1886: 305-306)

Through the lens of his own Victorian middle-class culture, the New Irelanders seemed like "wild beasts." To Rickard, their women were immoral, not assertive. "We were scarcely anchored [at Nusa] when a chief's wife came aboard alone - a thing never dared in our parts of the group, but corroborative of much of the immorality of the people of those parts, and which was shockingly apparent to us." (Rickard Letters 1886: 304-305)

German Annexation Changes the Missionary Approach

After the German annexation of the Bismarck Archipelago on November 3, 1884, a proclamation was issued forbidding fighting, the carrying of guns, unauthorized purchases of land by whites, and overbearing conduct by whites towards natives. (Deane 1933:279) To replace the Fijian and Samoan teachers with locally trained New Irelanders, the Methodist Synod in Sydney recommended in 1885 that a district training institute be set up on New Ireland. However, such teachers would need to be separated from their own villages and surrounded by the "superior moral atmosphere" of the training institution. Before this could come about, Rev. and Mrs. Danks were forced to leave the Bismarcks in August 1886 because of Mrs. Danks' poor health.

Discussion

While traders attempted to involve the New Irelanders in the capitalist economic system, which was foreign to them, missionaries came to New Ireland with the goal of totally transforming their lives. The missionary enterprise was to save the souls of the New Irelanders from eternal damnation and in the process to civilize and Westernize them.

Conversion does not necessitate "a deeply systematic reorganization of personal meanings but an adjustment in self-identification through the at least nominal acceptance of religious actions or beliefs deemed more fitting, useful, or true...a new locus of self-definition, a new, though not necessarily exclusive, reference point for one's identity." (Hefner 1993:17) Some like Horton (1971) see the dissolution of the boundaries of the microcosmic world of local community and spirits as the motive force moving people towards more universal doctrines and idea systems. Hefner points out how incorporation into a larger social order acts as a catalyst for both conversion and the reformulation of indigenous religion.

What propelled the New Irelanders who accepted Christianity towards a redefinition of their self-identity? By the time Rev. Brown arrived, the New Irelanders had already begun opening up to the outside world. They had regularized their exchange of supplies for goods with these outsiders, and some even learned Pidgin English; but they were still in control of the relationship. The consequent familiarity with Europeans made them more receptive to the message of the missionaries, especially since, at first, they were able to recast it in their own terms.

Pre-existing ideas and belief systems formed the framework for the acceptance of new ideas and institutions. For the Maisins, of Collingwood

Bay, Papua New Guinea, Barker notes "...the tendency of people to comprehend new things in terms of what they already know; and the tendency of people to assimilate new ideas into preexisting frameworks." (Barker 1992:210) The New Irelanders themselves at first visualized the acceptance of Christianity and the setting up of mission stations as "buying a cult" and leaders went to other villages to "purchase a church." As a Bakan villager related to us in 1987,

> An *orong* [big man] from Pire went to Kudukudu and bought a church from Kudukudu to bring it back to Pire, and then from Pire it came here. The people didn't understand what the church was, but they had heard stories that it stopped warfare. That was a good thing. They thought, 'I must go and buy the church' and they gave shell money to the Fijian ministers to get the church. The Fijian minister stayed at Kudukudu but he visited Pire and other places. People then built churches in each of the villages. (Rubel and Rosman, 1987 Field Notes, pp. 106, 125)

"Buying the church" was similar to "buying" a cult from another district or another island: that is, paying shell money for the secret esoteric knowledge which cult leaders hold[5]. *Sokopana* and *dukduk* cults moved from place to place in the same way. Neumann notes, "Tolai oral traditions emphasize that the lotu was first thought to be a powerful magic." (1992: 90) New Ireland leaders "bought the church" because they wanted access to the supernatural power of the missionaries, especially that of the charismatic Rev. Brown, who was able to move freely between warring groups as no native New Irelander could and whose oratory, directly addressed to his deity, was very powerful.

The New Irelanders at this early point seem to have taken a very pragmatic approach, without recognizing the changes that acceptance of

Christianity would ultimately involve. While they were willing to attend church services, they continued to pursue their own way of life. They did not accept wearing European clothing or ending war against their enemies or ceasing what the missionaries saw as sexual promiscuity. The missionaries had no way of knowing that ceremonial sexual promiscuity was connected symbolically to the all-important religious ritual through which society was reproduced. Despite the fact that the Christian message, directed towards the saving of individual souls, bore no resemblance to their own religious practices, which emphasized the reproduction of clan and community, the New Irelanders nominally accepted Methodist Christianity. The temporal advantages of civilization which conversion would bring were continually held out in the forefront. The attitudes of the New Irelanders towards the new religion became intertwined with their attitudes towards the Europeans, intruding with greater and greater frequency as the nineteenth century wore on.

By the mid-1880s, the missionary enterprise set up by the Methodists still had not engaged the New Irelanders to the extent that the Methodist mission had done in Africa with the Tshidis, where the latter slowly began to internalize ..".a set of values, an ineffable manner of seeing and being," which enabled them subsequently to be incorporated "into the industrial capitalist world." (Comaroff and Comaroff 1986:1-2) Though the exclusivity of Christian religious affiliation demanded that all previous religious beliefs and ceremonies be disavowed, in New Ireland Christianity was still being incorporated into an already existing religious matrix.

NOTES

1. As Whiteman notes, in order to properly contextualize missionaries' diaries, autobiographies, letters, popular articles and other kinds of writings, it is

necessary to understand the missionaries' theological suppositions, their "missiological" paradigm and "theology of culture." (1985: 305)

2. This incident was reported to Rev. Brown by the Fijian teacher at Kalil. The "selling" of human flesh in this manner would seem to be counter to the cultural rules that only the flesh of one's enemy who was in the opposite moiety could be eaten. Rev. Brown states this rule in his book *Melanesians and Polynesians*. (1910)

3. Rev. Danks gives us further information on Kaplen, indicating that Kaplen is the son of Tamantinut, Topulu's brother. ('Son' and 'brother's son' are called by the same term in the kinship terminology of the Duke of York.) Kaplen later became one of the first preachers from the Duke of York Islands (Paula Kiaplin in Danks' account). (Deane 1933: 197)

4. Rev. Brown left the Bismarck Archipelago at the end of 1880. He eventually became the General Secretary of Missions for the Methodist Church in Sydney. He wrote many articles from 1883 to 1907 opposing German colonial rule in the Pacific, under a pseudonym.

5. Neumann has described the same phenomenon on New Britain. The transference of the *Lotu* by purchase from one village to another is recalled in Tolai oral traditions, which emphasizes that the *Lotu* was, at first, thought to be powerful magic. (1992: 81-82, 90)

9. PACIFICATION AND ADMINISTRATION: THE IMPOSITION OF GERMAN RULE

Increasing pressures by German commercial interests in the Pacific to have the government protect their investments resulted in German annexation of northeastern New Guinea and the Bismarck Archipelago in 1884. British and Australian moves to take over Papua -- the southeastern part of the island of New Guinea -- were also factors in German annexation. G. von Oertzen was initially appointed as Imperial Commissioner and stationed in Mioko, in the Duke of York Islands, which had been renamed Neu Lauenberg. New Ireland became Neu Mecklenberg and New Britain became Neu Pommern. The Neuguinea Kompagnie, formed by the financier von Hansemann, absorbed the former Deutsche Handels- und Plantagen-Gesellschaft (previously Godeffroy & Son) and was granted the Imperial charter for German Neuguinea and the Bismarcks on May 17, 1885. The charter gave the company rights of sovereignty over the land, with the mandate to establish and maintain administrative institutions. All future land purchases required government authorization. Supplying liquor and firearms to the local people and recruiting them for work outside of the colony were prohibited. After an initial economically unsuccessful focus of development on Kaiser Willhelmsland, northeastern New Guinea, the Kompagnie shifted its emphasis to the development of the Bismarck Archipelago in 1892 and 1893.

The first step in the transfer of control of the colony from the Neuguinea Kompagnie to the German government in 1899 was the appointment of Albert Hahl as the new Imperial Judge. Hahl was born in 1866 in Bavaria, earned a Doctorate in Law, and worked for a year in the Bavarian civil service. In 1896, at the age of 27, he came to Herbertshohe, the capital which had been established in New Britain, as the sole representative of the German Reich. His charge was to establish a colonial government in the Bismarck Archipelago and the Solomon Islands. Hahl learned both Pidgin English and Tolai.

Continuation of Punitive Expeditions

One of the first actions of the Board of Directors of the Neuguinea Kompagnie had been to form an "…armed police troop, on the assumption that the rank and file can be recruited from among the natives of Neu Mecklenburg or from the Solomon Islands." (Neuguinea Kompagnie, Annual Report for 1886-87: 12) In 1895, there were 24 "police boys," soon to be augmented by a reserve force of 75 men, under Hahl's command. He observed that they could not be adequately trained because they were forced to work on the Neuguinea Kompagnie plantation after 8 a.m. every morning. The pattern of raids by New Irelanders on trading stations continued as before, and the colonial government's response, punitive expeditions, was much like the impromptu expedition formed by Rev. George Brown to punish those who killed his Fijian teachers. However, the colonial government now had a trained police force always available when such punitive expeditions were necessary.

Though a judge, Hahl seems to have spent very little time hearing both sides in disputes involving New Irelanders or rendering legal judgements. His trips to New Ireland were primarily to conduct punitive expeditions, since there was no representative of the German government living on New Ireland at the time. The only foreigners living there were men manning the trading stations and Fijian missionary teachers. Punitive expeditions of the German colonial government were intended to terrorize the New Irelanders into submission. The German government felt it was necessary to eradicate the bellicose activities of New Irelanders so that commerce could prosper.

The first punitive expedition which Hahl undertook to "pacify" New Irelanders, in May 1896, was to Mankai (Manggai) on the east coast, where a trading station had been attacked and robbed. The Europeans in the area petitioned him "…to appear there with a troop of a hundred men, to shoot down thirty or forty natives without inquiring after the individual culprits and to destroy their gardens," in order to deter future acts of this kind. (Hahl 1980: 15) He landed at Mankai, some 30 miles down the coast from Nusa, and found both the coastal and inland villages deserted. He recovered the stolen trade goods from the houses of the inland villages but made no contact with the local people, who had fled. (Hahl 1980: 15) In this instance the Europeans called Hahl in to make a show of force and wanted him to indiscriminately kill people to deter the New Irelanders from raiding trading stations, but he was able to recover the stolen trade goods without having recourse to such drastic measures.

Hahl led another punitive expedition to Kuras on the west coast of New Ireland in the summer of 1896. A cutter belonging to one of the traders had been driven ashore there. "The local natives attacked the vessel, killed the crew and devoured them." (Hahl 1980: 17) The Neu Guinea Kompagnie trading post manned by a Chinese man and the Wesleyan mission station to the south of Kuras were in danger, in Hahl's view, unless retaliatory action was taken. Hahl took eleven men with him and, unable to find reliable guides, marched inland with his small troop. After an eight-hour march, they encountered warriors. He observed,

> Every attempt to approach peacefully was rejected with contumely by the other side.... the two opposing forces, hidden behind the trees in the forest, were barely thirty meters apart. Any man who exposed himself was bound to be hit by a well-aimed spear or slingstone. Two of my soldiers had skillfully worked their way to the rear and were able to aim at the enemy from the flank. No sooner had two shots been fired and two men fallen than the whole lot took flight with such a will that pursuit was pointless. When the huts were searched, the goods from the boat were found neatly stacked there. (Hahl 1980: 17)

Hahl's police force included men from New Ireland. In September 1896, Gamelle, a sentry posted outside the armory at Herbertshohe, from Madine (Madina) on the east coast of New Ireland, broke into the armory with fourteen of his fellow "tribesmen" and stole five rifles and five hundred cartridges. They escaped to the west coast of New Ireland, north of Kuras, in a cutter, and crossed the mountains to Madina. Hahl pursued them by boat but was unable to catch them. He observed that they "…had absconded to help their home village which was reported to have engaged in a fight with a neighboring district." (1980: 18) By October they were "carrying out extensive raids of pillage and vengeance, bringing recruitment, trade and communications to a complete standstill." (Hahl 1980: 18)

In the ensuing retaliatory action, Hahl took 38 men with him, landed at Lamusmus on the west coast, and crossed over the mountains, where he was greeted with a great ovation by the local people, who had been attacked by Madina in the rampage and were obviously their enemies. A band of warriors from Lamusmus, armed with spears, joined Hahl and his forces. He attacked Madina at seven in the morning, noting that,

> The inhabitants, taken by surprise, at first tried to resist. There was bitter fighting but after a few minutes the enemy fled.... When the houses were searched we found that by chance Gamelle and his men had been busy cleaning the guns at the time of the attack so that they had been unable to make use of the firearms. They had taken the guns with them as they fled but two hundred cartridges fell into my hands.... The allied force had collected the bodies of all their fallen enemies and were bringing them to the sea, each one laid on a bamboo pole and carried by two men. When I asked the significance of this I was told that the bodies of their enemies were now to be brought home and consumed. I forbade this and ordered the warriors to board their boats and to return home immediately.... Next morning I was told that my allies had returned in their canoes to make sure of their booty and that the drumming was a signal to invite all their friends to partake of the feast. (Hahl 1980: 18-19)

Hahl was later informed that the actions taken against Madina had been successful, enabling trade and labor recruiting to start up again. However, this situation was not to last very long, since the people of Madina had once again raided a trading station newly established by Hernsheim & Company at the village of Leineru, their traditional enemies. According to Hahl, "...This station was robbed and destroyed by natives from the village of Madine when they avenged themselves on the natives of Leineru, their hereditary enemies for their assistance they had rendered to me." (1980: 30) Once again, Hahl had gotten involved in an ongoing conflict between traditional enemies. Firth further observes, "In the fights between the Medina people and their enemies on the opposite coastline of New Ireland both sides were led by men who had served with the German police." (Firth 1978: 33)

Despite the presence of Hahl and his police troops, traders continued to be murdered. Firth states, "...The traders Anat and Clark, employees of Queen Emma on Simberi Island [Tabar], were killed by the islanders after Anat shot one of them in a drunken rage...." (1978: 32) Anat's brutish drunken act was much like those acts of Europeans which we described in Chapter 6. Hahl never considered the response of New Irelanders to have been justified. Nor did he sit in judgement over non-New Irelanders like Anat for their unlawful acts.

Later in 1897, Hahl went to the village of Kabien, on the far northwest tip of New Ireland, because "of the long catalogue of crimes committed by these recalcitrant people." (Hahl 1980:36) They had killed a trader in Kabien, stolen a cutter and killed the crew, and were now raiding villages to the south. The day before he went, he sent a message through the people of Bagail village, "to tell them to wait for us",

> ...For I was coming not to fight them but to hear the complaints and grievances which they must surely have to lay before me. The natives received us peacefully and there followed a discussion in the course of which I had to listen to an account of all the wrongs done them by their neighbors and also by individual Europeans. They maintained that the men responsible for the crimes which had been committed were not living with them but in Kableman on the east coast of Neu Mecklenburg.... It was of course not possible to decide how much of their story was to be believed. But here too I attempted to gain some influence over the natives by a peaceful approach. (Hahl 1980: 36)

Misunderstanding New Irelanders' Conflicts

Hahl sought to establish the colonial government as the supreme authority by hearing local grievances. He wished to prevent New Irelanders from taking things into their own hands and seeking vengeance. Firth notes that the Kabien people continued their belligerence and attacked Lamusmus, to the south, because Lamusmus had been "...weakened by the loss of men to the labor recruiters." (1978: 32)

Though Hahl made reference to "blood feuds" between New Ireland groups, he did not seem to understand the relationship between enemies. He was constantly being drawn into conflicts between traditional enemies, when one side in a continuing "blood feud" came to him with a complaint that they had been attacked.

Hahl, using his own European frame of reference, thought that he could subdue a village and force it to make peace with its traditional enemies. His attempt to make peace, by the European method of ascertaining the facts and determining the guilty parties whom he could then punish was unsuccessful. This method was very different from the New Ireland way of making peace -- of which Hahl seemed unaware -- by means of exchange. The New Ireland method of making peace had been used by Hernsheim at Nusa some thirteen years earlier. Hahl did not grasp that, when there is a long history of ongoing feuding, you cannot simply punish the most recent violator.

Mouton, the plantation owner from New Britain, was drawn into ongoing conflicts just as Hahl was. While recruiting at Labur, a Patpatar-speaking village on the West Coast of New Ireland in 1892, Mouton was asked by the villagers to go with them to the next district, where their allies were engaged in fighting a third party. Mouton noted, "They wanted the protection of our firearms to protect them in their raid they were making in the next district to revenge themselves of a similar raid. One of the enemis [*sic*] has a shneider rifle and they were afraid of him and thought of using us as protection.... They [Mouton's allies] had killed a man and his wife and brought the child to be eaten... those victims were innocently working in their taros patch when they were massacred, it is their way and the enemies had done the same some time ago, with the protection of the chief who had a rifle, so it was eye for eye and blood for blood." (Mouton 1974:95)

On the following morning, Mouton was startled by "...about twenty or thirty natives all painted white from head to foot, brandishing spears and tomahawks dancing and coming towards us, ... a native came to me and told me that there would be no harm coming that it was an acknowledgement for the service we did in enabling them to have a revenge against their enemies, in fact as those warriors reached us they said, malumalum malumalum and throw their spears at my feet sticking them in the ground." (Mouton 1974: 95)

Shifts in Local Power Relations

The period of constant warfare during the last two decades of the nineteenth century is called "the period of *romtoday*" by the Patpatar-speaking people. (Rubel and Rosman, 1987 Field Notes, pp. 106, 128) New Irelanders see this period as one of great turbulence and upheaval. The cause of this efflorescence of fighting is attributed to the increasing number of weapons such as wooden-handled war axes with iron ax heads that were introduced by Europeans. During *rom*, one side invariably attempted to use the Germans to its advantage against its traditional enemies. In the late nineteenth century, New Irelanders saw themselves as still retaining sufficient political autonomy to be able to pursue their traditional rivalries, though Europeans were living among them. However, they surely must have wondered how long they could continue to determine their own destiny.

As the New Irelanders suggest, the introduction of new weapons was certainly a factor in the increase in conflict during *rom*. However, it seems more likely that the increase in warfare was due to the imbalance caused by Europeans' becoming involved on one side or the other in the relationships between traditional enemies. Before contact, no one village, district or clan was much more powerful than any other, over time. While one clan, through good fortune, might have grown larger in population than its surrounding enemies, it was never able to turn short-term advantage into long-term conquest and domination of its enemies.

With European contact, however, the balance of relations between groups was seriously tipped in favor of clans and villages which had more contact with Europeans and used these contacts to obtain weapons. These became more powerful than their more isolated traditional enemies. Often, the stronger group would act on its newly acquired advantage and attack its enemies. Just as the newly strengthened group might be motivated into action, the weaker party might also be prompted to attack, since, unless they did, their enemies might become so powerful that they could never be overcome. The weaker group also could try to acquire what the enemy had -- guns, trade goods, a mission station -- and also become more powerful. A village could also be severely weakened when many young men were recruited to work on plantations away from New Ireland. This left it exposed to the possibility of attack by its enemies. For example, Lamusmus was weakened by labor recruiting, and both Kabien and Madina took advantage of this weakness to raid it.

Not only were Europeans drawn into the pattern of traditional enmity between groups, but when they wanted to retaliate against New Irelanders for the killing of one of their traders, they often drew the traditional enemies of the group into the action. Douglas's research in New Caledonia has revealed a very similar situation. The New Caledonians had the same kind of checkerboard pattern, in which "each tribe is the enemy of those adjacent to it." (Douglas 1992: 94-95) Opposing sides were even organized into "…two mutually hostile, ritually opposed groupings known as Hoot and Waap…." in Tanga. (Douglas 1992: 94) The French were co-opted by the New Caledonians to fight their traditional enemies in the same way that the Germans were co-opted by the New Irelanders. (Douglas 1992: 101-102)

If a colonial administrative structure had not been imposed, it is possible that men with access to foreign goods might have developed into true chiefs, *i.e.*, men with differential access to resources, power and authority over their followers and the ability to pass their positions on to their heirs. However, this did not occur. In other parts of Pacific, however, contact did bring about significant changes in the political structure. Hawaii and Fiji both had chieftainships before contact, and these later developed into proto-states before a colonial administrative structure was finally imposed.

Changes in the Colonial "Pacification" Approach

Hahl recognized during his stay in the Bismarck Archipelago that a deterrent policy for dealing with violence through retaliatory raids would be unsuccessful. He noted, "The only recourse was to extend the power of the Administration geographically as far as possible by means of permanent stations, which would constitute visible sources of protection for both sides. Hand in hand with this, the natives must be carefully organized into an administrative system based on their own participation." (Hahl 1980: 24) Hahl's real agenda, of course, was to destroy the capacity that New Ireland villages had for warfare and resistance to the colonial government, to end their political autonomy, and to impose colonial rule.

In 1899 the German government took authority over the colony from the Neuguinea Kompagnie, with Hahl serving as Vice Governor, and Rudolph von Bennigsen as Governor. That year, Vice Governor Hahl advanced his proposal to establish a district office in northern New Ireland. At that time there were 16 trading stations, with 13 white men, seven Chinese, two Indians, and one Malay in New Ireland. There were three more stations on Tabar, another on New Hanover, and two on the smaller islands north of New Hanover, manned by Europeans and Chinese. (German Imperial Government Annual Report for 1898-99: 176)

Franz Boluminski, formerly a manager for the Astrolabe Company at Stephansort, on New Guinea, was chosen to be the District Officer. He moved to New Ireland to set up a district headquarters at Kavieng, in Nusa Harbor, in 1900. One of Boluminski's first moves to bring about the "pacification" of northern New Ireland was to confiscate all firearms from New Irelanders.

While the indigenous populations of the east and north coasts of New Ireland were subject to the jurisdiction of Boluminski, the District Officer in Nusa, jurisdiction over Europeans remained the responsibility of the Imperial Judge in Herbertshoe, the capital of the colony on New Britain. (German Imperial Government Annual Report for 1900-1901: 211-212) From Hahl's point of view, "Only in a few rare instances was it necessary to use armed force. It may be that the way had already been well prepared for the establishment of public peace in that area, as there was scarcely a single village where the young men had not already been employed by Europeans and had not only by observation and experience become accustomed to peaceful intercourse but also actively wished for it to be introduced." (Hahl 1980: 90) Whether or not New Irelanders "actively wished" for colonial rule, the presence of German armed force was certainly a factor.

Creation of a Territorially-based Administrative System

Early in his stay in the Bismarcks, Hahl decided that he would establish a system of native administration, based on a form of indirect rule, to assist him in governing the colony. This system, first set up in the Gazelle Peninsula and in the Duke of York Islands in the 1890s, was put into effect in New Ireland by Boluminski after the district headquarters office was established in 1900. "The north and northeast of Neu Mecklenburg as far as Mandine [Madina] have been almost completely counted and subdivided into fixed districts retaining their traditional chiefs in a magisterial capacity.... The chiefs have been issued with the insignia of authority [hat and stick]." (German Imperial Government Annual Report for 1901-1902: 228) Hahl noted that, "It was not difficult to persuade the inhabitants of the nearest villages to choose one of the clan elders of their district as their *luluai* or acknowledged chief, responsible to me. The natives were to submit their disputes to him, and the *luluai* was to report important matters to me immediately, or at the major court sittings, which took place in public from time to time. This meant that the chief with the assistance of some respected clan elders could regulate all family affairs and minor disputes peacefully at his discretion, without troubling me in the matter." (Hahl 1980: 18)[1].

Village political autonomy was effectively destroyed with the colonial government's establishment of a territorially based administrative system. Traditional justice, in which the wronged party exacted vengeance, was abolished. Clan members put forth their leaders as *luluais*. By investing colonial authority in these traditional leaders, power of these leaders was greatly increased. However, not every Big Man was made into a *luluai*, and there often were men in a village who were more influential than the appointed *luluai*. Feasts and mortuary rites, organized by Big Men, continued without direct interference from the colonial administration.

Problems developed with this system by the following year. The German Imperial Government Annual Report for 1902-1903 stated that, "The use of these chiefs to assist in the administration of justice appears to give rise to the greatest difficulty. Self-interest, excessive zeal and lack of understanding repeatedly interfered with the course of justice." (p. 237) Earlier, Big Men did not have the authority to settle disputes and determine guilt, but could only use their influence to resolve disputes. When the German administration gave *luluais* power to administer Western style justice in the adjudication of disputes, they responded with "self-interest, excessive zeal and lack of understanding."

Continuation of Village Warfare in the South

Though northern New Ireland had been "pacified," intervillage warfare continued in the south between interior and coastal peoples, who had been traditional enemies. Trading stations and plantations had not yet been set up in this area. This fighting, taking place in areas not yet under German colonial control, seems to represent local communities' proclaiming their political autonomy, perhaps their last attempt to assert their independence. They had never known a political structure more encompassing than that of their autonomous villages.

The Germans began to realize that merely sending punitive expeditions into these areas did not end warfare. "The application of military force is useful only when the advantage gained by intimidating the natives is followed up by a permanent government station which suppresses the feuds of the natives, gradually reconciles the warring factions, and guarantees the security of both person and property simply by its presence.... It must be remembered that Papuans have no conception of subjection to a territorial power." (German Imperial Government Annual Report 1902-1903: 236)

The policy presaged in this Report was for a government station to be established in this southern area and in 1903, a Police Station was established at Namatanai under the command of Wilhelm Wostrack, the District Officer. During the first year, the imposition of colonial control was met with resistance and attacks on colonial troops. "Particularly stubborn resistance was shown by the inhabitants of Mesi in the northern section of the area and the hill people round Muliama in the south. The latter had banded together under the leadership of a much-feared man named Wodschi and pillaged the land far and wide." (German Imperial Government Annual Report for 1904-1905: 251) Groups of allied villages under a single strong leader had attacked the police troop and resisted German attempts to incorporate them into the colonial structure. This violent activity was soon redirected, probably against traditional enemies, resulting in "pillaging of the land."

The imposition of an administrative system based on districts and localities disrupted the system of relations between autonomous village communities, in which they were either enemies and allies to one another. Administrative units based on "common locality" would often bring together villages which were enemies to one another within a single administrative district. In 1929 the village of Lesu, for example, was composed of two villages which in the past had constantly fought one another. (Powdermaker 1933: 32, fn.1)

PACIFICATION AND ADMINISTRATION

Despite the establishment of the Namatanai station in the central part of the island, as late as 1906 warfare between interior and coastal people persisted in the south near Morukon, where the influence of the district station was minimal. Hahl noted that,

> There was unrest among the mountain people when they observed that the coastal communities were disposed to espouse the new order. They joined together under the leadership of a mighty warrior from Buntur named Gagas and conducted a campaign of fighting and plunder against the coastal districts. Early in 1906 they had attacked Morkon [Morukon] and carried away large quantities of human flesh into the mountains. Now their leader was threatening to visit vengeance and punishment on any village and any chief who joined the administrative system.... District Officer Wostrack ... [broke] Gagas' hold over the people in March 1906. Immediately after his overthrow the mountain people inland from Muliama, relying on the protection of the Namatanai Station, settled on the coast. (Hahl 1980: 111-112)[2]

Gagas was the leader of an anti-colonial movement, showing his opposition to colonial rule by attacking those villages which had agreed to the extension of German colonial rule. After attacking Morkon, he threatened to do the same to any other village which accepted the German administrative structure. Beginning in 1901, the Colonial Administration had imposed a grid system of districts, each district comprising several villages[3]. The District, a purely territorial unit, had no counterpart in New Ireland culture. This administrative system was gradually extended over the whole island and outward to the off-islands. However, in many cases, villages were included in districts only on paper.

Road Construction

One of the earliest activities to which District Head Boluminski directed his attention was the construction of a road. Villagers today still talk about this monumental undertaking; and the road today is called the Boluminski Highway. The construction of roads is a most important symbol used by a colonial power to show the world that they are bringing progress and civilization to a "backward" area. Like the Romans, who brought law, administration, and roads to the barbarians of Germania, the German Imperial Government was intent on bringing the same improvements to New Ireland. In their Annual Report, the colonial administration claimed that, "the natives have worked willingly under their chiefs," though fines had to be imposed on two villages whose men refused to work, indicating that this form of corvee labor was resented by the local people. (German Imperial Government Annual Report for 1900-1901: 215-216) Corvee labor for road building, which was organized under *luluais*, was not as disruptive as the gap left by young men spirited away by labor recruiters, but it surely had an effect on the internal organization of work within the village. The only recompense for corvee labor was tobacco and pipes. This was a continuation by the German Administration of the old practice of giving tobacco, begun by the whalers in the mid-nineteenth century. Labor on the road as well as on other projects was considered a substitute for taxes, which had not yet been introduced. The German Administration's road-building endeavor enabled them to establish control at the local village level.

Nusa, earlier an *entrepôt* for trading and labor recruiting, became Kavieng, the location of Boluminski's district office. Hahl, who had become governor, went to Kavieng in 1902 and described Boluminski's accomplishments there:

...A fine residence had been built on the steep crag dropping down to the narrow coastal plain. The land in front had been turned into gardens and contained the necessary farm buildings. Inland from the house Boluminski had cleared the land of trees and undergrowth and commenced a coconut plantation.... Trading stations and plantations were then established one after another in rapid succession along this communication route [Boluminski's road], as the introduction of motor trucks for carrying passengers and freight gradually superseded slow transportation by sailing boat. The natives called the automobiles bush steamships (titimer na pui)." (Hahl 1980: 91)

Within a few years Kavieng developed into a bustling, heterogenous colonial community, having not only the amenities of Western civilization, such as eating houses, but also a prison and a hospital, all signifiers of modern Western life. It was the seat of government as well as the economic hub of the island.

Discussion

Once the Germans established the colony of German Neuguinea, they began to try to extend their control over the whole of this region. Trading stations were already dotting New Ireland, and the first extension of their colonial control was in the form of punitive expeditions. When this did not succeed in "pacifying" the area, they set up the first district office on the island, and tried to establish a system of indirect control- the *luluai* system. As the juggernaut of colonial control slowly moved south over the island, the Germans saw "peaceful relations established." New Irelanders' warfare against the German administration, as well as against their own enemies, was their last gasp of political independence in the face of encroaching German power and control. Like all colonial powers, the Germans had convinced themselves that the native population welcomed them as bringers of order and peace. Though written documents present these events primarily from the German point of view, resistance of the New Irelanders to colonial control is clearly evident in the German government reports.

During the last two decades of the nineteenth century, New Irelanders had seen an increasing encroachment upon their way of life. As the number of trading stations increased, New Irelanders responded with frequent attacks on those stations. Among the provocations for such attacks were the shooting and killing of villagers by drunken traders or sea captains and cheating in copra trading. There was an efflorescence of warfare against traditional enemies; but by the time New Ireland leaders realized that their real enemy was the Germans, it was too late. Increased conflict between New Ireland villages provided Hahl with an additional excuse to "pacify" the region, since continued hostilities threatened the expansion of the profitable copra enterprise.

With the failure of punitive expeditions, the Germans decided that district offices on the island and village control under government-appointed *luluais* was necessary for the colony to succeed. They had to be firmly in command of the political situation on the island. Before New Irelanders could turn around, they had lost their independence.

NOTES

1. The word *luluai* derives from the Tolai language family, which is found in the Gazelle Peninsula and in the southern part of New Ireland. It originally meant "a leader in battle." (Mihalic 1971: 125) As late as 1987, old-timers

still remembered use of the word "white-puss" to refer to *luluais*. (Rubel and Rosman, 1987 Field Notes) "White puss" is a corruption of the German words *weiss putz*, meaning the white decoration or insignia on the *luluai* hat issued by the German colonial government.

2. Albert identifies both the interior and coastal groups involved in this conflict as probably Lak. (1987: 38)

3. Districts of New Ireland in 1901-1902 were:

   a) Kaewieng District, including the islands of Nusa, Nusali and Nago, and the villages of Nag Siwusat, Bagail, Nauan, Mongall, Kulingit, Palkalle, Kulangen, Koblien, and Majum: 1,100 inhabitants.

   b) Bobsy District, comprising Kabelmann, Lowelei, Little Kaselok, Great Kaselok, Tintunuai, Butbut, Ulu and Nono: 1,200 inhabitants.

   c) Kapsu District, comprising Tiwingur, Kolopolpol, Losuk, Monkai Beach and Inland Monkai, and Liwitua: 850 inhabitants.

   d) Lauan District, comprising Sale, Parnai (Paruai), Nonapai: 1,240 inhabitants

   e) Lemagot District, comprising Lakurefange, Panegai, Liweru: 715 inhabitants.

   f) Lakuremau: 254 inhabitants.

   g) Rainbine, comprising Munewai and Lagugon: 324 inhabitants
   "The forest and mountain tribes have not been included in this list."
   (German Imperial Government Annual Report for 1901-1902:228)

ALIENS ON OUR SHORES

10. COPRA: VILLAGE TRADE AND THE ESTABLISHMENT OF PLANTATIONS

In New Britain, beginning in 1883, Europeans established a new form of exploitation, the plantation, which ultimately would spread throughout the Bismarck Archipelago. The operation of a plantation required forming a completely new type of relationship between local people and Europeans. Plantations required the "purchase" and permanent alienation of much larger tracts of land than were required for trading stations or missions. Plantations also required laborers who were paid for their work by the month or at the end of their term of service, especially if they came from other islands. The establishment of plantations near villages and the recruitment of local laborers represented much more of an intrusion into the life of New Irelanders than trading stations and the sale of copra had done.

Land for plantations had to be acquired from local clans who owned it. Since clan land traditionally was regarded as the dwelling place of the clan spirit or *masalai* and the burial place of clan members, it was never exchanged for valuables. A clan could only be displaced from its land by warfare. Clans transferring land to Europeans may have thought they were transferring temporary usufruct, since that did occur traditionally. Since the right to land was separate from the right to the produce of the trees on that land, the indigenous seller might have thought he still retained the right to harvest crops from those trees, as in the Kleinschmidt dispute. (See Chapter 6.) Whether the individuals who "sold" land to Europeans represented the members of their clan and therefore could transfer the land was also an issue[1]. Europeans purchasing land assumed that it was a commodity like any other commodity. After purchase, they thought they had absolute rights over the land and its disposition, including its further sale.

On two occasions before 1900, land was purchased on New Ireland with the intention of establishing plantations. When Hernsheim purchased 3,500 hectares opposite Nusa, his brother Franz intended to develop the land into a plantation. On May 5, 1885, Emma Forsayth and Thomas Farrell purchased two plots of land in New Ireland. In the Farrell-Forsayth transaction, parcels of land near "Cocalai," on the southwest coast, were transferred to "Thomas Farrell Pilot of the Steam Ship Golden Gate and Emma Eliza Forsayth of Ralum Plantation in the Island of New Britain" for eighty-two dollars in trade given to Tyese, Amoot, and Saibet. (Australian Archives G1 #6 series 210 file Kolbe vs Govt) The deed was signed by two European employees of Farrell, and the Xs of the New Irelanders. Included with the deed is a sketch-map of the plot. The text of this deed is in Appendix B.

In the second deed, Tatas senior, Tatas junior, and Brabucki received eighty-five dollars in trade from Forsayth and Farrell in exchange for "parcels of land situated on the South West coast of New Ireland including two villages -- including the foreshore... said pieces or parcels of land are called or known by the name Caruluka Targoo Miyi Aruven and Lavat." (*ibid*) The hand-drawn map locates "Rabihen," suggesting that these purchased plots were at Rebehen, on the west coast. Up to 1907 these two plots of land appear never to have been used for plantations. At that point, after much negotiation with the German colonial government, Emma Forsayth (Capt. Farrell had died by this time) renounced all claim to these lands, and they were given to the German government in exchange for Mrs. Forsayth's right to acquire land on the south coast of New Britain. (Sack 1973: 158)

Richard Parkinson: The First Plantation Manager

By 1883, Richard Parkinson, a surveyor on Samoa who was married to Emma's sister, Phebe, had joined them in New Britain and established the first plantation at Ralum, on Blanche Bay in New Britain. Parkinson was one of a larger coterie of exceptional individuals like George Brown, Eduard Hernsheim, and Emma Forsayth, who, each in his or her own way, interacted with the native population and influenced the evolving history of European/New Ireland contact. In addition to growing coconuts, Parkinson did agricultural experiments with cotton, maize, broom millet, sugar cane, cocoa, coffee and various tropical fruits and food plants. (Hernsheim 1983: 78, 148; Robson 1965: 128, 165) Workers for his plantation were recruited from Buka in the Solomon Islands. Parkinson's plantation was a success, and this had obvious repercussions for the establishment of plantations in New Ireland.

In addition to developing plantations, Parkinson also had an interest in the natural flora, fauna and the people around him. Robson notes, "Right from the beginning, as he explored the raw country and planned Emma's plantations, Parkinson examined and measured these new people, plants, birds, animals, insects, and made accurate records and collections of specimens; and he sent this priceless material to German museums." (Robson 1965:167) Parkinson received various medals in exchange for the artifacts he sent to German museums: masks, carvings, clubs, and canoes. Parkinson was so captivated by the environment and native life surrounding him that he soon gave up the tasks for which he had been brought to the Bismarcks, in order to devote himself to studying native peoples, languages, and beliefs.

His scientific interests brought him into conflict with Emma Forsayth, who insisted that he devote his energies to the care of her plantations. Mrs. Parkinson, Emma's sister Phebe, realized that her husband was bored by plantation management and so took over the work from him. Parkinson was then able to take up a position with the Neu Guinea Kompagnie in 1889 to plan their plantations, as well as to continue to recruit labor for them. This position gave him more time to pursue his research interests. Parkinson's detached "natural history" approach to the indigenous population was no doubt reflected in his interactions with them as a plantation manager and labor recruiter.

Dreiszig Jahre in der Sudsee is Parkinson's ethnographic compendium on all the areas of the Pacific with which he was familiar. Information on New Ireland is scattered throughout the book. His "natural history" approach was devoid of any concept of culture. However, he argued that rapid "salvage" ethnography was necessary because he thought that the native cultures would be completely transformed within a short time. Parkinson probably used interpreters, since Robson notes that he never spoke Pidgin English and scorned it. (1965: 168) *Dreiszig Jahre in der Sudsee*.

Frequently it was those Europeans with long term experience in trading who established plantations, beginning in 1900 when copra prices began to rise. In fact, the profits from trading were often used to establish these plantations. Despite the fact that the Forsayth Company had established its plantation at Ralum in New Britain in 1883, by 1897 the company was still making most of its profits from trading. It "...was estimated to be making an annual profit of up to M 200,000 [German marks], mainly from trading, and there were 49 trading stations spread throughout the islands in 1899." (Firth 1977: 14-15)

Plantation Laborers from Elsewhere

In the decade before plantations were established in New Ireland, labor recruiting there for work on plantations in New Britain and elsewhere in German Neuguinea continued. Those setting up plantations in New Ireland -- like Jean Baptiste Octave Mouton, a plantation owner in New Britain, who had come with the Marquis de Rays expedition -- preferred to obtain plantation laborers from other islands, because they felt they could get more work from them. Laborers from nearby villages were distracted by the presence of their families and by ceremonial events occurring in their villages. After their three-year term of service for Mouton, laborers from New Ireland were given boxes of trade goods when they returned to their villages. (Mouton 1974:119) This was the pattern of labor recruiting used earlier for workers taken to Queensland. By 1903 Mouton had 286 laborers working on his plantation. (Biskup, in Mouton 1974: 27)

In the late 1890s there was growing unrest on the Gazelle Peninsula due to the behavior of plantation workers from the Solomons and New Ireland towards the Tolai. According to Sack, "They misused the Sabbath rest to roam through the bush robbing the natives of their only wealth, their...(shell money) or committed even greater wrongs." (Mouton 1894,103, in Sack 1973: 107) Sack goes on to suggest that these "unnamed wrongs" were what Phebe Parkinson had described to Margaret Mead as "pulling bush maries," the raping of Tolai women who were traveling from the interior on their way to market. (Sack 1973: 107; see Mead 1960: 195.) Male labor recruits coming from other islands became sexually involved with local village women. Phebe Parkinson went on to mention that these plantation laborers "...would be killed by the bush natives and a retaliatory expedition would be necessary." (Mead 1960: 195)

For pragmatic reasons, Mouton thought it useful to learn as much as he could about the way of life of the people, in order to deal with them in their own terms when he bought land from them, or recruited them to work for him. In contrast to Hernsheim and Parkinson, his interaction with the local people was on a more equal basis. He learned Pidgin (Neomelanesian) and became fluent in Tolai. Mouton was even initiated into the *dukduk* society on New Britain and noted, "...It has helped me a great deal in my dealing with the natives...." (Mouton 1974:108) He lived with a Tolai woman as late as 1896, and referred to her as *"ma femme canaque."* (Biskup in Mouton 1974: 28)

Different Types of Plantations

The establishment of the District Office in Kavieng, which permitted the "pacification" of at least the northern part of New Ireland, allowed coconut plantations to be set up in New Ireland. As a pilot project, Boluminski, the District Officer, began a government coconut plantation of 12,000 palm trees inland from his house. Under local leadership, 9,000 trees were planted by the surrounding villagers and in exchange for weeding, they were allowed to plant and harvest their own crops between the rows of trees on the government plantation. (German Imperial Government Annual Report 1900-1901: 217-218) It is not clear whether the land for the plantation was purchased by the government, or seized by right of eminent domain. This program was seen as a prototype for village plantations if Europeans did not establish private plantations. The aim was to produce copra in the most efficient manner. If land were to be expropriated to form a village plantation run under the direction of the "chief," then profound changes in settlement pattern, land holding and leadership would have occurred. However, if, under German direction, copra became a cash crop grown on their own land, changes would not have been as great. Because the colonial government wished to turn the New Irelanders into cash croppers, they were prepared to go to great lengths to change the New Ireland way of life.

In 1900, private, European-owned plantations began to be set up in New Ireland. Coterminus with the setting up of Boluminski's 300-hectare government plantation at Kavieng, Hernsheim and Co. began to convert the island of Nusa, which Eduard Hernsheim had purchased in 1884, into their first plantation. (German Imperial Government Annual Report 1899-1900: 188) The government strongly supported the opening up of northern New Ireland to private plantation development according to the government report, "The opinion widely held among planters in Neu Pommern (New Britain), that the land in Neu Mecklenburg contained too much underground water to make farming economical, has been shown to be unfounded. In fact the country there is in some parts prairie land where it is possible to establish large-scale coconut plantations or it is forest country where the good rainfall observed so far suggests that it is suited to almost any crop." (German Imperial Government Annual Report of 1900-1901: 217)

In 1901, Julius Ruge, a local trader, received a government subsidy of $1,000 to develop a coconut plantation on Nusaum Island in Nusa Channel. Ruge did not have to pay rent on this land until his trees began to yield nuts. (Sack 1973: 101) Three locations, Kondalik and Kabotheron, owned by the Neuguinea Kompagnie, and Nusaum, owned by "Trader" Ruge, were characterized in 1900 as both trading stations and plantations. They were probably only future locations for plantations. (Blum 1900) Only Ruge developed his site into a plantation, however, planting 106 ha. the first year. (German Imperial Government Annual Report for 1901-1902: 226)

Table 1. Plantation Statistics for 1906-1907 for New Ireland

Company (Location)	Land, Inventory, Staff
Forsayth & Co.	125 ha. 12,500 palm trees also – 25 pigs, 2 sheep, 3 horses 3 white overseers, 36 native workers
J. Ruge (Nusaum)	200 ha. 20,500 palm trees also – 2 horses 21 workers
E. Macco (Kapsu)	120 ha. 12,068 palm trees also – 15 pigs, 8 cows, 2 horses 30 workers
E. Ostrum (Lakurafanga)	35 ha. 3000 palm trees 40 workers
Neuguinea Kompagnie (Fiosa and Ungan)	Fiosa - 200 ha. 10,000 palm trees Ungan - 347 ha. 95,776 palm trees Both plantations: 3 white overseers, 320 workers
Hernsheim & Co.-Kahyz (Nusa, Bagail, Lagagon)	381 ha. 45,500 palm trees 1 white overseer, 21 workers
Government Plantation (Kavieng)	(1) 400 ha. 40,000 palm trees 1 white overseer, 150 workers (2) 4 ha. 200 palm trees[2]
Source: Commonwealth Archives AA 63/83 B234; Forsayth & Co.	

Plantations owned by individuals who resided on them (Ostrum, Ruge and Macco) were different in size from those owned by firms such as Hernsheim, which had headquarters in New Britain, and were run by overseers. The latter tended to be larger (average size, 263 ha.) and to employ more workers (average number, 94) The average size of an individually owned plantation was 118 hectares, and it employed approximately 30 workers. There is no indication of whether workers came from areas close to the plantation, from other parts of New Ireland, or from other islands.

Based on their previous work experience in Neu Pommern (New Britain) and Kaiser Wilhelms land (New Guinea), the New Ireland labor force was thought of as "a most highly valued supply of labor." A good source of locally available labor for private plantations was thus being established on the island. (German Imperial Government Annual Report for 1900-1901: 218) Despite the difficulties discussed previously, workers from New Ireland continued to be recruited to work on plantations in New Britain (Neu Pommern). One New Ireland family history collected at Liandan indicated that the informant's father had come from Siar to work in a plantation near Lossu (Lesu), married his mother and remained living in Liandan. (Rubel and Rosman, 1987 Field Notes)

Demand continued for laborers from the Bismarck Archipelago to work on the German plantations of the D.H.P.G. in Samoa. D.H.P.G. had a monopoly on supplying labor for Samoa. (Firth 1977: 11-12) Firth notes that, "The D.H.P.G. reckoned that being able to employ New Guineans instead of Chinese saved them M 125,000 a year, and while the European price of copra doubled between 1900 and 1913, the cost of labour rose by less than half.". (1977: 12) Since New Guinea laborers knew little about the operation of the laws of supply and demand, they were willing to work for lower wages than others, like the Chinese. There were therefore a number of options for men willing to perform plantation labor- they could work in Samoa, New Britain, mainland German New Guinea (Kaiser Wilhelmsland), or on the newly established plantations on New Ireland itself, near their villages or in another part of the island.

Sabotage by Laborers and Local Populations

What was the nature of the interaction between the European owner living on his plantation and the surrounding population? H. Schluter, a trader living at Lauan, who had also planted coconut palms, complained 1n 1902 to Boluminski, the District Officer for New Ireland:

> A few days ago the natives of Lauan went and set fire to the grass plain. Thereby burning 100 coconut plants of mine. Therefore, I beg to you for advise how am I to set against such people, their pigs are also playing havoc with the coconuts, I have twenty people of Labangarurum [Lavongararum], working on the plain including some of Paruais but here are more of them doing nothing when the police boys comes they clear in the bush. The same with the Lauan people they are that lazy that they don't clear up the roads.... The natives here are in trouble again. The man by name Busimbas of Panafau is practicing some bad things again which the natives call poison.... The natives of Lauan and Nanapai [Nonopai] are positive that he is doing such things. Your boy Baren knows. The man he is causing much disturbances. I wish you will kindly give it your consideration also my land affair. With best wishes. H. Schluter." (October 3, 1902, Commonwealth Archives AA63/83 B203)

Schluter wrote again 12 days later:

> I beg to inform the court that, on my return from Nusa, I found that 400 coconut palms were destroyed by fire on my plantation. The fire was caused by a careless native setting fire to the grass plain. This is now the second time this has happened. Therefore I ask your honor to kindly take some

> proceedings to stop people from setting fire to plains which are already planted, for it is a great loss for such a one as me."
> (October 15, 1902 Commonwealth Archive AA63/83 B203)

The firing of Schluter's groves may have been the accidental spreading of a fire on land being cleared for gardens by the local people. However, gardens were usually located in the bush, an hour's walk from a village; and Schluter's plantation must have been close to the road and the coast, so this explanation seems unlikely. Instead, the fires probably were deliberately set by the local people as a protest against the intrusion of Schluter and his plantation. Once again, people are accused of laziness, although they probably just preferred to invest their productive labor in their own gardens, ceremonies, and crops, rather than work on the road to fulfill the corvee labor obligation of New Ireland men. Schluter's complaint is reminiscent of O'Keefe's complaint that the Yap people preferred to make stone money for ceremonies, rather than pick coconuts. (See Chapter 6.) The road assisted Schluter, the plantation owner, but he was not required to work on it. Schluter had hired twenty workers from the nearby villages of Lavongararum and Paruai, but he then complained that they were not working as hard as he wanted them to.

Regarding problems with local labor, the German Colonial Administration provided advice to planters as to how they should treat their laborers. The Annual Report stated that:

> ...The degree of loyalty to Europeans and the willingness to work of the local labourers depend entirely on the Europeans' skill and patience in handling them, and above all taking an interest in them. No manager can be in any doubt that it is quite impossible to demand of a detachment of local labourers anything approaching the

amount of work that can be asked of contract labourers recruited from elsewhere. Above all one must not insist on trying to force these people from the start into one's own work pattern. It is always advisable particularly in the beginning to let them work in their own way, and only gradually, with kindness and patience, if possible, always through a sensible and influential intermediary from their own village, to introduce European methods.... A plantation manager who knows how to treat the natives correctly, will always be able to obtain native labour and therefore have extraordinarily low operating costs. A knowledge of the language is absolutely essential. (German Imperial Government Annual Report 1901-1902: 229)

Schluter complained about the "practice of poison." (the Neomelanesian term for sorcery) and how it upset the village. This may have been a consequence of Schluter's intrusive presence in the area. The disruption in village life was clear from his report of their behavior. While some of the men in these villages may have been familiar with the experience of having worked as laborers on other islands or even in Australia, the experience of working on a plantation adjacent to one's own village was something else again. Working on Schluter's plantation meant that they would have less time to regularly work in their own gardens or deal with the important task of organizing feasts and ceremonies. European plantation owners were exploiting the New Irelanders from local villages immediately surrounding their plantations. The fires plaguing Schluter were a manifestation of the New Irelanders' response to such exploitation.

COPRA: VILLAGE TRADE AND THE ESTABLISHMENT OF PLANTATIONS

Trade and Payments

Since the European plantations which had been established were not yet in full production, most of the copra being exported was bought from villagers. In 1902, 600 tons came from plantations and 2200 tons, from trade with local people. Actual earnings from copra production fell that year because of a decline in the world price of copra and a decline in production because of drought. (German Imperial Government Annual Report for 1902-1903: 239)

By this time, a number of new trading practices had developed. Traders often used New Ireland intermediaries to buy copra for them. A. Jung, a trader at Ungan, wrote to Boluminski, saying, "I beg to inform you that my labour boy Kassili came to me this morning from Kabotheron and told me that two boys named Kalapos and Laboie of Bulgi stole his box that I gave him for buying copra whilst I am at Ungan.... [They] took all the tobacco about 250 sticks, two belts, two arm rings and two zinc mirrors.... So please inquire into the matter." (April 18, 1900, Commonwealth Archives AA63/83 B203)

Traders also gave villagers cases of goods in advance, with the understanding that copra would be delivered at a future date. However, according to the Annual Report, "In most cases the natives have no clear idea of the relationship between debit and credit. The District Administration is never in a position to clarify the issues in the disputes which frequently result, since the only record of the deliveries made by the two parties is always that kept by the trader, while the native hardly ever knows what he has undertaken to supply in return or what he has already supplied. It seems that the natives frequently accept the cases out of fear of the trader concerned." (German Imperial Government Annual Report for 1900-1901: 219) In an incident on New Britain, a "chief" who had received a box of goods from traders working for Farrell subsequently gave his copra to another trader. When the first traders returned, armed with weapons, to dispute with him, the "chief" killed them. Local people were taking advantage of competition between copra traders to get as much in European goods for their copra as they could.

In addition to barter of European goods for copra, traders up until 1901 also used local shell money, or *diwara*, as a medium of exchange in trade. Though *diwara* is the term for shell money on the Duke of York Islands, the German administration extended its usage to all indigenous shell money in the Bismarck Archipelago. Local people could use shell money to buy European goods, and traders could use it to pay for copra. As we discussed in Chapters 6 and 10 above, men like David Sean O'Keefe (referred to as His Majesty O'Keefe) had used their control of native currency to gain advantage in the trading of copra. In O'Keefe's case, it was by the manufacture of stone money.

The use of shell money as a medium of exchange was prohibited in 1901 in order to force New Irelanders to conform to European ideas about commercial transactions. The Annual Report of 1900-1901 noted,

> The use of shell money, which is obtained and manufactured on certain districts on the north coast of Neu Pommern, had been a great handicap to the development of trade. It was often very difficult for the European firms to obtain the shell money required to purchase copra. In this respect they were completely dependent on the natives, and at times the exchange rate for shell money was forced up absurdly high….Doubtless shell money will continue to maintain its role in transactions between natives for a considerable period. But as it will not be possible after 1 April 1902 to obtain European goods for shell money, the natives will be compelled, in order to obtain such goods, to devote their labors to the production of really useful goods,

suitable for export, such as copra etc., instead of to the acquisition of shell money. (German Imperial Government Annual Report: 220)

The objective of outlawing the use of shell money was to get the local people to produce more goods for export and to move them into a monetary economy. The German colonial government was also opposed to the long canoe voyages made by New Irelanders to obtain shell money in New Britain, because these trips took them away from more "productive" economic activities.

The New Irelanders were primarily interested in exchanging their copra for tobacco. According to one German Government report,

> The main reason, apart from weather conditions, why the natives allow part of their coconut harvest to rot in the interior, is that except for tobacco there is no article of consumption available capable of tempting them to work. Competition of a kind which often borders on the illicit has over five or six years forced the price of tobacco from 2.50 - 3.00 marks down to 1.25 marks per pound, so that the native now has to cut less than half as much copra as a few years ago in order to cover his tobacco requirements.... The only means of increasing trade and fully exploiting the supply of coconuts would appear to be a significant rise in the price of the most coveted consumer item, tobacco. However, it seems too much to hope that the traders concerned will come to an agreement on this. (German Imperial Government Annual Report for 1901-1902: 229-230)

By this time tobacco was being grown on plantations in mainland New Guinea (see Blum 1900: 157), and it is likely that some of the tobacco the traders were selling to New Irelanders came from there.

Plantation production of copra was still quite small, so the colonial administration instituted various ordinances to increase village copra production. However, production dropped, and this was blamed on "...cut-throat competition leading to the ruin of the traders in northern Neu Mecklenburg." (German Imperial Government Annual Report for 1903-1904: 247) The nature of competition among Europeans to establish trading stations in particular places is revealed in a complaint filed by Mouton. According to the complaint, Lanser, a trader, was given permission by the government to acquire a plot of land for a trading station at Mongol on March 26, 1900. He then sold the Mongol station to the firm of Mouton and Co. The firm of Hernsheim and Co. had established its own trading station in the midst of Mongol station, despite the protests of Mouton that he had a prior claim to this location. This Mongol location was close to Hernsheim's plantation at Bagail, and he probably did not want to have a competitor so nearby. Mouton wanted to be compensated for the loss of his Mongol station. (Commonwealth Archives G1 R6 series 231)

Friction Between Traders and Villagers

Though trading stations had been in existence for some time, friction between traders and villagers was common. Sometimes New Irelanders refused to trade with a particular European. A letter from A. Griffith at Lauen to Boluminski, dated Feb. 11, 1907, reads,

> ...It never occurred to me to believe for a moment that you had "tabooed" me? - no! But the men Barrasso and Lapuk have told the natives so and that is an insult to you and me and to me a severe loss as well. I have made careful inquiries through my boys and have also asked the Fijian Mission teacher and all say the same thing- that

Barrasso and Lapuk told the natives of [undecipherable] and Livitua that you had said I was not to get any more copra....

...What your boy Lapuk has against me I have not the slightest idea. The man Barrasso has generally been kept by me in tobacco ever since I have been here- and so far as I knew was quite friendly up to the time you returned from [undecipherable] Islands.

...I recognize of course the right of the natives to sell or not as he will but I am under the impression that he is wrong to prevent by any means other natives from doing so. I believe he will be punished for that. ...for a long time past, I have been as you know on the best of terms with all the natives here and am now for that matter. The whole trouble rises through Barrasso and Lapuk assuming an authority they neither possess and using you as an instigator. The whole thing is a barefaced attempt to make me raise my buying price for copra. This I will not do as the price I have to pay for my goods and the low price I get for my copra will not allow me to do so....the tabu now extends to both my trading boundaries and is causing me serious loss. (Commonwealth Archives AA63/83 B234)

In this case, two Big Men had placed a taboo on selling copra to Griffith, as they already had the power to impose a taboo on harvesting a crop in preparation for a large ceremony. Since Griffith refers to him as "your (Boluminski's) boy," Lapuk was also either a *luluai* or a "Police Boy." The use of Boluminski's name and authority to support the taboo indicates that the local people had probably accepted the rule of the German colonial administration to the point where Boluminski was seen as having the power to impose taboos.

There is no indication as to why trade with Griffith was placed under a taboo. Griffith's reasoning that this was simply a device to force him to increase the price he paid for copra may in fact have been correct. The mention of "trading boundaries" indicates that each copra trader was given a trading territory by the government, where he had a monopoly. As Firth notes, "Once demand itself had been created, competition was the trader's main problem and monopoly his best hope." (1977: 20)

If villagers wanted a higher price, they would have to move their goods elsewhere to get it. This might explain why they would resort to the action that they took in order to force Griffith to raise his price for copra. However, it is also possible that the local people did this to force him out of business and out of their area. While Griffith presented a favorable picture of his relations with the villagers, stating that he was "on the best of terms with all the natives here," their view of the relationship might have been totally different.

Regulation of Competition Between Traders

The Colonial Administration attempted to dampen down competition between traders with another series of ordinances. In order to beat out the competition, some traders had begun again to purchase whole nuts. The Ordinance of 18 October, 1900, prohibited this practice. It was argued that the purchase of whole coconuts "...relieved the natives of the labour of cutting the copra, reinforcing their natural tendency to indolence. The prohibition referred to is intended to put an end to this unsatisfactory state of affairs which militates against training the natives to habits of work." (German Imperial Government Annual Report for 1900-1901:217) The Colonial Government sought to encourage western oriented work habits, in order to increase the production of copra destined for sale on the world market.

COPRA: VILLAGE TRADE AND THE ESTABLISHMENT OF PLANTATIONS

Discussion

The primary aim of the German Colonial Administration was to make New Ireland a commercially productive area, though Firth notes that, "Like Germany's African colonies, the Pacific possessions were of little economic importance... Their trade was worth less than one seventh of one percent of total German trade in 1909....Copra from Germany's Pacific colonies- their main product- provided less than 8 1/2 percent of Germany's copra imports in 1910-1911 compared to 48 1/2 percent from British colonies and 40 percent from the Dutch East Indies." (Firth 1977: 3)

In order to make New Ireland economically productive, the Germans saw their task as one of "pacifying" the area first and then imposing a colonial administrative structure, which was to dominate and control villages that previously had been politically autonomous. The Germans were interested only in the commercial possibilities of the island; and New Irelanders were thought of as people to be exploited for economic gain. To the Germans, this aim required the introduction of "productive work habits," *i.e.*, adopting a Western work ethic. These newly formed work habits were meant not only to increase village production of copra, but also to make New Irelanders more amenable to daily work on European-owned plantations. These two aims would later come into conflict with one another. The western economic institutions, which the Germans attempted to introduce, treated each laborer as an individual wage-earner, paying no attention to the social aspects of a person's identity. In New Ireland society, however, membership in clans or localized sub-clans was a significant part of an individual's identity; and much labor was carried out collectively to accomplish clan purposes.

The reiteration in successive ordinances of the necessity of trying to get the local people to produce more copra indicates that the Germans' attempts to turn New Irelanders into cash crop producers had had little effect. Local people must have recognized that the German economic program would make serious inroads into the foundations of their culture. If the New Irelanders became cash crop producers of copra, as the Germans wished, their own productive system and its purposes would have been sacrificed to the colonialist cause. They normally produced copra only when they had an extrinsic need. Otherwise, they resisted colonial demands for increased copra production in the same way that they had resisted trading stations and other intrusions into their lives. At this time, most New Irelanders had no interest in becoming full-time employees on German plantations. In doing this, they would have had to forego their own organization of village work. Earlier, labor recruitment for work on other islands had affected the organization of labor and made serious inroads into village life. Similarly, the requirement of corvee labor for work on the road, Boluminski's great project, was pulling many men out of their villages, disrupting the local organization of work and clan members' livelihoods.

New Irelanders became involved in the market when they wanted Western goods, such as tobacco, and they sought the best price for copra when they wished to sell it. When the price of tobacco was reduced by competing traders, they sold less copra because they needed less to get sufficient tobacco to fill their needs. When the price they received for copra fell below what it had been in previous years, they probably attributed this to the niggardliness of the trader with whom they dealt, since they knew nothing about fluctuations of the world market. If the price for copra went down too low, they left the coconuts to rot rather than harvest them and produce copra.

Earlier, New Irelanders had chosen not to exchange supplies with the explorers when they felt they were not getting what they wanted in return. The

Germans thought that the desire for European goods and tobacco would become so strong, that New Irelanders would be motivated to increase copra production; but this did not occur. In all probability, this assumption caused a greater emphasis on the development of European plantations as a source of supply. New Irelanders, however, must have seen the efforts of the German administration to introduce a copra cash-crop economy as a threat to many aspects of their lives; and, as we have shown, they resisted these attempts in many ways.

NOTES

1. These issues have been considered by Peter Sack in his book, *Land Between Two Laws*. There, he discusses the confrontation between "primitive law and Western law" in regard to land acquisition in the early colonial period. (Sack 1973)

2. In making comparisons between plantations, one must keep in mind that they were at various stages of development. In the early stages, more labor was required to clear the land and plant sprouting coconuts. Hence, Ostrum was using 40 workers on his 35 hectares, while Ruge, whose plantation was established in 1901, had 20,500 trees but employed only 21 workers. Furthermore, a single entry may include several holdings. The entry for Hernsheim included holdings at Nusa, Bagail and Lagagon, supervised by one overseer.

11. THE EXPANSION AND SPREAD OF CHRISTIANITY DURING THE GERMAN COLONIAL PERIOD

New Ireland ceremonial life continued to be threatened by the expansion of Christianity, missionary activity into new areas, and the institutionalization of the churches already established. (as described in Chapter 8) Christianity had originally been introduced by Methodist missionaries. Somewhat later, as we shall describe in this chapter, Catholics arrived, resulting in competition between the two Christian sects. The Catholics, like the Methodists, objected to what they referred to as "pagan practices," and attempted to stamp them out. Some New Irelanders accepted Catholicism, while others became Methodists.

As we shall see, in time, villages in the northern part of the island, which had a social structure of dual organization, or moieties, continued to operate a form of moiety structure. Methodist and Catholic churches, in such cases, were found in the same village, and operated as competing opposites. We will first describe the activities of the Methodists since they arrived first, and then the Catholic missionary enterprise.

The details concerning the expansion of the missionary enterprise are found in works written by missionaries from their own point of view. The New Irelanders continued to be perceived, and described as "natives," "savages" or "heathens." The missionaries were not interested in the meanings that Christianity had for New Irelanders, and whether or not they were willing to completely give up their old religious beliefs to become Christians. Missionaries frequently wrote about their activities in order to elicit continuing financial aid from their supporters back home. To further this goal, their portrayal of missionary work emphasized the hardships they encountered and the progress they were making in spreading Christianity.

The Methodists

European ministers, few in number, were at the top of the mission hierarchy in the Bismarck Archipelago, and they were all stationed at the mission headquarters, first at the Duke of York Islands and then on the Gazelle Peninsula. They only occasionally visited stations elsewhere in the region. The Methodist mission continued to use Fijians, Samoans and Tongans (or South Sea Islanders, as they were called) as teachers and catechists in New Ireland through World War I. (See Latukefu 1978.) Despite illnesses and departures, by 1894, 81 South Sea Islanders, many accompanied by their families, had served in the Bismarck Archipelago. (Williams 1972: 116) Three of them were eventually made ministers, and in succession directed all the missionary work in New Ireland in the 1890s. By 1900, Methodist missionary activity in New Ireland extended on the west coast from Cape St. George to Kurumut, into the hill villages, and to Kudukudu on the east coast. (Threlfall 1975: 73)

The Methodist plan to indigenize the church in New Ireland began after the first decade of its establishment. By the middle of the 1880s, several New Ireland converts had become lay preachers and were teaching in the schools being set up. They were appointed as pastor teachers, though questions had been raised as to whether local villagers would accept them, since they did not carry with them the prestige and power of either the Europeans or the Fijians, the Europeans' surrogates. The New Ireland men who first moved into the Methodist Church hierarchy did not seem to be Big Men, those with local power and prestige. They probably were marginal to the New Ireland political structure. Though Big Men, existing political leaders, negotiated with the Methodists to bring churches to their villages, these leaders themselves did not seem to occupy positions in the church hierarchy.

Though many people attended church services, becoming a member of the Church was more complicated. According to Williams, "In preparing for membership, it became the normal practice for people to have a year of training and probation before baptism and being received as full members." (1972: 111) There were several categories of church adherents. The reported figures for 1886 indicate that throughout the area there were 3,983 people attending worship, but only 467 church members, with an additional 202 members on trial, and 32 receiving instruction. (Threlfall 1975: 62) The extent to which New Irelanders had to renounce indigenous beliefs about clan spirits, *masalais*, and important ritual practices in order to be permitted to attend church services or become members is not known; but surely, at this point, their behavior after conversion would not have continued to strongly support such beliefs and practices[1].

In the next decade, an increasing number of villagers became involved in the administration of Methodist churches, indicating greater success in the conversion process. Threlfall notes, "Each congregation appointed a church steward, who took care of the buildings and of the money raised for the Church; a congregation representative or spokesman; and several class leaders who helped in the instruction of members in the class meetings, and visited the sick." (1975: 64) Some of these individuals were women. The institutional structure of the Methodist church was slowly being replicated in New Ireland, while the pre-contact ceremonial structure of *malanggans* and *kaba*, and the supernatural belief system of *masalai* and ancestor spirits apparently continued to function at the same time. At this point in time, the two systems were probably compartmentalized.

Church plantations, worked by indigenous laborers, were set up in New Britain to make the church economically self-sufficient. They made the Methodist mission unmistakably part of the capitalist system. There is no indication as to how or whether the men working on plantations were paid. How could New Irelanders have distinguished plantation owners like Mouton and Parkinson, recruiting for their plantations, from missionaries like Rev. Fellmann, recruiting for the Methodist plantation?

It was important for the Australian Methodist Board to appoint German Methodists to work in the Bismarcks, in order to more easily enlist the support of the German colonial government in their endeavors. The first German, Rev. Heinrich Fellmann, arrived in 1897. However, control over the Methodist Mission in the Bismarck Archipelago remained in the hands of the Australian Methodist Mission Board even when Fellmann became Chairman. Because the Australian Methodist Mission Board had extended its missionary work to British New Guinea in the 1890s, there was a long delay in providing New Ireland with a European missionary, seen as necessary for the continued expansion of the church into new areas. Though New Ireland Methodists could staff existing churches, they were not seen as capable of being evangelists of its expansion.

The first European to man a mission station on New Ireland was George Pearson, a lay missionary appointed to Eratubu in 1901. The Rev. George Brown had paid compensation there in 1880 for killings carried out by his ally, Topulu. The strength of the church at that time was demonstrated by the fact that Pearson baptized 134 at a single service there, as 2,000 people looked on, in June 1902. (Threlfall 1975: 78)

Translating Christian Texts

The need to communicate the message of Christianity in a language which the local people could understand continued to be a central problem. Since the headquarters of the Methodist Mission were located in the Duke of York Islands, Brown and subsequently Danks and Rickard worked first on translating various religious texts into the Duke of York language. However, since greater numbers of people spoke Kuanua, the Tolai language, it was considered to be a more promising language for missionary activity.

Rev. Rickard began work on Kuanua in 1884. In 1896, it was decided that, "...All Methodists would then use Kuanua schoolbooks, the hymn book and scripture translations. All of the people among whom the Methodist Church was then working spoke Austronesian languages similar to Kuanua, and shared many words in their vocabulary; it would not be hard for these people to learn Kuanua, but it would obviously be impossible for the church to provide school-books and religious literature in every language of the District." (Threlfall 1975: 69) The Methodists made the decision to use Kuanua (Tolai), despite the fact that they recognized that religious texts in that language would not be completely understood even in the southern part of New Ireland, where the languages spoken belong to the same Patpatar-Tolai language family as Kuana. With Kuanua the official language of the church, both texts and religious services would have been unintelligible to the people of the northern part of New Ireland, as they spoke several different languages of the Northern New Ireland family.

This decision on the part of the Methodist Mission had important implications. It made it much easier for Tolai speakers to obtain an education in the Methodist-run schools and to have easier access to positions in the colonial government than others, as they have had even in the recent past. Missionaries working on New Ireland, however, found the use of Kuanua, the Tolai language, to be a problem in the areas into which the church had begun to expand; and they began to work on translations of scripture into other New Ireland languages. Revs. Schmidt, Wenzel, and Pratsch all worked on Patpatar and Susurunga translations, while Reddin and Boettcher worked in the Tigak language, spoken in the northern area around Kavieng. As Williams observed, "…The big number of languages used in New Ireland meant it was impossible to use these local languages as a common language. Pidgin became the main language spoken, but in the Church Kuanua remained the mission language and was persistently used right into the 1960s even though the Catholics had been using Pidgin for many years." (Williams 1972: 125)

During the first decade of the twentieth century the Methodist Mission extended its activities into central and northern New Ireland. Frequently, seeking new sites for mission stations was combined with labor recruitment for Methodist church plantations on New Britain. This practice was also used by the Catholic Church.

Rev. Fellmann, who had recently been made Chairman of the Methodist Mission for the entire Bismarck Archipelago, took the newly acquired sailing ship "Litia" northward along the west coast of New Ireland in 1902, "...to visit new areas and to seek workers for the plantation at Ulu." (Threlfall 1975: 79) The "Litia" ran aground at Kono while the missionaries were attempting to buy food there. Ligeremaluoga, a New Irelander who later became a pastor teacher, wrote that, "The people of Kono dragged it [the "Litia"] off the reef.

One of the men, Kasisie, wanted to kill the two missionaries and their schoolboys, but his brother, Timi, stopped him from doing so. Timi was the chieftain at that time, and the two missionaries stayed with him about two weeks. It was then that Timi asked the two missionaries to send him a teacher." (Ligeremaluoga 1932: 15)

Timi (or Simi, according to Threlfall) had worked as a plantation laborer in Samoa, where he became acquainted with the church. (Threlfall 1975: 79) The two brothers represent a contrast which probably characterized many villages. One brother saw the missionaries in their beached vessel as fair game to be killed as intruders, as Capt. Brodie's vessel, the "Lavinia," had been burned and its crew killed at Port Praslin 27 years earlier. The other brother, whose horizons had been broadened by his experience as a labor recruit in Samoa, saw advantages to be gained from the establishment of a mission station and a teacher in the village.

In connection with Methodist expansion in the northern part of the island, Reverends Cox and Doley were sent to buy blocks of land for the mission in villages near Kavieng in 1902. In 1905 Ernest Sprott, a lay missionary, came to man the Nusa station, accompanied by two Fijian pastor teachers and two local men, Ioap To Lulungan and Iosapat To Nunuar. In some villages labor recruits had gone to plantations on the Gazelle Peninsula, where they had been introduced to Christianity. These individuals were more receptive to the missionaries and their endeavors, and they might have encouraged their fellow villages to accept mission stations. Sprott soon began travelling to establish missionary stations elsewhere in the area. The Sprott party encountered Noa Pokpokat at Kaselok village and Hosea Kavuk at Munawai village. Both had become Christians while working on the Gazelle Peninsula. Williams (1972) notes that Noa Pokpok "…was a powerful force in urging the people to accept the new teaching. He was baptized himself and became a pastor to his own people."

Conversion was symbolically represented by the people bringing their old, ornately carved images used in ceremonies and burning them at the Church. "It was a pity that some of the best art in the area was thus lost, but there was no doubt that the action had great meaning for the people and indicated their desire to accept a new way of life." (Williams 1972: 127) The art being destroyed by the church was that associated with the *malanggan* mortuary ceremony, the focal religious institution which the Methodists were bent on eliminating. The Methodists assumed that the carvings represented "idols," and that the New Irelanders worshiped the *malanggans*. By destroying them they were renouncing "their religion and their gods." However, since these objects were always left to rot after the ceremony, the missionaries were destroying what was usually discarded anyway.

Despite the missionaries' assumptions that old beliefs had been renounced in favor of Christianity, other information indicates the continued coexistence of Christianity and indigenous religious beliefs at this time. The burning of "idols" by these missionaries is a sharp contrast to the avid collecting of such objects by Rev. George Brown some thirty years earlier.

The European missionaries continued to encounter divided opinions about conversion to Christianity among the villagers as they visited different parts of northern New Ireland, In January 1907 Revs. Fellmann and Pearson visited Mesi, which had been the site of an "uprising" several years earlier: "The people there had a bad reputation for fighting and had murdered traders, but the missionaries stayed two nights and selected a site for church work. Some Mesi men wanted to kill and eat the visitors, but others said, 'But how can we? They are missionaries!' and no harm was done to them." (Threlfall

1975: 80) Years after the first introduction of Christianity to other parts of New Ireland and the imposition of the colonial administrative structure, the polar positions of "resisters" and "accepters" of Christianity was still found in Mesi. The "resisters" represented people who wanted to continue with their traditions, and the "accepters" represented people who were willing to completely change their belief system.

The Methodist missionary enterprise expanded to the islands of Steffan Straights, Djaul, Simberi, and Tatau in the Tabar group. The establishment of the district office in Kavieng and plantations, coupled with already existing trading stations, had moved these New Irelanders beyond the horizons of their villages, and they saw benefits in having Christianity in their midst. The village leaders of Tabar requested a mission, as the villages on the east coast had twenty years earlier. The Annual Reports of the German Colonial Administration show an expansion in church numbers, membership and other activities[2].

Boarding Schools

The early efforts by Revs. Brown and Danks to translate various religious texts into vernacular languages was primarily to enable the mission to train local men to become preachers, catechists and teachers. They saw education as the key to making New Irelanders into Christians and "civilizing" them. The most efficient way of doing this was to set up boarding schools, removing children from their families and villages, and educating them in this created Western milieu. A minimal education was offered in the village schools that were beginning to be established. The curriculum there included reading, writing, arithmetic, geography, bible interpretation and singing. A very small number of children might then be sent to boarding schools, where the curriculum also included ten hours per week of instruction in the German language. Up to 1913, the number of students from New Ireland was very small, only eleven out of ninety-two. (German Imperial Government Annual Report for 1912-1913: 361) The missionaries also established a separate school for children of "mixed blood," who were considered by both missionaries and the government to form a separate category. The reports reveal the central role that institutions like the Omo Circuit Training Institute, established at Omo in 1907, played in training local people to become teachers, catechists, and eventually pastors. The purpose of educating the people of the Bismarck Archipelago in German, as well as other western subjects and practical skills, was to create a cadre of local individuals, an elite who could work for the benefit of the colonial administration.

Indigenizing the Church

Part of the policy of indigenizing the church was to move as rapidly as possible to village financial support of village churches. (Forman 1985) Various devices were adopted to pay church salaries, such as setting aside special coconut palms, whose nuts would be used to pay salaries, or collecting a few nuts from each member of the congregation at the end of every quarter for the same purpose.

The actions of New Irelanders reveal their attitudes towards the introduction of Christianity in the first years of the Methodist missionary effort. The ambivalence that they may have had about their own culture in the face of the Christian dogma emerges in the autobiography of Ligeremaluoga, a devout convert to Christianity and a teacher in the Methodist missionary school[3].

THE EXPANSION AND SPREAD OF CHRISTIANITY

Ligeramaluoga's Story

Ligeramaluoga begins his account with the statement that, "I was born into heathenism and confusion; war and cannibalism still reigned supreme. Perhaps God knew that I would later preach in His Name." (1932: 15) The events he described begin when he was eight or nine, with the coming of Christianity to his village of Kono in 1902. After attending primary school at Kono and Pinikindu, he was baptized in 1911 and sent to the college at Watnabara in the Duke of York Islands to become a teacher. In 1918, he was sent to teach at Omo, where he learned Tigak and married a woman from that area. Though Ligeremaluoga was a Christian, he married his wife according to local Tigak custom and lived uxorilocally for four years until he and his wife moved away from the village. He describes being involved in the social organization of the village to a greater degree than were Fijian or European missionaries. Eventually he became a teacher at the College at Watnabara.

He looked back upon his early life with mixed feelings, conveying to us how a New Irelander, who subsequently became a Christian, viewed the customs of his society as they operated in the period immediately preceding the large-scale adoption of Christianity. Ligeramaluoga's attitude is illustrated in his description of the "*A Qoqo*" rite associated with mortuary rituals. He noted, "They [men and women] sat together not only for singing, but for crying also; ...It was right to appeal to the synod to suppress this custom, for many bad men and women spoilt this ceremony of remembrance by making it a means of satisfying filthy inclinations." (1932: 59) "Satisfying filthy inclinations," referred to the sexual license which took place on ceremonial occasions, as we discussed in Chapter 2. This was a pattern of behavior that was a part of the larger fabric of social relationships in villages. When Ligeremaluoga accepted the teachings of Christianity, he also accepted a

Christian morality which encompassed a Western Victorian perspective on sex. Ligeremaluoga, the Christian, thus condemned these practices as "filthy" and in violation of Christian morality.

Ceremonial sexual license meant that sexual exclusivity was not an aspect of New Ireland marriage patterns. There was no concept of "adultery" as defined by the Ten Commandments, in pre-contact New Ireland life, as we have noted in Chapter 2. In fact, Powdermaker makes it very clear in her ethnography that, in Lesu neither husband nor wife had exclusive sexual rights over their spouses. The attempt of the Church to "civilize" New Irelanders involved a campaign directed against such "adulterous" practices, since they violated Victorian norms of sexual conduct. Ligeremaluoga's autobiography is an ambivalent account with its combination of pride in some aspects of the past, and condemnation of other practices which he labels as "heathenism."

Catholicism

By the first decades of the 19th century in France, enthusiasm for the Enlightenment and revolutionary fervor had waned, giving way to popular piety and the rise of a romanticized Catholicism[4]. Religious congregations increased in number in France, and many new orders with an interest in missionizing appeared, despite periodic bursts of anti-Clericalism.

Fr. Jules Chevalier founded the Society of the Missionaries of the Sacred Heart in 1854 in Issoudun, France. The mission was directly attached to the Catholic Church. Its representatives were emissaries of the Pope through the *Sacra Congregation de Propaganda Fide*, which directed all overseas missionaries and congregations. The proclaimed purpose of this order was the salvation of souls and the revitalization of the faith through dedication to the Sacred Heart of Jesus. Most of the missionaries of the Sacred Heart of Jesus grew up in religious households of modest socioeconomic means, raised by pious parents who typically were peasant farmers or artisans. Their parish priests often were the first to notice their exceptional piety and ability and steered them to the Sacred Heart Mission.

As Dupeyrat phrased it, this was an era of "religious romanticism." (Dupeyrat, in Langmore 1989:4) Though the salvation of souls was their goal, sanctity and holiness through suffering, even to the point of martyrdom, usually motivated men to join the Mission. Overseas missionary work had a romantic attraction and was seen as a means of achieving sanctity and martyrdom.

The Apostolic Vicarate of New Guinea (Melanesia and Micronesia) had been vacant for some years when the Pope indicated his wish that the Sacred Heart Mission be in charge of spreading the Gospel in this vast area. (Jouet 1887: 5) The Vatican's interest in sending missionaries into the Pacific was the result of the Marquis de Rays' request for missionaries for the area within which his ill-fated colony was to be located. (Langmore 1989: 201)

Fr. Joseph Durin, the mission Superior, Fr. Andre-Louis Navarre, and Fr. Theophile Cramaille, accompanied by Brother George Durin and Brother Mesmin Fromm, prepared to take up duties in the Bismarck Archipelago. The party arrived at Port Bretonon on the "Chandernagor" at the end of September 1882, finding barely a trace of the colony. They then proceeded to Matupi, on New Britain, visited Hernsheim's representative Mickelson (Michaelson) there, and went on to see Tolitoro, a local Big Man who was reported to be very devoted to Catholic missionaries. Fr. Navarre observes, "In each village the Protestants had already placed catechists: these were natives of the islands of Fiji and Tonga; they already had one in our village (Beridni) but he was due to leave. Tolitoro had always said he wanted Missionaries in full robes." (Fr.

Navarre in Jouet 1887: 35) Fr. Navarre notes that the Fijian catechists "are scorned and feared by the Kanaks." (Kanak was the term which the French used for all indigenous people in the Pacific.) Navarre's presentation of the scene was designed to emphasize the difficulties and the challenges facing his intrepid troop of Catholic missionaries. He stated, "Our Kanakas are like wasteland which has never been cultivated- all weeds grow there... their hearts are hardened by vicious habits, their spirits which do not rise above earthly joys are little able to receive supernatural impressions." (1889, quoted in Langmore 1989: 109) This characterization reveals a set of mind which would seem to make Fr. Navarre's professed goal of "civilizing" and converting the local population difficult to achieve. (Langmore 1989: 123) Fr. Lannuzel replaced Fr. Navarre, and the center of Catholic mission activities was soon shifted to Papua. (Sack 1973: 76) Unlike the Wesleyan missionaries, who constantly sought to expand their missionizing activities in New Ireland, the Catholic missionaries during this early period considered New Ireland to be *terra incognita*, perhaps because of what had happened to the abortive Marquis de Rays colony there. (See Chapter 6.)

The Catholic Mission of the Sacred Heart was rather dormant in the Bismarck Archipelago until the arrival of Fr. Louis Couppe in 1888 after the death of Fr. Navarre. Fr. Couppe was made head of the mission, subsequently Apostolic Vicar of New Britain, and later bishop. His head station at Vunapope, was later called Mioko. The German colonial government raised no objections to Catholic missionary activity, "...as long as these did not give rise to fears of a threat to the interests of the Reich and the Protectorate." (Neuguinea Kompagnie Annual Report for 1888-1889:42) At Bishop Coupe's request, Father Bernhard Bley, Father Hermann Kliem, Brother Jakob Winkler, and Brother Colestin Kayser arrived from Germany in 1890.

THE EXPANSION AND SPREAD OF CHRISTIANITY

(Zwinge 1932: 30) In 1901, Bishop Couppe traveled to Europe and returned with a number of young Dutch and German Catholic missionaries. (Peekel 1932:60)

Instead of concentrating primarily on spreading the Catholic message, Bishop Couppe insisted that the mission first must be economically self-sufficient. To achieve this, they established coconut plantations, as the Methodists had done, and set up a sawmill. (Zwinge 1932: 31) By 1901, the mission was operating several plantations.

The labor problem had become acute, and the mission vessel, instead of being used for religious purposes, was continually being used for the recruitment of laborers. Muller relates that, "Subsequently, recruiting became much easier as New Ireland workers became more familiar with Whites and everywhere pidgin English [*pidginenglisch*] was understood. The captains of the mission ships also act as recruiters and are involved in this business on their usual trips." (1932: 131-132)

The Catholic Mission recruited laborers from the west coast of New Ireland, along the stretch between Kalil and Kono, where Methodist missions had existed since the time of Rev. George Brown. After working on the Catholic Mission plantations in New Britain, many of these workers had become Catholics. They returned as the first New Ireland Catholics to areas that had been considered to be strongly Methodist. As Fr. Peekel optimistically stated, "The Catholic church and its headquarters at Vunapope were known in the countryside around Bom, Rapito, Kurumut, Nabumai, Bisapu long before a white [Catholic] missionary stepped on the coast of New Ireland and in the interior as well as on the coast, prayer houses were erected where they could serve God with prayer and song on Sundays." (Peekel 1932: 58)

The new Catholic ideas were spread by labor recruits, in contrast to ideas of Methodism, which were, for a long period of time, conveyed by South Seas Islanders and Europeans. Some of the workers from New Ireland on the Catholic plantations, who had become Catholics, stayed on after their period of service to attend the Catechist school set up at Vunapope by 1898. (German Imperial Government Annual Report for 1894-1895: 114) When they returned as catechists, they served to introduce Catholicism to their villages and to surrounding areas. Fr. Peekel notes, "In the northern area, Karl Konga and Jakob Bosbara who both attended the school in Vunapope as youths spread the Catholic religion in the surrounding areas of Langania and Lamasong with great perseverance and devotion. In order to make the work of the first catechists easier Bishop Couppe together with them translated the main prayers into the Pala (Patpatar) language of New Ireland." (1932:60) It is unclear why these men became Catholic catechists, since some of them came from areas which were already nominally Methodist.

In 1901, Father Johannes Eberlein was given the responsibility of selecting the location for a head station along the New Ireland coast. After traveling into the New Ireland mountains, he visited a catechist named To Mais at the village of Rachera. To Mais had been a labor recruit on the Catholic plantation in New Britain, had attended the Catechist school, and then returned home to work as a missionary. Some 200 people gathered on Sunday to celebrate Mass, though the church and the plaza in this village were too small for the audience. The large attendance proved to Eberlein that the catechists' teachings were effective.

Following his reconnaissance trip, Eberlein proposed that two Catholic mission stations be set up on the west coast of New Ireland, at Marianum and at Ulaputur (Rabuo). The choice of these locations represented a conjunction of several motives: their closeness to the headquarters of the mission at Vunapope, a suitable anchorage, and the fact that the east coast could easily be reached overland. (Peekel 1932: 60) The Catholic missionaries chose the west coast of New Ireland for their first mission stations for the same reasons that Rev. George Brown chose the same area for his catechists: its closeness to mission headquarters. However, by this time the colonial government had its New Ireland headquarters at Kavieng, in the far north, and Boluminski's road had already reached Fisoa along the east coast. The northeast region around Kavieng was to be the area that developed most rapidly as government control and trade expanded.

In June 1902, Frs. Anton de Jong and Josef Abel, the first European priests in New Ireland, opened the stations at Ulaputur and Marianum and were soon joined by two lay brothers. The responsibilities of lay brothers included the various practical activities necessary to keep the missions operating: carpentry and the erection of the mission buildings, operation of the sawmill on the Toriu River, running the coconut plantations at each mission, and building and running the ships necessary to periodically provision stations in outlying areas. (Baumann 1932: 112-125) The fathers tended to sacred concerns. In contrast, the Methodist South Sea Island catechists had to perform both secular and sacred tasks or rely on local people to help them.

When the government established its station at Namatanai in 1905, the Catholic Mission also prepared to open a station there, which would be located "...where the native catechist Sagal had erected a small church and had held Sunday services." (Peekel 1932: 61)

The establishment of churches or prayer houses by labor recruits turned catechists often formed the basis for founding Catholic mission stations staffed by European priests. The Catholic missionaries did not have to confront the problem faced by Rev. Brown, that of bringing their religion to people who knew nothing about it. New Ireland converts and catechists had already paved the way. In fact, a number of native catechists were appointed to be in charge of "outstations." Father Gerhard Peekel, who became a scholar of both the New Ireland languages and New Ireland cultures, was assigned to the station at Namatanai. A boarding school for young men which served as a quasi-catechist school was established at each mission station.

Catholic missionaries who worked in New Ireland, men such as Fr. Peekel, recognized the necessity of learning the language of the people and something about their way of life. In this, they were replicating what the Methodist missionaries had been doing. In his earlier reconnaissance, Fr. Eberlein had seen that the variety of languages spoken along the west coast of New Ireland presented a great problem for missionary work. He understood that seven different languages were spoken in the area he visited but that the same language was spoken on the west coast and at a parallel location on the east coast. (Eberlein 1902:218) The initial work on Patpatar (Pala), where the Catholics first worked, was done by Bishop Couppe when he brought students from the area back with him to attend school at Vunapope. It was continued by Father Peekel[5].

Confrontations Between Methodists and Catholics

Direct confrontation between Methodists and Catholics was bound to occur -- and it did, in northern New Ireland, where the Methodists had but recently begun to set up stations and the Catholics soon followed. Fr. Peekel noted, "Because of its favorable location and good harbor, Kavieng was considered central in the new territory." (1932:62) Catholic missiomary activity in the northern part of New Ireland was beset by a series of problems.

THE EXPANSION AND SPREAD OF CHRISTIANITY

As Fr. Peekel perceived the situation, "A white Wesleyan missionary had resided for some years at Omo and visited the sparse surrounding population providing them with Wesleyan service. The off islands of Nusa and Nusalik had their `Teacher' (a Wesleyan Black teacher) The leaders of the Wesleyan missionary establishment could not be kept uninformed of the plans of the Catholic mission. The unexpected establishment of the mission was like a warning shot across their bow. They saw their monopoly endangered since they believed that they would have a monopoly for a very long time." (Peekel 1932:63)

The Wesleyans had great initial advantages in the competition, since they had already been working in the Kavieng area. People knew their mission, and in many villages there were youths and young men who had been educated at the Omo Training Institute. In contrast, in most places in northern New Ireland the Catholic Mission and its goals were unknown.

Until 1912, the Catholics concentrated their expansion into the islands of Tabar, Tanga, and Lihir, setting up stations on the sites acquired by Bishop Couppe on his trip to New Ireland in 1909. In 1912, the Catholics established New Ireland stations at Lamekot, Bitanga, and Kamalu.

Wherever the Catholics set up a mission station, they brought an elaborate institutional structure with them. At Lamekot, a dwelling house for the Fathers, a boarding school for girls, and then a house for the Sisters, who would run the boarding school, were built. Sisters Theresa, Gabriele, and Agatha from the Hiltrup Mission soon arrived on the scene, the first sisters to serve in New Ireland. The European fathers, lay brothers and sisters who were part of the mission establishment had to be appropriately housed and cared for; and the European cultural setting from which they had come had to be recreated as much as possible. Though there were New Ireland catechists, they were subordinate to the European Catholic religious hierarchy.

To avoid direct competition, the German colonial government attempted to divide up the area into Catholic and Methodist districts, giving some the right to erect "Catholic prayer houses," in which they themselves could say the Catholic prayers and sing songs. (Bley 1925:29) When a dying Catholic requested a priest, the priest could not refuse to enter a Methodist district. The government later admitted that trying to divide up the area into Catholic and Methodist districts had been a mistake.

Discussion

It is clear that the Methodists and the Catholics organized very different kinds of missionary enterprises. Though the first Methodist mission stations in New Ireland were manned by South Sea Island converts, with European ministers appearing from time to time to supervise, by the middle of the 1880s some New Ireland converts to Methodism had become lay preachers and teachers, in line with the Methodist goal of the indigenization of the church. The Catholic Mission, in contrast, was dependent primarily on European personnel who were part of the Catholic hierarchy, including priests, lay brothers, and sisters. It was these individuals who manned the mission stations rather than indigenous converts. The Europeans lived somewhat apart from villages and represented islands of European culture. Native Catholic catechists manned the outstations but expatriates dominated the religious structure.

The figures for 1906-1912 show that the Catholics had more than ten times the number of Europeans serving on their staff than did the Methodists[6]. Local people were much more involved in the staffing of the Methodist mission than among the Catholics.

THE EXPANSION AND SPREAD OF CHRISTIANITY

From the beginning the Methodists tried to develop a staff of indigenous clergy, in contrast to the Catholics, who at first relied on a mostly European staff supplemented by native catechists. The Methodists insisted that villagers assume a role in the governance of local churches. The Catholics seem not to have had an equivalent organization. Methodists soon involved villagers in the financial support of the churches. The Catholics took a different route, supporting their mission work through outside economic endeavors not related to the life of the villagers.

The government's attempt to avoid competition by keeping one district purely Catholic and another purely Methodist proved impossible. Catholic and Methodist missionaries vigorously competed for adherents. The Catholics did not concede any area to the Methodists just because the latter were already established there. The colonial administration supported both missions, since village and boarding schools had always been important components of missionary activity, and this obviated the need for the government to establish its own school system.

Both Methodists and Catholics realized that the most effective way to "produce" Christians was to remove children from their families and villages and place them in boarding schools, where they could be indoctrinated in the Christian way of life, surrounded by an atmosphere which fostered this. Barker notes, "Through schooling and the application of imported arts, missionaries began to familiarize islanders with the orientations and organization of the hegemonic colonial system the Europeans were then building." (1990: 16)

The responses of the New Irelanders to the missionary activity of both the Catholics and the Methodists varied. There were numerous examples of headmen and village leaders who invited the church into their villages by "buying a church."[7] Sometimes villagers responded in a belligerent manner to visits by missionaries. At other times, villages were divided, with some villagers in favor and others opposed.

The rivalry between aspiring leaders and leaders of clans came into play in the introduction of Christianity. If a Big Man in a village was in favor of bringing in the *lotu*, his rival usually opposed it. Boutelier notes that, "the new religion offered a convenient vehicle for working out old rivalries, for gaining material wealth, and for advancing political ambitions." (1985: 14)

In other parts of the Pacific where the political system was of the chieftainship type, conversion of the chief immediately led to the seeming conversion of the populace. This was the case in Fiji, Tonga and elsewhere. Barker reports that, "The progress of the missions tended to be slower in Melanesia than in eastern and northern Oceania because of the absence in most places of large political units. Converts had to be won village by village." (Barker 1990: 3)

As time went on, converts to both Methodism and Catholicism were to be found in the same villages. The structure of relationships between New Ireland Catholics and New Ireland Methodists frequently took the form of the balanced opposition between moieties which characterizes the social structure found in many parts of New Ireland, as well as the opposition between "enemies." Lesu in 1929 was a single village, though it had been two villages which had been enemies in the past: Tagum and Lesu. After the abolition of warfare by the colonial government, the two villages were united. The Catholic mission was located in Tagum and the Methodist mission, in Lesu. (Powdermaker 1933) By 1954, the village again had split into two halves; Lesu I, which was Methodist, and Lesu II, which was Catholic. (Lewis 1959)

THE EXPANSION AND SPREAD OF CHRISTIANITY

Christianity was being presented to the New Irelanders in terms of an opposition between Methodism and Catholicism and their pattern of conversion seems to have been shaped by their own structure of oppositions: between moieties and between enemies and allies. This latter set of oppositions had earlier shaped the support of or opposition to traders and the colonial government. Neumann notes something similar for the Tolai: "Sometimes internal divisions led to the acceptance of both denominations in one village." (1992: 91) This illustrates what Barker refers to as "cultural continuity within Christian forms." (1990:8)

Christianity was a set of ideas brought back by returning labor recruits, along with some knowledge of Pidgin English and a box of trade items. Those who returned baptized as Catholics or Methodists often set up prayer houses and became proselytizers for the new faith. Just as the *Sokopana* cult had been brought back to Tanga by influential men, Christianity, as a new idea system, was brought back by an aspiring political leader to enhance his power.

From this distant vantage point, we cannot directly ask what New Irelanders thought about Christianity. Except for Ligeremaluoga, this can only be teased out of the divergent, extant European sources. One can only speculate about how these two different forms of Christianity were perceived by the New Irelanders, when first presented to them. Some New Ireland leaders clearly were receptive to Christianity for instrumental reasons, because it gave them economic and political advantages. Except for practices which the missionaries insisted on stamping out, Methodism or Catholicism as belief systems were added to existing beliefs. For individuals who accepted Christianity as adults, Christian beliefs at first formed only a superficial layer over earlier beliefs which were not rejected, according to Powdermaker (1933). Beliefs in magic and sorcery, clan spirits, and spiritual doubles, seem to have coexisted with Christianity in New Ireland without conflict. Though girls' initiation was eliminated, and boys' initiation was reduced in terms of time spent in seclusion, the focal institution of mortuary rites continued to be important. People like Ligeremaluoga, who wholeheartedly embraced Christianity, developed contempt for aspects of their own culture which they now saw as "depraved heathenism."

Christianity served to open up a complicated outside world to New Irelanders. However, in time, Christianity and New Ireland culture interpenetrated one another.

NOTES

1. [Editor's note:] According to an anonymous reviewer of this manuscript, documents in the Methodist Overseas Missions Archive (minutes, circuit reports, and regulations) specify what behaviors were forbidden or not. Furthermore, several New Ireland ethnographers "remark on widespread belief in *masalai* and other spirit beings despite conversion to Christianity. Given that the existence of *masalai* is closely bound up with land tenure, [such beliefs] are not so easily displaced."

2. Attendance at services, numbers of churches and preaching places, number of adults and children baptized, day schools and Sunday schools, numbers of church members and local catechists are all documented in the colonial records. (See German Imperial Government Annual Reports for 1906-1907: 269; 1907-1908: 299; 1909-1910: 312;1911-1912: 343; 1912-1913: 362; 1913-1914: 115-119.)

3. Ligeremaluoga, also known as Osea Lige, was a teacher in the Methodist missionary schools. Miss Ella Collins encouraged him to write the work, which she translated into English. The language in which the original

account was written is unknown. The translation presents real difficulties, especially with Miss Collins' use of the terms "tribe," "family," and "chief," since the terms Ligeremaluoga used are not given. He was approximately 38 or 39 when he wrote the book. The earlier events which he describes, both in his life and in the life of his people in Kono (Barok-speaking), refer to a time at the beginning of the twentieth century.

4. This material on the backgrounds of the Sacred Heart Mission personnel, and the conceptualization of their goals comes from Langmore's study of the European missionaries who worked in Papua between 1874 and 1914. (1959) The same Sacred Heart Mission personnel worked in both Papua and the Bismarck Archipelago.

5. Fr. Peekel's career as a missionary and scholar closely paralleled that of Reverend Brown's. He published a grammar of the Pala (Patpatar) language and wrote a manuscript on the language of Lamekot (Kara). His other publications included articles on kinship terminology, religion, magic, and *malanggan* rites of central and northern New Ireland.

6. For example, in 1906-1907, the Catholics had 95 Europeans on their staff, and 55 "native catechists." In comparison, the Methodists had nine Europeans on their staff, and 162 "colored helpers." In assessing these figures, it is important to know the number of stations that each mission maintained. In 1906-1907, the Catholics had 26 head stations and 64 outstations, a total of 90 stations; the Methodists had 189 stations. (German Imperial Government Annual Report for 1906-1907:269)

7. Neumann describes how Tolai Big Men negotiated the "spreading of the *lotu*" and became its leaders. (1992: 88ff.)

ALIENS ON OUR SHORES

12. CONSOLIDATON OF COLONIAL CONTROL: 1884-1914

Germany assumed control over "Neu Mecklenburg" in 1884. At that time, though missions and trading stations had been set up, villages were independent and autonomous. The occupying Germans viewed the New Irelanders as "naked, savage cannibals." Two decades later, the effects of their "civilizing" efforts were noticeable. A road had been built. Pacification was being enforced in many parts of the island. Christianity was taking hold. And New Irelanders were learning to speak German. The first decade of the twentieth century saw the tightening of the Germans' colonial grip over more and more areas of New Ireland life.

The head tax was a central feature in incorporating the local population into the colonial structure and attempting to force villagers into a monetary economy. The head tax, first instituted in 1904 on New Britain (Neu Pommern) and the Duke of York Islands (Neu Lauenburg), was extended to Kavieng District in 1906 and Namatanai District in 1907. (German New Guinea Draft Annual Report for 1913-1914: 165) Governor Hahl optimistically observed that the "natives" willingly paid the head tax, since they realized it was used to pay for medical treatment in hospitals, which they valued and freely used. He states, however, that,

...When I announced the introduction of the tax to a meeting of chiefs [*luluais*] in the Rossel Range, and asked the men sitting round me to express their opinion frankly, the reply was: 'We have the money ready, and will hand it over. But we have heard that the plantations anticipate that we will now have to send our young men into employment to earn money for the tax. This will not happen. The money drops down to us from the palms which we own and which we planted at your behest." (Hahl 1980: 112)

The *luluais* clearly saw the head tax as the means of forcing them either to sell their labor to the plantation owners or sell their copra to the traders, in order to get money to pay the tax. Though the plantation owners wanted labor recruits, the leaders were trying to prevent this, since it was most disruptive to the organization of work in the village. They preferred that the villagers sell their copra rather than their labor, even though it required an increase in copra production and additional labor. It is apparent, however, that the Germans had succeeded in getting the local people to plant coconut palms solely to produce copra for sale, becoming cash croppers. Funds from such sales could be used to pay the head tax.

Populations Relocate from Mountains to Coastal Settlements

Colonial control during this period was extended to the rugged Rossel and Schleinitz ranges, in the southern part of Namatanai District. One of the important consequences was that people moved from interior villages down to the coast. "...People from the mountains settled in uninhabited places along the shore and began to plant coconut palms. Mountain and coastal people are now living peacefully alongside each other, whereas there was bloodshed and fighting only a short time ago," according to the German Imperial

Government Annual Report for 1907-1908. (p. 278) The scene presented in this Report would seem to indicate that the "bloodshed and fighting" in the southern mountains a few years earlier had ceased with the imposition of tighter colonial control. However, as we will see below, outbreaks of violence did occur again. No doubt, the Germans had a hand in the movement of villages, since administrative control was easier when mountain people moved to the coast. (Patrol Report 10/1949-1950, MCW Rich, in Albert 1987: 39) Living on the coast made it possible to conduct commerce with other villages and off-shore islands, and made exchanges with traders of copra for Western goods easier. But people could only move to land not claimed by other clans, or where they had access by kinship connections.

The Germans had a very optimistic picture of what was happening. The German Imperial Government Annual Report applauds the establishment of coconut plantations by mountain people on the Siar Coast since these would appear to be geared towards the commercial sale of copra. (German Imperial Government Annual Report for 1908-1909: 290) The impression given is that the people of the southern part of New Ireland readily accepted German colonial rule and eagerly bought the idea of Westernization and economic progress. However, according to Albert, "The bulk of the interior people relocated because they were overawed by demonstrations of German military might, and because the offer of peace, church, and western goods was a powerful inducement to abandon the more band-like, warring patterns of the interior." (Albert 1987: 40)

By 1911-1912, administrative control had been extended over New Hanover, the islands of Tabar, Lihir, Tanga and Anir, though communication with those areas was poor. (German Imperial Government Annual Report for 1911-1912: 337-38) During the nineteenth century, the people of the off-islands had had frequent contacts with whalers, labor recruiters, and missionaries. However, from the point of view of the German colonial administration, these islands were peripheral and did not warrant government stations of their own. Though control was maintained from Namatanai, the colonial administration did not penetrate the lives of the people on the off-islands to the degree that it did on mainland New Ireland.

Individuals who, for one reason or another, wished to escape the authority of the colonial government fled to places beyond German control, such as the interior of New Hanover. In 1912 the Kavieng District Office sent an armed contingent to the interior of New Hanover "…against recalcitrant natives, mostly absconders and former labourers." (German Imperial Government Annual Report for 1912-1913: 355) Those "absconders and former labourers" were probably indentured workers who fled plantations where they were employed before their contracts terminated.

Although in other parts of the island economic penetration in the form of trading stations had occurred before the establishment of German colonial control, in Namatanai District, the two went hand in hand. The first plantation, which also served as a trading station, was set up in 1908. (German Imperial Government Annual Report for 1908-1909: 300) By 1913 other European and Chinese traders had established themselves there, and that year they bought 300 tons of copra from villages in the district and six to eight tons of shells. (German New Guinea Draft Report for 1913-1914: 58) Considering how recently the area had been brought under administrative control, copra production for cash and the sale of green snail shells by New Irelanders was quite active.

Increasing Numbers of Men Working for Europeans

By 1914, a large proportion of the adult male population of the island was either presently working for Europeans or had done so at some previous time. The Kavieng District Report for that year notes, "At the present time 4,000 natives have been recruited for labour, *i.e.* one-seventh of the total population.... In the village of Lemusmus on the west coast of Neu Mecklenburg (320 inhabitants), all the adult males (147) with the exception of one old man have been employed by whites or are at the present time employed." (German New Guinea Draft Annual Report for 1913-1914: 42) The report does not indicate whether men were employed locally or went elsewhere as contract laborers.

The village of Lemusmus had had a long involvement in the labor market. Earlier, we saw the village vulnerable to attack from its enemies because so many of its young men had been recruited for labor in other places. All plantation workers from local villages now worked daily for fixed wages and took orders from European bosses. As a consequence, almost all adult New Ireland men became aware of what Europeans expected from wage-laborers. The pace of work and its timing -- when it started and when it ended – these were culturally different, and New Ireland men had to learn to conform to the western structure of work. The removal of so many men from the day-to-day activities of the villages must have had repercussions on production for subsistence and ceremonies. It would also have increased production of copra as a cash crop, which the German colonial government was promoting. The New Irelanders thus were caught in a situation of competing activities and goals.

European-owned Plantations, Large and Small

European-owned plantations were increasing in number. Sack notes, "The small settlers kept pace with the [economic] development. Their ranks were swelled by a growing number of former members of the Imperial Navy and the merchant marine. "S.M.S. Cormoran" reported to the Emperor after a visit in 1911 that of the six plantations along the southeast coast of New Ireland [Namatanai District] two were owned by retired navy men and a third by a former engineer of the North German Lloyd." (Sack 1973: 104)

Little is known about the life of European owners and managers who lived on plantations on New Ireland at this time. A legal action brought in 1913, however, shows what a plantation owner had to do in order to staff his plantation in his absence. In 1913, J.O. Mouton brought suit against the German Exchequer, and the case record reveals information about the operation of C. Ostrom's plantation at Lakurafanga, which was described in Table 1 above. Mouton was asking for "restitution of the compulsory maintenance and return voyage costs of the Seaman Sandquist in the amount of 520 marks." (Commonwealth Archives G2 R6 N.55) Mouton had brought Sandquist, a Finnish seaman, out to the Pacific to work on one of his ships and was therefore liable for his passage back. Sandquist left Mouton's employment to work on the Lakurafanga plantation of Ostrom, his countryman. Sandquist, who was a heavy drinker, got into trouble; and the German government forced Mouton to pay Sandquist's return fare home. Mouton complained that Sandquist had managed Ostrom's plantation for the months of March and April 1912, while Ostrom was in Rabaul and Herbertshohe, and was therefore responsible to pay for his own fare home. An owner who managed his own plantation on New Ireland could not leave his plantation unless he hired someone to take his place temporarily. Going to conduct business in Rabaul and Herbertshohe meant an absence of two months, and the plantation could not be left without a manager for that period of time. Ostrom preferred to hire a European, and since few were available, he had to lure Sandquist away from Mouton. The heavy-drinking Sandquist was very much like the captains and traders about whom Hernsheim had constantly complained, indicating that the character of Europeans available for work in the Pacific had not changed from the 1880s. The characters of the plantation owners and managers had an effect not only on men who worked on the plantation, but also on the surrounding villages. While colonial officials and missionaries were bringing one side of Western civilization, some ship captains and plantation mangers were bringing a darker side.

Tension in New Irelanders' Relationship with the Colonial Government

Just as the American government tried to control the behavior of American Indians, the German colonial government passed several ordinances in order to control the behavior of New Irelanders. These reaffirmed the prohibitions against issuing firearms and ammunition to local people, serving of alcohol to them, and granting of credit to them. These edicts did not apply to Europeans and Chinese on the island. Refusal of credit to New Irelanders implied that they were untrustworthy. New Irelanders were not allowed to be served alcohol because the colonial government considered them less than mature persons who could not control their behavior when under the influence of alcohol. However, no such limitations were placed on the Europeans, who already had shown by their violent behavior during drunken binges that they could not control their alcohol consumption.

The copra being exported from the Protectorate continued to come primarily from the sale of village-grown coconuts to traders. The government continued to encourage people to clear away old palms and establish new coconut plantations. Villagers were shifting to the use of cash. "In those parts where cash is beginning to become the regular medium of exchange, the natives prefer to sell their copra only for shiny new one mark pieces. These are therefore highly prized and the companies and plantations, practically all of which buy copra directly or through agents from natives in addition to their other regular business, do their best to obtain stocks of this coin or of other silver coins. As, however, the natives have few wants and spend little money, and as they like hoarding coins, it is difficult to keep up the supply of cash. According to very reliable sources, there are chiefs who have in their possession 10,000 marks in silver coins, especially in one mark coins, in fact some individuals own even more." (German Imperial Government Annual Report for 1909-1910: 313)

Though the people of northern New Ireland were incorporated into the capitalist market system, they treated the shiny new silver marks which they received for their copra as they did shell valuables. They did not spend the coins to buy Western goods as the Germans anticipated they would, but hoarded them as they did shell valuables. Coins were taken out of circulation, creating a problem which the government did not seem to know how to solve. New Irelanders valued the marks in terms of shininess as they valued shell money according to color. The Government Report states that "chiefs" were the repositories of large amounts of silver coinage. Just as Big Men held shell money belonging to an entire clan, these "chiefs" were holding hordes of coins belonging to their clans.

The campaign on the part of the colonial administration to persuade local people to expand their groves of coconut palms and increase copra production was apparently successful. New Irelanders, however, were still tabooing coconuts, when they wanted to hoard them for the ceremonies they continued to hold. "…They cannot be persuaded by any means to abandon old traditional customs and practices in connection with the harvesting of their coconut groves," said one Report. "From time to time certain trees or whole groves are 'made taboo' for a certain time, *i.e.* proscribed. Then it is quite impossible to persuade them to gather nuts from these palms for the preparation of copra." (German Imperial Government Annual Report for 1910-1911: 329)

From the German point of view, the New Irelanders had not completely "rationalized" their harvesting of the nuts. They continued to harvest the nuts only when they needed money for head taxes or some other purpose for which cash was necessary, and to taboo the harvesting of nuts when they needed to accumulate food for a feast, a pre-contact practice continued up to the present time. Local villagers were still hulling the coconuts and bringing in the fresh coconut undried for sale. "Administrative officials have been instructed to advise the natives and urge them to improve their methods of preparing copra.... It is also intended to urge the natives to set up copra driers," demanded the German Imperial Government Annual Report for 1911-1912 (p. 345).

A significant innovation was begun in the village of Munuwai, near Kavieng, in 1913. The Draft Annual Report observes that, "…The natives have, without any inducement on the part of the authorities, formed a kind of co-operative under the freely acknowledged leadership of an intelligent former police trooper. Their aim is to co-operate in the cutting and drying of the coconuts belonging to the members and then to sell the. They have built two copra dryers and one copra shed." (1913-1914: 45) A former police trooper who had come back to his village brought about changes in the copra production process. The term "co-operative" probably referred to members of a clan pooling labor and resources to set up a non-traditional operation

Most of the European planters were recruiting their labor from within the district in which their plantations were situated. It had now become apparent that there was a conflict between two of the important aims of the administration. The European-owned plantation system was set up in New Ireland with the assumption that there would be a plentiful supply of labor, either indentured laborers coming from elsewhere in New Ireland or in the Protectorate, or local laborers coming from the area surrounding the plantation. By 1913, the availability of laborers from the German Solomon Islands, in particular from Bougainville and Buka, which had been a source of indentured laborers for the Bismarck Archipelago in the past, was seriously cut back. Plantations were being set up by Australians such as William Lever in these two areas of the German Protectorate. As in New Ireland, in the Solomon Islands men preferred to work locally rather than hire out to work in the Bismarcks. Despite this, the Draft Report for 1914 indicates that some laborers continued to be recruited from the Solomon Islands to work on Tingwon (Portland Islands) and Kavieng. Plantation owners were beginning to experience labor shortages; and at the same time, there seemed not to be enough men remaining in the villages to sustain the level of copra production desired by colonial authorities. The increase in the number of European-owned plantations was probably the reason[1].

The German colonial government recognized that this curtailment in the availability of labor for plantations would have a profound effect on the development of European-owned plantations and consequently adjusted its land policy. People buying land had to pay "a greatly increased price" per hectare, and they were informed that they could no longer expect to have a steady labor supply. This change in government policy made the plantation owner responsible for finding adequate labor to work his plantation at a time when it might be in short supply.

Nevertheless, Europeans continued to speculatively invest in land holdings, which were not taxed[2]. The German colonial administration controlled the purchase price of land and increased it at this time to encourage those holding land for speculative purposes to sell it to others interested in exploiting it for cultivation. Europeans, motivated by the rising price of copra on the world market, were purchasing increasing amounts of land from New Irelanders. By this time, however, the German colonial administration was more carefully regulating and controlling such land transfers[3]. Because land suitable for cultivation was still abundant, these sales of land to Europeans did not create a landless population of New Ireland villagers.

Chinese Traders

From the beginning of the establishment of the German Protectorate, Chinese people had come to New Ireland as artisans and traders. Chinese traders ran trading stations located away from plantations, as agents for European companies. (German Imperial Government Annual Report for 1910-1911: 330) Hahl noted that the Chinese "…had become quite indispensable."

> Those who did well in their employment brought their relations out after them, so that towards the end Chinese were immigrating in increasing numbers at their own expense and looking for work opportunities in the country.... I proceeded to grant land on long lease at cheap rates to Chinese with experience in the country, and Chinese farms sprang up on the thinly populated west coast of southern Neu

Mecklenburg. My policy was in most cases disapproved. No one wished to or was able to do without the Chinese, but no one wanted to have them in the country. The ban imposed by our near neighbour Australia on Asiatic immigration influenced public opinion." (Hahl 1980: 144-145)

Most of the Chinese who came to New Ireland remained there as traders. Some married New Ireland women. By World War II, most of the trade stores in New Ireland were owned by the descendants of these Chinese immigrants.

In the first decade of the twentieth century, the network of Chinese-run trade stores was quite extensive in the Tigak-speaking area of northern New Ireland. Chinese traders had stores at Butbut, Kableman, Maium, Kasselok, Ululnono, and Lamangan.

The following is a picture of economic arrangements at Kasselok from the Tigak point of view:

> The Kasselok plantation was owned by Germans. I didn't work there, but I played there. When the Germans were here, the Chinese managed the station. There were no trucks or tractors to pick up copra. Instead, sailing boats came down here, passed through the reef, and took it back to Nusa. The Chinese bought the copra, and the people got back rice and tobacco. The Chinese trader [Kongkong] had a big house on the beach here, on land bought from the Makatitien [a local clan]. There was no *mai-mai* [Big Man, leader]. They got food in exchange for the land. They traded their copra for axes and knives, not guns. The Chinese trader also bought green snail shell and *kalvu* [a larger snail] shell. The Chinese traders did not have native wives. (Etwat of Kasselok, Rubel and Rosman, 1987 Field Notes, p. 12)

Health Services

By the end of the nineteenth century, it was clear that increasing contact had introduced new forms of diseases damaging the population's health in several areas of New Ireland. European, Chinese, and Malay traders had spread gonorrhea in New Ireland and adjacent islands, where sexual intercourse outside of marriage was not interdicted. On the Gazelle Peninsula, where all sexual transgressions were forbidden, the incidence of gonorrhea was low. (Neuguinea Kompagnie Annual Report for 1898-99)[4] Colonial governments the world over have introduced western medical practices and hospitals, which they considered superior to the people's "...superstition, homesickness and an aversion to the treatment of internal diseases...." (Annual Report for 1909-1910: 311) In 1909 a program of treatment for venereal disease among the local people was instituted. (Annual Report for 1909-1910: 311) By 1910, a hospital had been established in Namatanai; and in the following year, a health care system in the villages manned by local people was introduced[5].

Health concerns also affected the heart of the colonial enterprise - the plantation system. Laborers, fed a daily diet predominantly of rice because it was cheap, soon contracted beriberi in epidemic proportions. When the Germans recognized the connection between diet and beriberi, they prevented the occurrence of the disease by adding beans (pigeon peas) to the laborers' diets.

Infrastructure Development

The development of transportation was very important for the economic life of the colony. Imports to and exports from New Ireland were shipped through Rabaul, which succeeded Herbertshoe as the capital, until 1914. At this point, Kavieng became the terminus of the Norddeutscher Lloyd Singapore-New Guinea Line[6]. European-owned plantations had become much more productive, and by 1914, about half of the 3,600 tons of copra exported from Kavieng District came from them, the remainder coming from villages. The European plantations-maintained communications by sea with Kavieng via small coastal steamers; and two boatyards for the construction of small sailing vessels were established. (German New Guinea Draft Annual Report for 1913-1914: 47-48) Work continued to improve the main East Coast road, which was made suitable for travel by motor vehicles up to Lokon by 1913. However, the main users of the road were horse-drawn vehicles and ox carts.

As patterns of colonial domination were accepted and regularized, Kavieng expanded as the urban, administrative center of New Ireland, in an area where there had only been autonomous villages before colonial penetration. Commercial buildings were erected by housing companies such as Hernsheim & Co. and Forsayth, Kirchner & Co. A European-style hotel and a Chinese public house and retail shop were built for the ethnically diverse population. Europeans had their own cemetery, on the other side of town from the New Irelanders' cemetery. The latter must have been for New Irelanders dying far from their homes, whose bodies could not be returned to their villages and buried in the usual way. The government plantation set up by Boluminski became the Agricultural Establishment for the Kavieng District Office, with much of its acreage worked by a labor force of 25 prisoners.

The Last Anti-Colonial Uprisings

In the period just before the Germans lost control of New Ireland, the colonial government saw many people welcoming its administration because of its benefits -- particularly health services -- to the point where they were seen as eagerly paying head taxes. However, this was clearly not the case everywhere. As late as 1913-1914, some mountain people still strongly resisted the imposition of a colonial administrative structure with its district organization, *luluais,* and *tultuls.* When an expedition entered the mountains and was attacked, the government reasoned that,

> ...The mountain people were against the introduction of the native organisation [the *luluai* and *tultul* system] and the attendant controls. The more powerful chiefs were afraid that the spread of the native organization would put an end to the standing feuds and associated cannibal practices and that their own influence would be weakened. As they had scarcely any previous contact with Europeans they believed that by wiping out an expedition they could dissuade the Europeans from visiting their mountain region. (German New Guinea Draft Annual Report for 1913-1914: 57)[7]

An expedition led by Head Forester Deininger went into the mountain region inland from Hilalon, an area not really penetrated by the German colonial administration, to study forestry resources for their commercial potential. On the second day they were attacked near the village of Poronsuan (Poronzuan). Deininger was injured, five of his troopers and four carriers were killed, and all of the equipment was taken. "The bodies of those killed were consumed by the rebels." (German New Guinea Draft Report for 1913-1914: 5, 56)

This attack led to a wider uprising involving the attack and looting of several Chinese plantations. The Namatanai District Officer launched a punitive expedition with thirty troopers and four carriers. A number of "rebels" were captured, and much of the stolen equipment, including three of the nine rifles which had been taken, was recovered. Eight of the "rebels" were killed, but the colonial troops suffered no casualties. Further punitive measures were taken, many more New Irelanders were killed, and "the Expeditionary troop succeeded in suppressing the uprising." (German New Guinea Draft Annual Report for 1913-1914: 5)

Though the mountain people who participated in this uprising may have been visited by German officials and probably had some knowledge of Europeans, they certainly were not yet under the complete control of the German colonial administration. Their villages were still autonomous and politically independent; and they could still carry out warfare under the leadership of clan warriors when this was politically warranted. These mountain people had seen what happened when villages on the coast were forced to submit to German colonial rule, with appointed *luluais* and *tultuls*. They, no doubt, attacked the German expedition because they did not want this colonially manufactured "native organization" imposed on them. And they surely thought that Head Forester Deininger represented the beginning of a series of irreversible steps toward domination. The report sees the chiefs seeking to retain their power. Since the attack on the Forestry Expedition was the signal for other attacks on Chinese plantations, the mountain people also still appear intent on driving out other intrusive foreigners as well. This seems to have been the last anti-colonial uprising on New Ireland.

The End of German Control

By 1914, the German Colonial Administration had stabilized its control over New Ireland and was continuing to try to penetrate many areas of the life of New Irelanders, though much of their colonial agenda already had been accomplished. German political control was more or less secure. New Irelanders were producing copra for sale. German marks had become a widely accepted form of currency. Even New Irelanders' health and education were coming under the aegis of the colonial government.

All this was to come to an abrupt end in July 1914. When shots were fired in Sarajevo in the Austro-Hungarian Empire, beginning World War I, the repercussions were felt quickly in Rabaul and Kavieng. The German colonial government immediately turned German planters and civilians into soldiers under military control. Mouton, who was a Belgian national, noted, "My manager Mueller was a German and was held responsible for us." (1974: 140) In September 1914 an Australian Expeditionary Force arrived, and the Germans quickly surrendered.

As Mouton witnessed the events, "…The "Australia" and the "Brisbane" arrived and a couple of days later the first convoy with soldiers arrived, they landed some of them at Kabakaul and proceeded to Bitapaka the wireless station on the road they were met by the police and all the German force available, and in the action a few men were killed and wounded…. Now we were under the Australian military control." (Mouton 1974: 140-141)

Mueller, Mouton's manager, like other Germans, was taken prisoner, but he was released almost immediately by the Australians. The terms of the armistice were very generous. German laws were retained during the period of Australian military occupation, and some German officials who declared their neutrality even retained their posts. In accordance with the provisions of the Treaty of Versailles, German New Guinea was entrusted to Australia in 1919 as a mandated territory, to be administered as an integral part of Australia.

Discussion

While these momentous events were earth-shaking for Europeans, they probably had little or no impact on the life of New Irelanders. To them, the new colonial administration differed little from the former one. And. their political autonomy and full control over their own lives already had been irretrievably lost before World War I.

NOTES

1. The Draft Annual Report for 1913-1914 observes, "In many parts [of Kavieng District] the natives are not even sufficiently numerous to cut all their nuts.... Many older married natives also hired themselves out as day-laborers and by the month in both Neu Mecklenburg and Neu Hannover." (German New Guinea Draft Annual Report for 1913-1914:45-46)

2. Emma Forsayth's purchases of land on New Ireland and elsewhere, which she never put into production represent a case in point.

3. The Annual Report for 1911-1912 states, "Every purchaser is obliged to commence cultivation within one year and to bring three-quarters of his land area under cultivation within fifteen years and to keep it cultivated. In principle, land at a particular place is sold only when all preliminary queries as to existing property rights held by natives, landing facilities, public interest etc. have been dealt with fully.... The transfer of ownership takes place after the land has been surveyed.... The demand has been almost entirely for land for the establishment of coconut palm plantations. This is explained by the favorable prices and the apparently stable long term market prospects for copra...." (German Imperial Government Annual Report 344) There were 3.5 times as many hectares in production in 1913 than in 1906.

CONSOLIDATON OF COLONIAL CONTROL: 1884-1914

4. The German colonial administration and the succeeding Australian administration exhibited increasing concern over the declining population of New Ireland which was later determined to have been caused by venereal disease.

5. The plan was to train men who had been orderlies in hospitals for three months and then to appoint them as "medical *tultuls*" for their villages, to treat injuries and minor illnesses. Every village had a small house built with the assistance of the authorities in which dressings, bandages and medicines were stored, and patients accommodated when necessary. (Annual Report for 1911-1912: 341)

6. It was not until 1914 that the direct export from Kavieng of copra (750 tons), tortoise shell (116 kg.), and mother of pearl (4 tons) consigned to Germany took place. (German New Guinea Draft Annual Report for 1913-1914: 47)

7. "According to information obtained by the station... those taking part in the attack were the inhabitants of the inland area bounded in the north by a line drawn from Suralil to Cape Reis and in the south by a line from the mouth of the Mandaru to the mouth of the Danfu River." (German New Guinea Draft Annual Report for 1913-1914: 57)

ALIENS ON OUR SHORES

13. CONCLUSIONS

For the first 250 years after contact with Europeans, New Irelanders maintained their culture and controlled their destiny, taking what they wanted from the explorers and traders who came to their island. Visits by Europeans had little permanent impact on them. Europeans came only to renew their supplies of food and water. From 1875 onward, however, after the first missionaries arrived, maintaining their independence became more and more difficult.

The Bismarck Archipelago, along with the rest of Melanesia, thus was one of the last places in the Pacific where missionary activity and colonization began. Missionaries and traders were already established in such areas of Polynesia as Fiji, Samoa, Tahiti, the Marquesas, and Hawaii, well as Micronesia, by the middle of the nineteenth century. European powers jockeying for position there. In Melanesia, however, multiple encounters had reinforced earlier explorers' picture of Melanesia as an exceedingly dangerous region for Europeans. Even "castaways and beachcombers" tended to stay away from Melanesian islands, preferring the more inviting shores of Polynesia and Micronesia.

Although New Irelanders still were completely in control of the situation, contacts with Europeans became increasingly frequent in the early decades of the nineteenth century. By that time a pattern of exchanging fresh supplies for goods that the New Irelanders wanted had developed. They brought the food stuffs that they knew the Europeans wanted to the liminal area -- the shallow water or the beach -- between the land, which was controlled by the New Irelanders, and the European ships. The Europeans in return had come to know that New Irelanders wanted hoop iron, iron axes and later, tobacco, and that they also accepted buttons, bottles and cloth. Only the iron, however, had an impact on their way of life at this time. It enabled them to rapidly and skillfully cut down trees, to clear land for horticulture, to manufacture canoes and bows (where they had them), to build houses, and to carve sculptures, clubs and canoe prows.

The rules of exchange between New Irelanders and Europeans continued to be the same when European traders came solely to get tortoise-shell and bêche-de-mer in the 1870s. Providing these commodities began to draw the New Irelanders inexorably into the capitalist world trade system. Though they had hunted sea turtles and were aware of trepang, European demand for these items probably resulted in an increase in their production. This in turn had some effect on the organization of work and economic activities of New Irelanders.

One could argue that a shift to commodity production, though of a minimal sort, had occurred. But the new kinds of exchanges now taking place were still entirely under New Irelanders' control. They continued to be transacted in the liminal areas, with European guns protecting European trading vessels. Should the European traders be caught off guard or a ship induced to come too close to the land, it could be overrun and sacked.

The Bismarcks soon became a source for copra, which had become a much sought-after product on the world market. German trading companies had already set up stations in Samoa and in parts of Micronesia, and the search for additional supplies of copra to supply European factories with raw material for soaps and oils led them to the Bismarcks. Since the early trade in copra was the same as for tortoise shell and trepang, the New Irelanders could still dictate where and when it would take place.

The setting-up of trading stations on New Ireland, however, enabled Europeans to extract more copra and collect it in a more systematic way. New Irelanders, for the first time, found intruders in their midst whose behavior they were not able to understand or control. At first, they acquiesced to stations being set up in their villages. They probably saw an advantage in being close to a source of supply of goods they desired. They clearly did not immediately recognize the consequences. However, the lonely European traders, often drunk, and their Solomon Islands assistants frequently clashed with the villagers. New Irelanders often burned down stations to rid themselves of the European intruders. The traders were still bartering for copra, but they also were teaching the New Irelanders that, if they wanted iron axes, knives, and tobacco, they would have to bring a steady supply of coconuts, tortoise shell, green snail shell, and trepang.

New Irelanders were being introduced to the capitalist laws of supply and demand. As a consequence, the economic aspects of their way of life were the first to be subjected to change. When more than one trader appeared in the same location, they learned that the price was not fixed. The price they received for copra could vary, and they could sell copra to the trader who would give them the best price- better axes, more beads, and even guns. This was in contrast to the value of pigs and canoes, which had specific equivalents in shell money, and which did not fluctuate unless amounts were increased to enhance the prestige of the giver.

The New Irelanders had little notion of the price which the trader received when he sold the copra on the world market, or what the beads and the other trade goods cost the trader. These were factors relating to the world economic system, of which the villagers on the local level were completely unaware. If they had known the prices of the beads, tobacco, and other items that they were receiving and the price of copra in Europe, they would have been able to bargain much intelligently. This information was not part of their cultural knowledge. Their own economic system was completely different: there was little price fluctuation and no concept of bargaining.

Credit often was extended by traders competing with one another to gain access to copra. The traders would sometimes leave trade goods in anticipation of obtaining the equivalent in copra at a later time. This idea of extending credit, characteristic of the capitalist system, fit with New Ireland ideas of delayed exchange. Sometimes, villagers receiving trade goods gave their crops to other traders anyway, just as a delayed exchange might not be completed in their indigenous exchange system, and a pig one was counting on might be given to another "creditor." Later, the German government prohibited the extension of credit.

The introduction of western money also incorporated New Irelanders into the market system. At first, shell money, which was an integral part of their exchange system, was given to them in lieu of goods by traders in exchange for copra. Traders were soon handicapped by an insufficient supply of shell money, since they were dependent on the indigenous manufacturers of it and did not try to manufacture it themselves, as O'Keefe had done earlier on Yap. After the use of shell money was prohibited in 1901, the German colonial administrators sought to convince the villagers to use German marks. They anticipated that, when villagers were paid in marks for their goods or labor, they would use the marks to buy western goods. However, New Irelanders treated the shiny new silver marks, which they received for their copra, as they would shell valuables, and hoarded them in a similar fashion. They imposed

CONCLUSIONS

their own system of value on the marks and ranked them in terms of shininess, paralleling the color-based value placed on shell money. Clan leaders, who held the clan's supply of marks as they had held the clan's supply of shell money, might have up to 10,000 marks in their possession. German marks became necessary when a head tax was instituted, and when villagers needed to pay marks for the trade goods they desired.

The New Irelanders had gotten the point about copra production, since they were producing hundreds of thousands of pounds of copra for collection by trading stations. The German colonial government continued to encourage villagers to plant more groves of coconut palms, in order to produce copra for sale. while also encouraging Europeans to establish coconut plantations on New Ireland. Until 1913, the bulk of the copra exported from New Ireland still came from village sources.

The organization of labor in New Ireland villages must have changed significantly with the increase of copra production in villages, since harvesting and removal of husks required labor inputs, as did the planting of new trees to increase production. New Irelanders had labored in their villages to provide themselves with food and also to accumulate surplus resources to be used for feasting in connection with their focal mortuary rites and other ceremonies. The distribution of the pigs, yams, and other items on such occasions enhanced the importance and prestige of a clan and its leader. Labor normally was a social responsibility, not something to be sold or even exchanged for something else. One was under an obligation to contribute one's labor to a kinsman, to one's Big Man, or to one's clan. This way of life was, of course, totally different from the "aliens'" Western market system, in which labor is seen as a commodity that can be bought and sold.

Under Western impact, when labor became a commodity, each individual received compensation, monetary or otherwise, for his or her work. This new system undermined traditional social networks within which labor was embedded.

New Irelanders working on Australian plantations received objects as payment. When labor recruitment for the sugar plantations in Queensland, Fiji, and Samoa began in New Ireland in 1882, the New Irelanders had only a hazy idea that they were exchanging their labor for three years in a foreign place for the box of goods they would receive at the end of their period of service. Sometimes they were enticed onboard and kidnapped. Sometimes they sought adventure. And sometimes village leaders received goods, or even arms, so that they would induce their young men to go aboard the ships and become labor recruits. The effect of labor recruitment on the organization of village work was much greater than was the increase in copra production. A large percentage of men were removed from participation in the economic life of some villages.

The ritual process, with its attendant feasts and celebrations was also disrupted, since the labor required to produce the necessary surpluses of food was seriously depleted. The dearth of young men in certain villages also disrupted the balance of power between villages, making some subject to attack by others which had retained their strength.

When plantations were established in close proximity to villages, European plantation owners expected that a local supply of labor on a regular basis would be available to work on them. However, they soon found that local laborers did not perform according to their expectations. Working on a local plantation on a regular basis interfered with subsistence and ceremonial labor demands made on laborers by families and clan members in their own villages.

CONCLUSIONS

In this conflict between the capitalist system's need for labor and the expectations and needs of New Irelanders, the New Irelanders won out at first. Since laborers recruited from far away proved to be better workers, the plantation system initially depended on them.

Under the capitalist system, land can be bought and sold like any other commodity. It can be purchased for use as a trading station, a church or missionary station, and held for speculation, to be sold when its value increases. The land owned by New Ireland clans, however, was not a commodity in this sense. It was not alienable. The purchases of relatively small plots of land for trading stations and missions had little impact on the village. As the world market for copra expanded and the price rose, however, the colonial government encouraged the development of European-owned plantations, in order to increase copra production, since the copra being purchased by traders from villagers was not deemed sufficient. Though the plantations being set up were large, land shortages do not seem to have initially harmed New Ireland villages.

The New Ireland local economy went through a process of being increasingly drawn into the world trade system. Initially, tortoise shell and trepang were commodities to be bartered, and later copra was as well. Money as a medium of exchange eventually was introduced, replacing barter. Labor became a commodity. Finally, land became a commodity as well -- something to be bought by Europeans and sold by New Irelanders.

Cash cropping of copra was only partially adopted by New Irelanders, and this remains true today. New Irelanders not only maintained their self-sufficiency; they also continued to produce enough for ritual and ceremonial purposes. If they needed cash to pay the head tax, they could choose to increase village production by planting more coconut palms in their villages, and sell copra as a cash crop. Or they could work as wage laborers. Each of these choices involved a different allocation of labor. When the villagers, encouraged by the German colonial government to expand their "village plantations," did so, they would stay home and divide their labor between copra production and more traditional pursuits.

If many men chose to work on nearby plantations, not only would the production of copra from village plantations suffer, but there would not be sufficient labor to produce surpluses for feasting and ceremonial purposes. The New Irelanders were still agents, making choices in how they allocated their labor and the degree to which they wished to involve themselves in the capitalist economy.

Increasing contact with Europeans was transforming the leadership pattern in New Ireland even before the colonial administration imposed its own political structure on local villages with the appointment of *luluais* and *tultuls*. Labor recruits used the goods in the boxes which they received in return for their labor to further their careers within the New Ireland political structure. Similarly, village leaders who made close connections with traders and missionaries were able to greatly enhance their status, making them much more powerful than other leaders in this formerly egalitarian society. The Europeans looked for "chiefs" when they first encountered New Irelanders. Big Men who sustained contact with Europeans became more powerful than the rest, and were fitted into the chiefly category by Europeans. Europeans looked to these "chiefs" for assistance in labor recruiting, for help in securing copra for purchase, and for help acquiring land for trade stations and, later on, plantations. One example was Nanati, Romilly's host, who was able to amass a fighting force of 1,500 men and seemed to have power over large numbers of people.

CONCLUSIONS

The independence and political autonomy of New Ireland villages was eroded, as increasing numbers of New Ireland villagers were drawn into the German colonial empire's orbit. From an early point, certain villages had relationships with Europeans -- traders, blackbirders and missionaries, while others did not. A village in such a position had enormous strategic advantages, making it more powerful than its more isolated traditional enemies. Through these connections, many villages were able to obtain the European goods they desired, especially iron ax heads, which were turned into war axes. They sometimes even got rifles.

Nusa was such a strategically located village. Hernsheim established the first trading station on New Ireland there because of its dense population. Within a short time, Nusa had become the center of the copra trade, with other traders competing with Hernsheim there. The people of Nusa enlisted Hernsheim as their ally when they went to war against their traditional enemies, and he called on them for assistance. Recruiting ships would stop at Nusa to pick up interpreters who knew Pidgin English to help with recruiting, when the blackbirding trade shifted to the off-islands of Tabar, Lihir, and Tanga. Nusa had become an *entrepot* where Pidgin English was widely understood. Understandably, Boluminski established the first government station at Nusa, renamed Kavieng. Nusa had been transformed from just another New Ireland village into an urban colonial center with a heterogeneous population.

For a time, the New Irelanders were able to manipulate the Europeans, fitting them into the indigenous pattern of alternation of enemy and ally villages, which we have referred to as the checkerboard pattern. Traders like Hernsheim would set up trading stations in villages, which then might be attacked by traditional enemies. The erratic unpredictability and cruelty of traders also provoked villagers to attack them. The trader would then use his

New Ireland allies to retaliate. Villages allied with traders had a source of arms which gave them great advantages over traditional enemies having no such source, causing shifts in the balance of power. Sometimes only a single rifle had this effect. Someone recruiting plantation laborers, as Mouton was, might be enlisted in traditional feuds between enemies in the same manner.

The punitive expeditions launched by the German colonial government in order to make peace also fed into the checkerboard pattern of enemies and allies. A village that had been attacked would enlist the help of Hahl, the future governor, and his police boys to seek retribution. The enlistment of Europeans on one side or the other and the introduction of European weaponry led to imbalances in power relations between enemy groups and an efflorescence of warfare between what were still relatively autonomous villages during the first two centuries of contact.

The full impact of the German colonial administration on the indigenous political structure was felt only when a district office was set up in Kavieng. The colonial government, with its headquarters at Herbertshohe in New Britain, recognized the ineffectiveness of punitive expeditions intended to control the New Ireland population. In order to truly transform the New Ireland way of life and make the New Irelanders "civilized" copra cash-croppers who would fulfill the colony's commercial goals. the Germans decided that the continuous presence of the colonial administration with its District Officer and "Police Boys" at a station right on the island was necessary.

The aim of the German colonial government was to bring about the end of the political autonomy of the villages. This was accomplished by the building of a road, which acted as a conduit not only for trade and commerce, but also for police action when necessary; the establishment of a village administration, which co-opted village leaders when possible, who were responsible for the actions of their villagers, corvee labor; and the imposition of a head tax. The colonial government also passed a series of edicts to control copra production and move the New Irelanders into as much of a cash economy as possible.

As the colonial administration widened its area of control on New Ireland, it began to entice whole villages to move out of the mountainous interior and down to the coast, where it would be possible to bring them into the colonial orbit and better control their activities. In the more remote areas, some villages fought to retain their independence by attacking not only the German authorities, but also other villages who had agreed to submit to German authority. By 1914, when the Australians took over, however, the political system had been inexorably altered.

With the final termination of warfare, war leaders disappeared. Village and clan leaders continued to organize focal rituals like the *malanggan* and *kaba* ceremonies, as they still do up to the present. In fact, the cessation of warfare enabled these ceremonies to take place more easily, since guests from other villages could attend without fear of attack. In fact, a broadening of the network of ceremonial attendance and exchanges occurred. The internal political structure continued, despite the fact that some clan leaders became officials of the colonial government when they were made *luluais*. Government appointments made such clan leaders still more powerful because they could now order villagers to perform corvee labor. Foster's research shows how Tangan clan big men who became *luluais* continued to operate according to Tangan custom. (Foster 1995) However, although their power as intermediaries of the colonial government might have been considerable, they were no longer acting as independent political agents.

Of the many types of Europeans who came to New Ireland, those who came to missionize were the most intent on completely changing the New Irelanders' way of life and "civilizing" them. Paradoxically, though New Irelanders were receptive and often wanted missionaries to send teachers to their villages, on the whole they strongly resisted the efforts of the missionaries to transform their culture into an Oceanic Christian version of Victorian England. In the fundamental life cycle ceremonies of birth, marriage and death, New Irelanders steadfastly maintained the core aspects of their own cultural practices. However, under the influence of missionaries, they became members of churches, attended Sunday services, and incorporated such things as cement gravestones for dead clan members into their mortuary ceremonies. Institutions such the *kaba* and *malanggan* ceremonies nonetheless continued to remain central and significant.

In the minds of the New Irelanders, when a Big Man gave shell money to a Fijian teacher to bring the church to his village, he was making a decision about "buying a church." At first, the addition of Christian belief and practice was similar to "buying" the esoteric knowledge of any other cult and adding it to existing belief systems.

Despite the persuasive powers of the missionaries, and the examples provided by the Fijian catechists, the "Pacific Christian gentlemen," new church institutions grew slowly, though Christian teaching against nudity, cannibalism and ceremonial sexual license did have some effect, resulting in modifications of cultural practice. Much later, there was an interpenetration of the two belief systems. For example, at the initiation ceremony in Lesu in 1929, after a shortened period of seclusion, the boys received religious instruction from their Catholic priest[1].

CONCLUSIONS

The entry of Catholic missionaries, competing with the Methodists who had arrived some twenty-five years earlier, enabled New Irelanders to fit the Christian denominations into the structure of opposition found in parts of the island -- the dual organization, including the moiety structure. Indeed, this oppositional structure may have aided the Catholics in increasing their numbers and catching up to the Methodists in the success of their church. While European Catholic and Methodist missionaries saw each other as misguided heretics, New Irelanders viewed these two denominations as both oppositional and complementary, like two sides of a moiety-based society.

The Methodist missionary enterprise aimed to indigenize the church. This involved making a local language into the language of the church, training a clergy composed of New Irelanders, and having the governance and financing of the church in the hands of local villagers. The Catholics, in contrast, relied primarily on European staff, though they recognized the necessity of translating prayers and the catechism into local languages and used New Ireland catechists to man outstations.

Early explorers and travelers had no way of communicating with the local populations they encountered, other than misunderstood forms of sign language; and even basic greetings were misinterpreted. As contacts became more frequent in the middle of the nineteenth century, a system of intercultural communication between Europeans, local people, Malays, and Chinese began to develop. Prior to 1860, there were "…a number of unstable varieties of jargon English in various parts of the Pacific Ocean." (Muhlhausler, in Keesing 1988: 24) Belcher, a visitor during the 1840s, was able to communicate with New Irelanders on shore in what must have been one of these forms of "jargon English."

The Bismarck Archipelago saw the development of one of the major forms of Pidgin English in the Pacific. Keesing notes, "I read the evidence as indicating that the pidgin spoken on the German plantations in Samoa and in some parts of the Bismarck Archipelago as of the first half of the 1880s was essentially the same as that spoken in Queensland, the New Hebrides, and the Solomons: these areas were part of a single, dispersed speech community." (Keesing 1988: 3)

During the early 1880s, when the Bismarck Archipelago was a center of blackbirding and labor recruiting, vocabulary from Tolai-Patpatar languages was introduced in heavy doses to replace earlier vocabulary, giving the present version of Pidgin English, Tok Pisin, its Tolai emphasis. Fifteen percent of the vocabulary of the Tok Pisin vocabulary is of Tolai-Patpatar derivation. (Mihalic 1971: 56) When labor recruits returned, their knowledge of Pidgin enabled them to act as interpreters for labor recruiters and traders. The diversity of languages on New Ireland had presented problems in communication between people of different areas. The development of Pidgin English as a *lingua franca* not only allowed communication between Europeans and local people, but it also made it possible for Pacific islanders of different areas to communicate with one another.

From the very beginning of contact with Europeans, New Irelanders tried to control their own destiny. Forces beyond their island ultimately determined the extent to which they could continue to do so. In some respects, they acquiesced to the Europeans' intrusion, and might even at times have welcomed them because of their interest in the goods they had. The sheer power of the colonial administration and its military strength enabled the Germans to finally take over the island. But the New Irelanders still maintained their cultural autonomy, their family and clan organization, their moiety and village structure, their ceremonies, as well as the ability to decide the extent to which they wished to participate in the cash economy.

Our story ends in 1914. From that time until today, New Irelanders have gone through two World Wars and the Australian colonial period. They are now part of the independent nation of Papua New Guinea, in whose politics they fully participate. They did not choose to go the route of a complete cash economy based on mono-cropping of coconuts, palm oil, cocoa, or other cash crops which Europeans tried to introduce. Nor did they engage in exploitation of the rich fish resources around the island on a full-time basis for cash. They chose to maintain their multiplicity of languages, along with Neomelanesian, the language of the nation-state of Papua New Guinea. Although changes have occurred, they have been able to maintain most of their rich ceremonial life. Native sons have left New Ireland to go out into the world to work at various occupations, but some have chosen to return, opting for life in villages and participation in their ceremonies rather than submitting to the pressures of life in Rabaul and Port Moresby.

NOTES

1. Editor's Note: The authors did not provide a source for this information, but it probably comes from Powdermaker (1933).

ALIENS ON OUR SHORES

APPENDIX A. THE ARCHEOLOGY AND LINGUISTICS OF NEW IRELAND

A.1 Hunters and Foragers

Recent archeological investigations at four cave sites, Matenkupkum, Balof 2, Matenbek and Panakiwuk, support a late Pleistocene occupation of New Ireland. (Allen *et al.,* 1989) Matenkupkum, on the east coast, in the southern part of New Ireland, a cave 50 meters from the shore has the earliest material. There are four dates from shell material from the lowest level of the cave, ranging from 31,350 +/- 550 b.p. to 33,300 +/- 950 b.p. This consists of a dense marine shell midden, with more than 200 flake stone tools, consisting for the most part of large flakes detached from river cobbles, with little or no retouching. The shell midden continued to accumulate up to c. 21,000 b.p. According to Allen, Gosden and White, "The fish bones at Matenkupkum at this date are the earliest evidence known to us of the human capture of marine fish anywhere in the world." (1989:552) Since there was no archeological evidence of fish hooks, the authors infer that fish traps, or possibly nets, spears, or poisoning were used. These bones were of reef fish species. The stone tools from these four sites are not easily placed into readily recognized tool types.

Obsidian deposits are not found on New Ireland, and the source of the material from which the artifacts were made is Talasea or Mopir in West New

Britain, some 300 kilometers away, indicating a regional exchange network at this early period. Matenbek, another cave site located quite close to Matankupkum, was occupied from 19,000 - 20,000 b.p. Obsidian from New Britain was found in the lowest levels of Matenbek, giving the obsidian trade between New Ireland and New Britain a date of 19,000-20,00 b.p. The lowest levels at Panikiwuk and Balof 2 date to approximately 14,000 b.p. Allen, Gosden and White have summarized the results of their excavations at these sites, concluding "In Pacific prehistory, New Ireland represents an early example of humans colonizing an Oceanic island possessing a restricted range of natural food resources. Broad spectrum hunting and collecting, followed by manipulations of the food supply (whether deliberate or accidental) and transfer of useful materials was, in formula, the same strategy which, some 20 millennia later, was the basis of the successful colonization of Remote Oceania." (1989: 559) The early New Ireland hunters and foragers encountered an environment rich in marine resources but fairly impoverished in land fauna. It has been suggested that the human colonizers introduced species of rat and phalanger, just as later colonizers introduced the pig.

In 1985, another shelter, Balof 2, a few meters away from Balof 1 was excavated, which yielded dates of 14,000 b.p. The cultural deposits from Balof 2 include stone tools, marine shells and animal bones, as well as a hearth site from which the early dates were obtained.

Balof 1 contains cultural material from a later period, with the earliest radiocarbon date of 6,800 +/- 410 b.p. Downie and White view the 7,000 year development at Balof 1 as a series of "clear changes through time in the artifactual content." (1978: 797) They use this material to support a gradualist model of Melanesian development, that is, a series of internal cultural changes without major cultural influences from outside the island. (White, Downie and

APPENDIX A. THE ARCHEOLOGY AND LINGUISTICS OF NEW IRELAND

Ambrose 1978: 877) In the material itself, however, there is a distinction between the adaptation or mode of life of the earlier and the later inhabitants of Balof 1 cave. In the lowest levels (6, 7, and 8) pottery, pig and fish bones, ground stone and shell arm rings are all absent. A wide range of stone materials is present, coming from other parts of New Ireland as well as from Talasea in New Britain and islands to the northeast, documenting the presence of exchange networks between communities in different parts of the islands and with other islands. The flaked stones of this period are not worked in a bipolar fashion (with the exception of some obsidian) The stones are worked with a technique in which "stone is knapped in a more ad hoc" fashion.... (which) seems to be common to New Guinea, Melanesia and beyond and probably represents the original form of stone use in the area." (Downie and White 1978: 799) The shellfish used by these people were gathered from "rocks at the high tide splash level." (Downie and White 1978: 771) The presence of animal remains and bone barbs indicate that they hunted land animals (cuscus, flying foxes and monitor lizards) using arrows or spears. Shark teeth, though not in abundance, are found suggesting that they went beyond the reef to fish for shark (shark teeth are also found in the upper levels).

As part of the Lapita Homeland Project, excavations were conducted by Jim Allen at Panakiwuk cave, 3.5 Km inland from Mangai village on the east coast. (Allen *et al.*. 1989) This cave is located 40 km. north of the Balof rock shelter. It contains two units which are distinct stratigraphically and artifactually. The early material dates from around 15,000 to 9,000 b.p. and included a stone assemblage of predominantly small, thin, squarish flakes (Allen *et al.*. 1989: 554), numbers of animal bones, and the remains of terrestrial snails. The chert and dolerite from which the flakes were made "must all be exotic." (Allen 1985:8), and appear to indicate the long-distance transportation of these raw materials at this very early period. Allen suggests that these are the remains of a population of hunters and foragers. At Panakiwuk there is a temporal gap between the earlier Pleistocene material and the upper strata which begin again at around 1,700 b.p. (Allen *et al.*. 1988) In this upper deposit, there were fewer bones, but marine shell and crustacea were present, as well as pottery, obsidian and some small chert flakes. According to Allen, this upper deposit contains the remains of a horticultural population.

A.2 Agriculturalists including the Lapita People

The more recent inhabitants of Balof 1 cave, whose remains are found in levels 1 through 5, seem to have had a somewhat different adaptation. Fish bones signify that they exploited the lagoon for fishing. The number of shellfish collected from the mangrove swamps increases and the reef and lagoon are also exploited now for shellfish. Hunting of land-based animals continued to be important. Pottery appears for the first time in level 5. The amount found was too small for detailed comparative analysis, but there were general similarities between the sherds at Balof 1 and those from other New Ireland sites (to be discussed below). (Downie and White 1978: 799) Pig bones appear in level 4. Fragments of trochus shell arm rings were found in levels 2 and 3, and ground stone artifacts were recovered from levels 3 and 4. In this later period, some obsidian comes from Talasea, as it did earlier, but beginning with level 5, obsidian from Lou Island, in the Admiralty Islands, makes its appearance. There is also a reduction in the amount of stone for tools deriving from other outside sources.

Downie and White state that, "The material excavated demonstrates, to a limited degree, that whereas early inhabitants drew on a wide range of stone sources, (including Talasea obsidian), hunted land animals (one to extinction?), and collected most shell fish from a particular environment, later users were in possession of pottery and also made use of a wider variety of marine resources, but drew on a narrower range of stone resources, particularly Lou Island obsidian. Small bipoints may be linked to hunting or to some activity no longer current, but whether arm rings, ground stone axes and the possession of pigs are all restricted to the later users remains to be determined by research on a larger scale." (Downie and White 1978: 800) This quote would seem to indicate that the possibility that external influences resulting from the migration of other peoples into the area must also be considered, since the differences between the two sets of levels is fairly sharp.

The people with pottery occupying the upper levels of the cave sites we have just discussed appear contemporaneous with the earliest levels in the excavations at Lesu. A radiocarbon date of 2,460 +/- 120 b.p. for these lowest levels at Lesu is based on charcoal found 4 m. below the surface of one of the mounds excavated. The present-day village of Lesu, which is strung along the seashore, overlies part of the site. The faunal fragments indicate "The dominance of presumably domestic animals (pig, dog) and fish ..., and is in sharp contrast to the inland site of Balof [Balof 1] where none of these animals were common, being replaced by marsupials that were presumably hunted." (White and Downie 1980: 197) It is not clear from the archeological evidence whether or not Balof 1 was a habitation site. It is possible that village horticulturalists, like the people from Lesu, used the Balof 1 rock shelter as a temporary hunting camp. The few pig bones found at Balof 1 may either be those of domestic pigs or feral wild pigs that were hunted. Human bone fragments (of skulls) are much more common than pig bones at Lesu, but pigs' teeth greatly outnumber human teeth. Fish were also important and they account for two-thirds of the identifiable bone. The skeletal material from 88 varieties of shellfish, from reef, lagoon and brackish-water (mangrove) environments, were found, demonstrating an extensive dependence on marine resources which parallels that found in the upper levels at Balof 1.

There is only a minimal amount of bone artifactual material at Lesu, in contrast to Balof 1. Bone spatulas which may have been used in chewing betel nuts were found. Several worked human bones and teeth suggest that they may have been used as ornaments. One premolar has two holes drilled through the root. There are several trochus shell arm ring fragments (which were also found in the upper levels at Balof cave), adze-blades made of tridacna shell, and mangrove bivalve shells which may be scrapers. Stone artifacts include adze-blades whose stone is local rock (one comes from Lihir), and 300 grams of obsidian flakes some of which were probably used as drills. The obsidian appears to have come from Lou Island. Seven slingstones made of coralline limestone and of different weights and shapes were found in the top horizons of two mounds.

A large number of potsherds were found scattered throughout the excavation. White and Downie note, "Among the 22kg of pottery recovered, 332 pieces were decorated... with a combination of incision and applied relief." (1980: 205) One potsherd similar to "classic" Lapita was found. Two types of temper, one a calcareous temper of shell and sand, and the other of black volcanic sand, were used in the manufacture of the pottery at Lesu. The analysis by Dickinson states that these tempers are of local origin. (White and Downie 1980: 218) The pottery found at Lesu is similar to that found at the nearby site of Pinikindu, and seems to belong to the Mangaasi type described for Vanuatu. Though Mangaasi is different from Lapita, "...an approximate contemporaneity between the two traditions seems likely...." (White and

APPENDIX A. THE ARCHEOLOGY AND LINGUISTICS OF NEW IRELAND

Downie 1980: 215) The site of Pinikindu is located on the east coast, 20 miles south of Lesu on a small peninsula, where the present village of Pinikindu is found. Surface material was collected, and a test excavation was carried out at one mound. (Clay 1972) Trochus shell armbands and tridacna adze blades were found, along with reef shellfish remains. Pig bones were found at all levels, but there were no obsidian or other stone artifacts. Clay notes that there are three types of temper used in the pottery sherds found at Pinikindu. They are all probably contemporaneous, although the temper consisting primarily of crushed shell may be the oldest, according to Clay, since it was preponderant in the lowest levels excavated. Only two sherds are decorated with pinched applique strips, and two of the six rim sherds are crenulated. The bulk of the sherds are plain. As noted, this pottery resembles that excavated by White and Downie at Lesu, and the plain ware described by Specht from Watom, near Rabaul on New Britain. The tempers of the Pinikindu ceramics are also found at Watom. The applique strip decoration and crenulation found on several of the sherds from Pinikindu are also found on Watom, suggesting a relationship between the peoples represented at these sites, another village site on New Ireland, at Lasigi, was excavated in 1984 as part of the Lapita Homeland project. (Gosden *et al..* 1989) Lasigi is located 30 km. southeast of Pinikindu. Excavation of a mound, the Dori site, revealed an occupation layer (phase 4) containing marine shell refuse, cooking stones, and potsherds, below which were found two large postholes (phase 3) In a corner of the lowest layer (phase 1) were the remains of a burial which was not excavated. The body was in a seated or squatting position. In that same layer were the remains of two individuals who had been cremated there. Another area, the Mission site, was also excavated at Lasigi, in which potsherds were more plentiful, and marine shells less plentiful than at the Dori site. Two small fishhooks were found here, the first on record for New Ireland according to Golson. Small amounts of obsidian and volcanic stone in pebble form were found. Most of the obsidian came from Lou Island, in the Admiralty Islands, but five pieces came from Talasea. The pottery found at Lasigi is similar to that from Lesu. (Gosden *et al.* 1989: 571)

As a result of the work done on the Lapita Homeland Project, the upper levels of several sites- Balof, Lasigi, Lesu and Pinikindu, have been identified as being related to the Lapita complex, though none of the classic dentate-stamped pottery has been found at these sites. The Lapita cultural complex was first identified through its pottery, which has a distinctive dentate-stamped design. According to Green, "However, other types of impressing, as well as incising, modelling, applique, and cut-away relief, were also used as decorative techniques.... The Lapita ceramic series consists of vessel forms such as various shouldered pots, open-mouthed jars, and flat-bottomed dishes.... [and] a range of infrequently decorated bowls of simple shapes and varying sizes." (1979: 40) Despite the diversity of form and decoration, Green argues for a cultural unity. He states, "The restricted number of rules needed to generate the Lapita style from its elements, and the demonstration of a substantial corpus of early motifs spread from Watom (off New Britain) to Samoa, are the most convincing evidence available that the style reflects a unified system known to the makers of the pots everywhere. The likelihood that we are dealing with a series of closely related communities is therefore great." (Green 1979: 40)

In some sites, the Lapita pottery is associated with pig and chicken bones, and the evidence for horticulture is "indirect but persuasive." (Green 1979: 37) Several sites have indicated the presence of arboriculture, involving coconut palm, canarium and pandanus (Gosden *et al..* 1989: 573) Hunting was not an important part of the Lapita economy. Marine resources of reef and shallow

APPENDIX A. THE ARCHEOLOGY AND LINGUISTICS OF NEW IRELAND

water lagoons were exploited extensively. Green notes, "Thus the majority of the fish are those most easily taken with nets, traps, and spears, data that are consistent with only minimal representation of one-piece fishhooks and no specialized gear such as lures for taking surface-feeding fish offshore." (1979: 36-37) Adze blades made of the giant clam, sling stones with pointed ends of shell and ground stone, trochus shell arm rings and conus shell bracelets are also associated with the Lapita pottery. Obsidian, chert and other types of stone found in Lapita sites far from the original sources of these materials indicate extensive inter-island exchange. With respect to settlements, Green states, "Despite the limited evidence available, it seems certain that the Lapita settlements were internally differentiated, self-sufficient villages occupied by sedentary populations...." (Green 1979: 34) These settlements are found on the beach, with clustered, rather than dispersed, households. In a recent article, a tentative regional chronology for the Bismarck Archipelago was proposed. The Lapita material at Lolmo Cave site (Arawes Islands off New Britain), dated at 3,473 b.p., and the Nissan Island site, dated 3,200 b.p., both overlay pre-Lapita levels containing obsidian, worked bone, shell artifacts, evidence of pig and a range of domesticated fruits and nuts (Nissan), but no pottery. (Gosden *et al.,* 1989: 569)

At present, the earliest known Lapita site producing a sizeable assemblage, including classic dentate-stamped pottery, is at Eloaua, in the St. Matthias group (Mussau), north of New Ireland in the Bismarck archipelago. The Bismarck Archipelago is the westernmost area where Lapita is found. This site is dated at 3500 b.p. (Kirch and Hunt 1988) Lapita sites have been found in island groups to the east and south of the Bismarcks including Reef Islands, Santa Cruz, New Hebrides, New Caledonia, Fiji, Samoa and Tonga. Green notes that the earliest dates for Lapita sites in these island groups are more or less contemporaneous. (1979: 34) Lapita represents a widespread cultural horizon within which Eastern and Western Lapita traditions can be clearly distinguished. (Green 1979: 34) A recent study of 78 carbon-14 age determinations from Lapita sites throughout the Pacific area, from the Bismarcks to Tonga and Samoa revealed that Lapita populations very rapidly moved into the vast island area they came to occupy, being dispersed within a period of c.300 years. (Kirch and Hunt 1988: 165)

Only two examples of Lapita pottery have been found on New Ireland itself, a potsherd found at Lesu by White, and a partially complete pot found in situ at Lamau by Gorecki. (Gosden *et al.*. 1989: 571) However, a number of sites on islands off the coast of New Ireland or nearby have been clearly identified as Lapita. A collection of potsherds from the north end of Ambittle Island in the Feni group was analyzed by White and Specht, who concluded that some of the sherds were of the classical Lapita style, with its dentate stamping, while the decoration on others resembled the relief decoration of slashed and pinched bands and nubbins found on some of the pottery White uncovered at the upper level of Lesu. (White and Specht 1971: 92-93)

Watom Island, off Rabaul in New Britain, reveals extensive evidence of Lapita occupation dating from 2720 b.p. to 2033 b.p.. (excavations conducted by Meyer, Specht, Green and Anson) Classic dentate stamped pottery was found in the lower levels, while a thinner plain ware, believed by Specht (1974) to be derived from Lapita, characterized the upper levels. (Green and Anson 1985: 44) The extensive remains of marine fish and shellfish seemed to point to a marine oriented economy with domesticated pigs and fowl and arboriculture, including coconuts and canarium nuts. (Specht 1974, Green and Anson 1985) Obsidian flakes from Lou and Mopir and later, in much greater quantities from Talasea, give evidence of inter-island trade. Burials in round or oval pits were also found. (SAC site, Green and Anson 1985)

The three Lapita sites excavated on Eloaua and Emanunus Islands in the Mussau group north of New Ireland represent the earliest known Lapita material as well as one of the largest assemblages of classic Lapita material. Along with numerous examples of Lapita dentate-stamped pottery there were also ceramics which have been characterized as "simplified" Lapitoid similar to that excavated at Lasigi. The Eloaua sites also yielded large numbers of shell scrapers and peelers, one-piece fishhooks of pearl shell and trochus, and a collection of shell and bone objects of an ornamental nature. The latter included rings and beads of conus shell, spondylus shell beads and necklace segments, conus shell plaques, perforated pig tusks and flying fox teeth and a small, finely carved anthropomorphic figure made of bone. (Kirch 1987: 174-175)

In addition, abundant faunal remains including fish (making up 75% of the total), turtle, bird, fruit bat, cuscus, and pig were found. There were many examples of well-preserved seeds and seed cases, representing 19 taxa of the fruit and nut species important in the arboriculture of most Pacific Islands including coconut palm, and canarium. Kirch argues that this information demonstrates that the Lapita colonizers came into the area with these tree crops 3,500 years ago, rather than the reverse- arboriculture following in the wake of horticulture. (Kirch 1987: 167)

The two areas, A and B, of site ECA on Eloaua Island are seen as providing information on internal differentiation. (Gosden *et al.*. 1989: 572) Area B, with a large collection of classic dentate-stamped sherds, obsidian, shell and bone artifacts, and preserved plant material, represents the remains of a stilt house built over shallow water. Area A, contemporaneous with it, includes a large number of undecorated sherds, with few shell artifacts.

Gosden *et al.*. note, "Whether this indicates that Area B was the focus of unusual activities practiced by the whole community or whether the differences between Areas A and B reflect social differentiation within the community cannot be determined at present." (1989: 572) Social differentiation clearly has import for the nature of social structure. No mortuary goods which would support the hypothesis of hierarchical social structures have been found in Mussau. However, the separate spatial distribution of the two kinds of pottery and the production of certain kinds of shell objects which indicate craft specialization has led Kirch to conclude that some form of social differentiation existed. (Kirch 1988a: 164)

A.3 Linguistics

Linguistic evidence also sheds light on the successive settlements of New Ireland. According to Wurm, Kuot (also known as Panaras), the only Papuan language spoken on New Ireland, is a stock level isolate of the East Papuan Phylum. (Wurm 1975) Kuot today is spoken in a narrow band from the east coast (from the village of Lesu) to the west coast (the village of Panaras). Wurm believes that the ancestral speakers of the East Papuan Phylum may represent a remnant of the first Papuan migration into mainland New Guinea, which he dated at 10,000 to 15,000 b.p. They were subsequently displaced into the islands east of mainland New Guinea by the main migration of Papuan speakers of the Trans-New Guinea Phylum. Wurm proposed these dates before the archeological dating of the earliest human occupation of New Ireland had been pushed back to 32,000 b.p. No suggestions regarding the possible linguistic affiliations of these earliest immigrants have been put forth.

The speakers of languages of the East Papuan Phylum, such as Kuot, have lived in close proximity to Austronesian speakers and as a result their languages have been strongly influenced by Austronesian. Tryon notes that,

APPENDIX A. THE ARCHEOLOGY AND LINGUISTICS OF NEW IRELAND

"The resultant pidgin languages, then, retained a largely Austronesian grammar but a considerably Papuan vocabulary." (Tryon 1982:243)

The Austronesian speakers of New Ireland all speak languages which are members of a single family (or subgroup), Tolai-New Ireland, one of 27 sub-groups of the Oceanic language group. (Pawley 1985) Pawley hypothesizes several stages in the development of the Oceanic languages. After a relatively unified development of the proto-Oceanic branch of Eastern Malayo-Polynesian along the north coast of New Guinea to a point east of Saera Bay for several centuries, speakers of Proto-Oceanic settled the Bismarcks and the Solomons and moved southeast to Vanuatu. Speakers of this unified language, or dialect chain, inhabited the string of mutually visible islands from New Guinea to Malaita and San Cristobal, in the Solomons. After several centuries, Proto-Oceanic broke up into the 27 sub-groups of which it is made up today. Pawley suggests a connection between the Lapita cultural complex and the speakers of this Proto-Oceanic language community and notes that, by 2000 BC significant local variation in material culture and dialect diversity existed within the Proto-Oceanic community. (Pawley 1985: 172-177)

APPENDIX B. DEED OF LAND PURCHASE ON NEW IRELAND, MAY 5, 1885

"This Indenture made the fifth day of May one thousand eight hundred and eighty-five Between Tyese, Amoot, and Saibet of the first part and Thomas Farrell Pilot of the Steam Ship Golden Gate and Emma Eliza Forsayth of Ralum Plantation in the Island of New Britain of the second part Witnesseth that the said parties of the first part for and in consideration of the sum of Eighty two dollars in Trade_____ to them in hand paid by the parties of the second part the receipt whereof is hereby acknowledged have bargained and sold and by these presents do bargain and sell unto the said parties of the second part their heirs successors and assigns forever All those certain pieces or parcels of land situated on the South West coast of New Ireland, including the foreshore being the true and lawful owners thereof Which said pieces or parcels known by the name of Masalam - Conari - Leroro - Comilose - and Mapulipum (generally known as "Cocalai") and are more particularly described as follows: comprising the land at right angles to the Beach to about a mile inland which said pieces of land will be more fully described when surveyed "Together with all and singular the hereditaments and appurtenances thereunto belonging or in anywise appertaining And also all the right title interest claim and demand whatsoever of the said parties of the first part either at law or in equity of in and to the above bargained premises and every part and parcel thereof To have and to hold to the said parties of the second part their heirs successors and assigns for ever "In witness whereof the said parties to these presents have hereunto set their hands and seals the day and the year first before written

his mark

"Signed (by affixing their & seal marks) sealed and delivered Tyese X part in the presence of Saibet X Agostino Stalio Master of S S Golden Gate T. Dalutte Clerk to Farrell

"We the undersigned hereby certify that the above instrument was read translated and fully explained to the above mentioned parties of the first part and who in our presence declared their perfect knowledge of the contents of such instrument and expressed their entire satisfaction Witness to the mark of Seena"

Her Seena X

T. Dalutte mark Agostino Stalio [registered as sub No 124 in Matupi, March 27, 1888- in German]. (Australian Archives G1 #6 series 210 file Kolbe vs Govt) Included with the deed is a sketch-map of the plot.

APPENDIX C. THE POPULATION OF NEW IRELAND BEFORE 1914

Attempts were made between 1905 and 1910 to determine the size of the population of New Ireland. Kavieng District was "...inhabited by from 20,000 to 22,000 free natives. In the south Neu Mecklenburg District, 11,206 natives were counted in those localities where a count could be conducted. These counts did not include the localities from Cape Matanatamberan as far as Cape St. George or the Lihir, Tanga and Anir groups of islands. About five thousand inhabitants of these areas should be added to the figure given above, so that the total population of the Namatanai District comes to sixteen thousand natives. Unfortunately there are still signs of a rapid decline in population in the whole of Neu Mecklenburg." (German Imperial Government Annual Report for 1910-1911: 324) In 1913-1914, the Draft Annual Report notes, "Only the future can show whether the doctor's efforts can halt the decline in the population [of Namatanai District] previously observed." (pp. 59-60) This theme of the declining population of New Ireland, which could not be explained, was taken up in later years by the Australian administration. The anthropologists Chinnery and Groves investigated this problem in the 1930s, and eventually the cause was traced to venereal disease.

The Draft Report for 1913-1914, the final report of the German colonial administration, gives a figure of 28,000 as the population of Kavieng District. By this time Kavieng District had been enlarged to include the northwest islands of Musau (St. Mathias), Emirau (Sturm Island) and Enus (Tench Island), and the southern border of the district had been extended to Karu. Comparison with earlier population figures for the district therefore reveals little. The population of Namatanai District at that time was 16,140 persons in the "organized areas," which included the area north of Cape Matamatamberan on the east coast and Suralil on the west coast, and Lihir Islands. (German New Guinea Draft Annual Report for 1913-1914: 58) The total population for the areas of New Ireland included in the census in 1913-1914 was 44,000. .LS2

The population figures for Kavieng District reveal a great disparity between the sexes. Of the adult population, 12,350 were men and only 8,660 were women. The reason for the disparity between the number of males and females is unclear. Female infanticide has never been reported for New Ireland and indeed would make no sense in these matrilineal societies where the size of a clan is dependent on its female members producing children.

BIBLIOGRAPHY

Adams, Percy G. 1980. *Travelers and Travel Liars, 1660-1800*. New York: Dover Publications.

Albert, Steven. 1987. *The Work of Marriage and of Death: Ritual and Political Process among the Lak, Southern New Ireland, Papua New Guinea*. PhD dissertation, University of Chicago.

-----. n.d. Swilil and The Marquis de Rays. Paper presented at the American Anthropological Association Meeting, 1988, Phoenix, Arizona.

Allen, Jim. 1985. *Lapita Homeland Project: Report of the 1985 Field Season.*

Allen, J.J., C. Gosden, R. Jones, and J. Peter White. 1989. "Human Pleistocene Adaptations in the Tropical Pacific: Recent Evidence from New Ireland, a Greater Australian Outlier." *Antiquity* 63:548-61.

Barker, Francis and Peter Hulme, Margaret Iversen, and Diana Loxley. 1985. Europe and Its Others. *Vol. 1. Proceedings of the Essex Conference on the Sociology of Literature,* July 1984. Colchester: University of Essex.

Barker, John. 1990. "Introduction: Ethnographic Perspectives on Christianity in Oceanic Societies." In *Christianity in Oceania: Ethnographic Perspectives*. John Barker, ed. ASAO Monograph No. 12. Lanham: University Press of America.

-----. 1992. "Christianity in Western Melanesian Ethnography." In *History and Tradition in Melanesian Anthropology*. James G. Carrier, ed. Berkeley: University of California Press.

Baudet, Henri. 1965. *Paradise On Earth: Some Thoughts on European Images of Non-European Men*. New Haven: Yale University Press.

Baudouin, A. 1885. *L'Aventure de Port Breton et la Colonie Libre dite Nouvelle-France*. Paris. [Editor's note: reference from Biskup 1965-1991]

Baumann, P. Matthias. 1932. "Die Laienbruder in der Mission." In *Pioniers Der Sudsee*. Hiltrup: Missionare vom Hlst Herzen Jesu.

Beaglehole, J.C. 1966. *The Exploration of the Pacific*. Stanford: Stanford University Press.

Beale, Thomas. 1839. *The Natural History of the Sperm Whale... to which is added a sketch of a South-Sea Whaling Voyage*. Reprinted 1973. London: Holland Press.

Beaumont, C.H. 1972. "New Ireland Languages: A Review." In Beaumont, C.H., D. Tryon and S.A. Wurm, eds.. *Papers in Linguistics of Melanesia* #3. Research School of Pacific Studies. Australian National University.

Belcher, Captain Sir Edward. 1983. *Narrative of a Voyage Round The World Performed in Her Majesty's Ship "Sulphur" During the Years 1836-1842.* 2 volumes.

Bell. F.L.S. 1933. Report on Fieldwork in Tanga. *Oceania* 4:290-309.

----- 1934. "Warfare Among the Tanga." *Oceania* 5:253-76.

----- 1935a. "The Avoidance Situation in Tanga." *Oceania* 6:175-198, 306-322.

----- 1935b. "The Social Significance of Amfat among the Tanga of New Ireland." *Journal of the Polynesian Society* 44: 97-11.

----- 1936. "Dafal." *Journal of the Polynesian Society* 45:83-98.

----- 1946. "The Place of Food in the Social Life of the Tanga." *Oceania* 17:139-172.

Bennett, Judith A. 1987. *Wealth of the Solomons: a History of a Pacific Archipelago 1800-1978*. Pacific Islands Monograph Series #3. Honolulu: University of Hawaii Press.

Biersack, Aletta. 1991. "Introduction: History and Theory in Anthropology." In *Clio in Oceania: Towards a Historical Anthropology*. Aletta Biersack, ed. Washington: Smithsonian Institution Press.

Biskup, Peter, ed. 1965-1991. *The New Guinea Memoirs of Jean Baptiste Octave Mouton*. Pacific History Series No. 7. Published by Australia National University Press as an open access document.

Bley, Bernard P. 1925. "Die Herz-Jesu Mission in der Sudsee." *Geschichtliche Stizze uber das Apostoliche Vikariate Rabaul*. Hiltrup.

Blum, Hans. 1900. *Neu-Guinea und der Bismarck Archipel: Ein Wirtschaftiche Studie*. Berlin: Schoenfeldt & Co. Verlag.

Bolyanatz, Alexander H. 2000. *Mortuary Feasting on New Ireland: The Activation of Matriliny Among the Sursurnga*. Westport: Bergin and Garvey.

Bougainville, Lewis de. 1772. *A Voyage Round The World Performed by Order of His Most Christian Majesty In the years 1766, 1767, 1768 and 1769*. Translated from the French by John Reinhold Forster. London: J. Nourse.

Bougainville, Louis de. 1967 [1769]. "A Voyage Round the World 1766-1769." *Bibliothecca Australiana* #12. Amsterdam: N. Israel.

Boutilier, J.A., D.T. Hughes, and S.W. Tiffany, eds. 1978. *Mission, Church, and Sect in Oceania. ASAO Monograph* #6 Lanham, MD: University Press of America.

Boutilier, J.A. 1985. "We Fear Not the Ultimate Triumph: Factors Effecting the Conversion Phase of Nineteenth-Century Missionary Enterprises." In *Missions and Missionaries in the Pacific*. Char Miller, ed. *Symposium Series* V.14. New York: The Edwin Mellen Press.

Brettel, Caroline B. 1986. "Introduction: Travel Literature, Ethnography and Ethnohistory." *Ethnohistory* 33: 127 - 138.

Brouwer, Elizabeth C. 1980. *A Malagan to Cover the Grave: Funerary Ceremonies in Manda*. Ph.D. Thesis. University of Queensland.

Brown, Reverend George. 1881. "A Journey Along the Coasts of New Ireland and Neighboring Islands." *Royal Geographical Society, Proceedings.* London. New Series 3:213-240.

------ 1908. *Pioneer Missionary and Explorer. an Autobiography: A narrative of 48 years' residence and travel in Samoa, New Britain, New Ireland, New Guinea and the Solomon Islands,* London: Hodder & Stoughton.

Buschmann, Rainer F., ed. 2008. *Anthropology's Global Histories: The Ethnographic Frontier in German New Guinea, 1870-1935*. University of Hawaii Press.

------ 1910. *Melanesians and Polynesians*.

Carrier, James G. 1992. "Introduction." In *History and Tradition in Melanesian Anthropology*. James G. Carrier, ed. Berkeley: University of California Press.

BIBLIOGRAPHY

Carteret. Philip. 1965. "Carteret's Voyage Round the World 1766-1769," *Hakluyt Society, 2nd Series No. CXXIV*. Cambridge: Cambridge University Press.

Chatterton, E. Keble. 1925. *Whalers and Whaling: The Story of the Whaling Ships up to the Present Day.* T.F. Unwin. [Editor's note: The author's original text refers to "Chatterton n.d.," but this seems likely to be the citation intended.]

Chinnery, E.W. Pearson. 1929. "Studies of the Native Population of The East Coast of New Ireland." *Territory of New Guinea Anthropological Report*. No.6

Clay, Brenda. 1975. *Pinikindu: Maternal Nurture, Paternal Substance.* Chicago: University of Chicago Press.

----- 1986. *Mandak Realities: Person and Power in Central New Ireland.* New Brunswick: Rutgers University Press.

Clay, R. Berle. 1972. "The Persistence of Traditional Settlement Pattern: An Example from Central New Ireland." *Oceania* 9:1-17.

Cohn, Bernard. 1981. "Anthropology and History in the 1890s." *Journal of Interdisciplinary History* 12:227 - 252.

Columbus, Christopher. 1960. *The Journal of Christopher Columbus.* Revised and annotated by L. A. Vigneras with and appendix by R.A. Skelton. London: The Hakluyt Society.

Comaroff, Jean and John Comaroff. 1986. "Christianity and Colonialism in South Africa." *American Ethnologist*. 13:1-22.

Corris, Peter. 1968. "Blackbirding in the New Guinea Waters,1883-4: An episode in the Queensland labour Trade." *Journal of Pacific History* 3.

----- 1973. *Passage, Port and Plantation: A History of the Solomon Islands Labour Migration. 1870-1914.* Melbourne: Melbourne University Press.

Coulter, John. 1847. *Adventures on the Western Coast of S. America & the Interior of California: including a narrative of incidents at the Kingsmill Islands, New Ireland, New Britain. New Guinea and other Islands in the Pacific Ocean.* Reprinted 1972. Boston: Milford House, Inc.

Cro, Stelio. 1989. *The Noble Savage: Allegory of Freedom.* Montreal: Wilfred Laurier University Press.

Crocombe, Ron, and Marjorie Crocombe, eds. 1982. *Polynesian Missions in Melanesia: from Samoa, Cook Islands and Tonga to Papua New Guinea and New Caledonia.* Suva: Institute of Pacific Studies, University of the South Pacific.

Dampier, William. 1770. *The Voyages and Discoveries of Captain William Dampier in the South Seas and Round the World.* London.

--------1886 [1770]. "The Voyages and Discoveries of Capt. William Dampier in the South Seas and Round the World." In Pinkerton, John. *Early Australian Voyages.* Melbourne: Cassell & Co.

----- 1981. *A Voyage to New Holland: The English Voyage of Discovery to the South Seas in 1699.* James Spencer. Gloucester, ed.: Alan Sutton Publishing Ltd.

d'Urville, M.J. Dumont. 1832 *Voyage de la Courvette L'Astrolabe Execute [ar prde du Roi pendant Les Annees 1826-1827-1828-1829 sous le commandement De M.J. Dumont d'Urville. Histoire du Voyage.* Vol.4 Paris: J. Tastu.

BIBLIOGRAPHY

----- 1988. *An Account in Two Volumes of Two Voyages to the South Seas.* translated from the French and edited by Helen Rosenman. Honolulu: University of Hawaii Press.

Davidson, James W. 1966. "The Problem of Pacific History." *Journal of Pacific History* 1: 5 - 21.

Davis, Natalie Zemon, 2001. "Polarities, Hybridities: What Strategies for Decentring?" In *Decentring the Renaissance: Canada and Europe in Multidisciplinary Perspective, 1500-1700*. Toronto: University of Toronto Press. pp. 19-32.

--------.2006. "What Is Universal About History?" In *Transnationale Geschichte. Themen, Tendenzen und Theorien*, Gunilla Budde, Sebastian Conrad, and Oliver Janz, eds. Göttingen: Vandenhoeck & Ruprecht. pp. 15-20.

Daws, Gavan. 1980. *A Dream of Islands: Voyages of Self Discovery in the South Seas.* New York: W.W. Norton & Company.

Day, G.M. 1972. "Oral Tradition as Complement." *Ethnohistory* 19: 99-108.

Deane, Wallace, ed. 1933. *In Wild New Britain: The Story of Benjamin Danks, Pioneer Missionary.* Sydney: *Angus,* Robertson, Ltd.

Defert, Daniel. 1982. "The Collection of the World: Account of Voyages from the 16th to the 18th Centuries." *Dialectical Anthropology* 7:11-20.

Dening, Greg.1966. "Ethnohistory in Polynesia." *Journal of Pacific History* 1:23-42.

------1996. *Performances.* Chicago: University of Chicago Press.

------1980. *Islands and Beaches: Discourse on a Silent Land -Marquesas 1774 - 1880.* Honolulu: University of Hawaii Press.

------2004. Beach *Crossings: Voyaging Across Times, Cultures, and Self.* Philadelphia: University of Pennsylvania Press.

Diderot, Denis. 1964. "Supplement to Bougainville's Voyage" In *Rameau's Nephew and Other Works*. New York: Bobbs Merrill & Company.

Dispatches to the Governor of New South Wales. In *Dispatches of Secretary of State, 1840. January - July.* Manuscript Division, Mitchell Library, Sydney.

Docker, Edward Wybergh. 1970. *The Blackbirders*. Sydney: Angus, Robertson, Ltd.

Dodge, Ernest S. 1965 *New England and the South Seas*. Cambridge: Harvard University Press.

Douglas, Bronwen. 1992. "Doing Ethnographic History: The Case of Fighting in New Caledonia." In *History and Tradition in Melanesian Anthropology. James* G. Carrier, ed. Berkeley: University of California Press.

------1998. *Across the Great Divide: Journeys in History and Anthropology.* Amsterdam: Harwood Academic Publishers.

Downie, J. E. and J. Peter White. 1978. "Balof Shelter, New Ireland - Report on a Small Excavation." *Records of the Australian Museum* 31:762 - 802.

Dudley, Edward and Maximillian E. Novak, eds. 1973. *The Wild Man Within: An Image in Western Though from the Renaissance to Romanticism.* Pittsburgh : University of Pittsburg Press.

Duffield, A.J. 1884. *What I Know of the Labour Traffic*. Brisbane.

----- 1889 *Recollections of Travels Abroad*. London.

Dunmore, John. 1965. *French Explorers in the Pacific. Vol I.The Eighteenth Century*. Oxford: Clarendon Press.

Duperrey, M.L.I. 1826-30. *Voyage autour du monde execute par ordre du Roi sur la corvette la Coquille pendant les annees 1822, 1823, 1824 et 1825*. Zoologie par M.M. Lessonet Garnot et F.E. Guerin-Meneville. Paris: A. Bertrand.

Eberlein, Johannes. 1902. "Missionreise nach Neu Mecklenburg." *Gott Will Es* pp. 183-191: 216-224; 245-256.

Elliot, J.H. 1970. *The Old World and the New - 1492-1650*. Cambridge.

Errington, Frederick K. 1974. *Karavar: Masks and Power in a Melanesian Ritual*. Ithaca: Cornell University Press.

Fairchild, Hoxie Neale. 1961. *The Noble Savage - A Study in Romantic Naturalism*. New York: Russell & Russell.

Fergie, Deane J. 1985. *Being and Becoming: Ritual and Reproduction in an Island Melanesian Society*. Ph.D. dissertation, University of Adelaide.

Finsch, O. 1893. *Ethnologische Erfahrungen und Belegstucke aus der Sudsee*. Wien: Alfred Holder.

Firth, Stewart G. 1977. "German Firms in the Pacific Islands, 1857-1914." In *Germany in the Pacific and Far East, 1870-1914*. J.A. Moses and P.M. Kennedy, eds. University of Queensland Press.

----- 1978. Albert Hahl: Governor of German New Guinea. In *Papua New Guinea Portraits: The Expatriate Experiences*. James Griffen, ed. Canberra: Australian National University Press.

Forman, Charles W. 1985. "Playing Catch-Up Ball: The History of Financial Dependence in Pacific Island Churches." In *Missions and Missionaries in the Pacific.* Char Miller, ed. Symposium Series V. 14. New York: The Edward Mellen Press.

Foster, Robert J. 1987. "Komine and Tanga: A Note on Writing the History of German New Guinea." *Journal of Pacific History* 22:56-64.

_____. 1995 *Social Reproduction and History in Melanesia.* Cambridge: Cambridge University Press.

Frantz, R.W. 1934. *The English Traveller and the Movement of Ideas, 1660-1732.* Lincoln: University of Nebraska Press.

Friederici, Georg. 1912. *Beitrage zur Volker-und Sprachenkundevon Deutsch-Neuguinea.* Berlin: Mittler.

Frost, Alan. 1976. "The Pacific Ocean: the Eighteenth Century's New World." In *Studies on Voltaire and the Eighteenth Century.* Theodore Besterman, ed. Vol.152 Oxford: The Voltaire Foundation at The Taylor Institute.

Fyshe, Eldred. 1837-1839. *Log - A Journal of a Voyage to the South Seas during the years 1837-April 1839, on the Barque Cornet Whaler.* Pacific Manuscript Bureau #375. Nantucket Whaling Museum.

Garrett, John. 1982. *To Live Among the Stars: Christian Origins in Oceania.* Geneva and Suva: World Council of Churches and The University of the South Pacific.

Gay, Peter. 1969. *The Enlightenment: An Interpretation. Vol. II: The Science of Freedom.* New York: Alfred A. Knopf.

German Imperial Government Annual Reports 1898-1913. In *German New Guinea: The Annual Reports.* Edited and translated by Peter Sacks and Dymphna Clark, 1979. Canberra: Australian National University Press.

BIBLIOGRAPHY

German New Guinea. *The Draft Annual Report for 1913* - 1914. Edited and translated by Peter Sack and Dymphna Clark, 1980. Dept. of Law, Research School of Social Sciences, Australian National University.

Gosden, C. J. Allen, W. Ambrose, D. Anson, J. Goldon, R. Green, P. Kirch, I. Lilley, J. Specht, and M. Spriggs. 1989. "Lapita Sites of the Bismarck Archipelago." *Antiquity* 63: 561-86.

Green, Roger. 1979 "Lapita." In *Prehistory of Polynesia.* J. Jennings, ed. Cambridge: Harvard University Press. pp.27-60.

Green, Roger, and D. Anson. 1985 "Report on Watom." In *Lapita Homeland Project.*

Greenblatt, Stephen J. 1990. *Learning to Curse: Essays in Early Modern Culture.* New York: Routledge Press

Groves, William C. 1934-1935. "Tabar Today: A Study of a Melanesian Community in Contact with Non-Primitive Influences." *Oceania* 5: 224-40, 346-60 and *Oceania* 6: 147-158.

----- n.d. (1965) *Kinship and Social Organization in a New Ireland Community.* Research School of Pacific Studies, Australian National University.

Gunson, Niel. 1978. *Messengers of Grace, Evangelical Missionaries in the South Seas, 1797-1860.* Melbourne: Oxford University Press.

Hahl, Albert. 1980. *Governor in New Guinea.* Edited and translated by Peter Sack and Dymphna Clark. Canberra: Australian National University Press.

Hakluyt, Richard. 1904. *The Principal Navigations, Voyages, Traffiques and Discoveries of the English Nation* Vol.7 Glasgow: James MacLehose & Sons.

Hawesworthy, John. 1773. *An Account of the Voyages undertaken by the order of his present majesty for making Discoveries in the Southern Hemisphere and successively performed by Commodore Byron. Captain Wallis, Captain Carteret and Captain Cook in the Dolphi, the Swallow and the Endeavour.* Drawn up from the Journals which were kept and from the papers of Joseph Banks, Esq. . Vol. 1. London: W. Strahan and T. Caldell

Hefner, Robert W. 1993. "World Building and the Rationality of Conversion." In *Conversion to Christianity: Historical and Anthropological Perspectives on a Great Transformation.* Robert W. Hefner, ed. Berkeley: University of California Press

Hernsheim, Eduard. 1983. *South Sea Merchant.* Edited and translated by Peter Sack and Dymphna Clark. Port Moresby: Institute for Papua New Guinea Studies

Hill, Jonathan D. 1988. "Introduction." In *Rethinking History and Myth: Indigenous South American Perspectives on the Past.* Jonathan D. Hill, ed. Urbana: University of Illinois Press. pp. 1-18

Hornborg, Alf and Jonathan D. Hill, ed. *Ethnicity in Ancient Amazonia: Reconstructing Past Identities from Archaeology, Linguistics and Ethnohistory.* Boulder: University Press of Colorado, 2011.

Horton, Robin. 1971. "African Conversion." *Africa* 41:85-108.

Howe, Kerry. 1977. "The Fate of the Savage in Pacific Historiography." *New Zealand Journal of History* 11:137-154.

Hulme, Peter. 1986. *Colonial Encounters: Europe and the native Caribbean, 1492-1797.* New York: Methuan & Company.

Hulme, Peter, and Ludmilla Jordanova, eds. 1990. *The Enlightenment and its Shadows*. London: Routledge.

Hunt, Lynn. 1989. "Introduction: History, Culture, and Text." In *The New Cultural History*. Lynn Hunt, ed. Berkeley: University of California Press.

Java II. *Log. 1869-1870*. Old Dartmouth Whaling Museum. New Bedford, Pacific Manuscript Bureau #281.

Jessop. Owen D. *Land Tenure in a New Ireland Village*. Ph.D. dissertation, Australian National University, 1977.

Jouet, Father Victor. 1887. *La Societe des Missionaires du Sacre-Coeur dans les Vicariats Apostolique de la Medlanesie et de la Micronesie*. Issoudun.

Kalb, Don, and Herman Tak, eds. 2006. *Critical Junctions; Anthropology and History Beyond the Cultural Turn*. Oxford and New York: Berghan Books.

Keesing, Roger. 1986."The Young Dick Attack: Oral and Documentary History on the Colonial Frontier." *Ethnohistory* 23: 268-292.

----- 1988 Melanesian Pidgin and the Oceanic Substrate. Palo Alto: Stanford University Press.

------ 1992 "Kwaisulia as Culture Hero." In *History and Tradition in Melanesian Anthropology*. James G. Carrier, ed. Berkeley: University of California Press.

Kent, Mrs. William. 1803. Mrs. William Kent's Journal. May 13-Oct. 13, 1803. Voyage of HMS Buffalo, Captain William Kent. *Kent Family Papers* Vol IV. Manuscript Division. Mitchell Library, Sydney.

Keppel, Henry. 1853. *A Visit to the Indian Archipelago in HM Ship Maeander*. London: Richard Bently.

Kirch, Patrick V. 1987. "*Lapita and Oceanic Cultural Origins: Excavations in the Mussau Islands, Bismarck Archipelago, 1985.*" Journal of Field Archaelogy 14: 163-180.

----- 1988a. "Problems and Issues in Lapita Archeology." In *Archeology of the Lapita Cultural Complex: A Critical Review*. Patrick V. Kirch and Terry L. Hunt, eds. Thomas Burke Memorial Washington State Museum Report No.5

----- 1988b. "The Talepakemalai Lapita Site and Oceanic Prehistory." *National Geographic Research* 4:328-342.

Kirch, Patrick V. and Terry L. Hunt 1988. "Radiocarbon Dates From The Mussau Islands and the Lapita Colonization of the South-western Pacific." *Radiocarbon*. 30: 161-169.

Kirch, Patrick V., Daris Swindler and Christy G. Turner III 1989. "Human Skeletal and Dental Remains from Lapita Sites (1600-500B.C.) in the Mussau Islands, Melanesia." *American Journal of Physical Anthropology*. 79: 63-76.

Langmore, Diane. 1989. *Missionary Lives: Papua, 1874-1914*. Pacific Islands Monograph Series No.6. Honolulu: University of Hawaii Press.

Lanyon-Orgill, Peter. 1960. *A Dictionary of the Raluana Language.* Victoria, the author.

Latukefu, S. 1978. "The Impact of South Seas Islands Missionaries on Melanesia." In *Mission, Church, and Sect in Oceania*. J. Boutilier, D. Hughes, and S. Tiffany, eds. pp.91-108. ASAO Monograph No. 6 Lanham, MD: University Press of America.

Latukefu, S., and Ruta Sinclair. 1982. "Pacific Islanders as International Missionaries." In *Polynesian Missions in Melanesia: From Samoa, Cook Island and Tonga to Papua New Guinea and New Caledonia*. Ron and Margery Crocombe, eds. Suva: Institute of Pacific Studies. pp.1-6.

LeBlanc, Steven. Constant Battles: *The Myth of the Peaceful, Noble Savage*. New York: St. Martins Press, 2003.

Lesson, R.P. 1829. "Memoire sur la Nouvelle Ireland et sur ses Habitans." *Journal des Voyages, decouvertes et navigations modern our Archive Geographique du XIX siecle* 41:179-211. 257-293.

----- 1839. *Voyage autour du Monde, entrepreis par ordre du government sur La Corvette La Coquille*. Paris: P. Pourrat Freres.

Lewis, Philip H. 1969. *The Social Context of Art in Northern New Ireland*. Anthropological Series 58. Chicago: Field Museum of Natural History.

Linneken, Jocelyn S. 1983. "Defining Tradition: Variations on the Hawaiian Identity." *American Ethnologist* 10:2:241-252.

Lutz, John Sutton, ed. 2007. *Myth and Memory: Stories of Indigenous-European Contact*. Vancouver: University of British Columbia Press.

Ligeremaluoga, 1932. *An Account of the Life of Ligeremaluoga (Osea): An Autobiography*. trans. by Ella Collins. Melbourne: F.W. Cheschire Pty, Ltd.

Marshall, P.J. and Glyn Williams. 1982. *The Great Map of Mankind: Perceptions of New Worlds in the Age of Enlightenment*. London: J.M. Dent & Sons, Ltd.

Maude, H. E. 1964. "Beachcombers and Castaways." *Journal of Polynesian Society*: 73: 254-63.

McPherson, Robert S. 2009. *Comb Ridge and Its People: The Ethnohistory of a Rock.* Logan, Utah: Utah University Press.

Mead, Margaret. 1960. "Weaver of the Border." In *In the Company of Man: Twenty Portraits by Anthropologists.* Joseph B. Casagrande, ed. New York: Harper and Brothers. pp.175-210.

Michner, James A., and A. Grove Day. 1957. *Rascals in Paradise: The Tales of High Adventure in the South Pacific.* New York: Random House.

Mihalic, F. 1971. *The Jacaranda Dictionary and Grammar of Melanesian Pidgin.* Port Moresby: The Jacaranda Press.

Montaigne, Michel Eyquem de. 1965. [1580]. *Essays.* Translated by John Florio. London: Dent, Everymans' Library.

Morrell, Captain Benjamin. 1832. *A Narrative of Four Voyages to the South Sea, North and South Pacific Ocean, Chinese Sea, Ethiopic and Southern Atlantic Oceans, Indian and Antarctic Oceans, From the Years 1822-1831.* New York: J. & J. Harper.

Morrell, Abby Jane. 1833. *Narrative of a Voyage...in the years1829, 1830, 1831.* New York: J.&J. Harper

Mouton, Jean Baptise. 1974. *The New Guinea Memoirs of Jean Baptist Octave Mouton.* Peter Biskup, ed. Canberra: Australian National University Press.

Muller, Herman. 1932. "Mission und Arbeiter." In *Pioniere Der Sudsee.* Hiltrup: Missionare vom Hlst. Herzen Jezu.

Neumann, Klaus. 1992. "Not the Way It Really Was: Constructing The Tolai Past." *Pacific Islands Monograph Series.* No.10. Honolulu: University of Hawaii Press.

BIBLIOGRAPHY

Neuguinea Kompagnie Annual Reports 1886-1899. In *German New Guinea: the Annual Reports*. Edited and translated by Peter Sack and Dymphna Clark. Canberra: Australian National University Press.

Niau, J.H. 1936. *The Phantom Paradise*. Sydney: Angus and Robertson.

Parkinson, Phebe. Correspondence. Mormon Genealogical Center, Salt Lake City, Utah.

Parkinson, Richard. 1926 [1907]. *Dreissig Jahre in der Sudsee*. Stuttgart: Strecker und Schroder.

Pawley, Andrew. 1985. "Proto-Oceanic Terms for 'Person': A Problem in Semantic Reconstruction." *Oceanic Linguistics*, Special Publication 20: 92-104.

Pawley, Andrew, and Roger C. Green. 1984. "The Proto-Oceanic Language Community." *The Journal of Pacific History* 19:123-146.

Peekel, Gerhard P. 1932. "Neuirland (Laur)" In *Pioniere Der Sudsee*. Hiltrup: Missionare vom Hlst Herzen Jesu.

Pollack, Donald K. 1993. "'Conversion and 'Community' in Amazonia." In *Conversion to Christianity: Historical and Anthropological Perspectives on a Great Transformation*. Robert W. Hefner, ed. Berkeley: University of California Press.

Powdermaker, Hortense. 1933. *Life in Lesu: The Study of a Melanesian Society in New Ireland*. London: Williams and Norgate.

Powell, Wilfred. 1883. *Wanderings in a Wild Country or Three Years amongst the Cannibals of New Britain*. London.

Quoy, Jean-Rene, and Joseph Gaimard. 1830. "Zoology," Vol.1. In *Voyage de la corvette l'Astrolabe, execute par ordre du Roi pendant les annees 1826,*

1827, 1828, 1829, sous le commandement de M. Jules S-C Dumont d'Urville. Paris: Tastu et Cie.

Rannie, Douglas. 1887-1888. "New Ireland." *Royal Geographic Society of Australia. Proceedings of the Queensland Branch* 3:72-92.

------1912. *My Adventures among South Sea Cannibals. An Account of the Experiences and Adventures of a Government Official among the natives of Oceania*. London: Seeley, Service & Co.

Retamar, Roberto Fernandez. 1989. *Caliban and Other Essays*. Minneapolis: University of Minnesota Press.

Richter, Daniel K. 2001. *Facing East from Indian Country; A Native History of Early America*. Cambridge, Mass.: Harvard University Press.

Rickard, Rev. R.H. 1882-1893. "Letters etc." *Methodist Overseas Mission (MOM328)*. Mitchell Library, Sydney.

Robe, Stanley L. 1972. "Wild Men and Spain's Brave New World." In *The Wild Man Within: An Image in Western Thought from the Renaissance to Romanticism*. Edward Dudley and Maximillian. E. Novak, eds. Pittsburgh: University of Pittsburgh Press.

Robson, R.W. 1965. *Queen Emma*. Sydney: Pacific Publications.

Romilly, Hugh Hastings. 1886. *The Western Pacific and New Guinea. Notes on the Natives, Christian and Cannibal, with some account of the Old Labour Trade*. London: John Murray.

-----1893. *Letters from the Western Pacific and Mashonaland,1878-1891*.London: David Nutt. Rosenau, Pauline Marie. 1992. *Post-Modernism and the Social Sciences: Insights, Inroads, and Intrusions*. Princeton: Princeton University Press.

Rosman, Abraham, and Paula G. Rubel. 1989. "Dual Organization and its Developmental Potential in two Contrasting Environments." In *The Attraction of Opposites*. David Maybury-Lewis and Uri Almagor, eds. (*Royal Society Philosophical Transactions* I.1665) Ann Arbor: University of Michigan Press.

-----2009. "Structure and Exchange." In *The Cambridge Companion to Lévi-Strauss*. Boris Wiseman, ed. New York: Cambridge University Press. pp. 59-69.

Rosman, Abraham, Paula G. Rubel, and Maxine Weisgrau. 2017. *The Tapestry of Culture; An Introduction to Cultural Anthropology*. Lanham, Boulder, New York, London: Rowman & Littlefield. 10th edition.

Rubel, Paula G., and Abraham Rosman. 1978. *Your Own Pigs You May Not Eat; A Comparative Study of New Guinea Societies*. Chicago and London: The University of Chicago Press.

----- 1991. "From Ceremonial Exchange to Capitalist Exchange: How the New Irelanders Coped with the Establishment of Trading Stations." In *Man and a Half; Essays in Pacific Anthropology and Ethnobiology in Honour of Ralph Bulmer*. Andrew Pawley, ed. Auckland: The Polynesian Society (*Journal of the Polynesian Society, Memoirs*, No. 48) pp. 336-343.

-----1996. "George Brown, Pioneer Missionary and Collector." *Museum Anthropology* 20:1:60-68.

-----2012. *Collecting Tribal Art: How Northwest Coast Masks and Eastern Island Lizard Men Become Art*. West Conshohocken, PA: Infinity Publishing.

Ryan, M.T. 1981. "Assimilating New Worlds in the 16th and 17th centuries." *Comparative Studies in Society and History* 23:519-538.

Sack, Peter G. 1973 *Land Between Two Laws: Early European Land Acquisitions in New Guinea.* Canberra: Australian National University Press.

Sahlins, Marshall. 1981. *Historical Metaphors and Mythical Realities: Structure in the Early History of the Sandwich Island Kingdom.* ASAO Special Publications, No.1. Ann Arbor: University of Michigan Press.

----- 1985. *Islands of History.* Chicago: University of Chicago Press.

Saunders, Kay. 1982. *Workers in Bondage: The Origins and Bases of Unfree Labour in Queensland 1824-1916.* University of Queensland Press, Scholar's Library.

Scarr, Deryck. 1967. *Fragments of Empire: A History of the Western Pacific High Commission 1877-1914.* Canberra: Australian National University Press.

-----1970. "Recruits and Recruiters: A Portrait of the Labour Trade." In *Pacific Island Portraits*. James W. Davidson and Deryck Scarr, eds. Canberra: Australian National University Press.

Schlaginhaufen, Otto. 1909. "Strifzuge in Neu-Mecklenburg und Fahrtennach benachbarten Insel-gruppen." *Zeitschrift fur Ethnologie* 40:952-957.

Schouten, William Cornelison. 1618a. *Journal Ofte Deschryvinghevan de wonderlicke reyse, ghedaen door Willem Cornelisz Schouten van Hoorne, in de Jaren 1615,1616, en 1617.* Amsterdam: Williem Jansz.

-----1618b *Journal, ou Description du Merveilleux voyage de Guillaume Schouten, Hollandaise etc.* Amsterdam; Guillaume Janson.

-----1618c *Warhaffte Beschreibung der Wunderbarlichen Rayseuns Schiffar. so Wilhelm Schout von Horn etc.* Arnheim: Jan Jansen.

BIBLIOGRAPHY

-----1619a *Novi Freti, a parte Meridionali, in Magnum Mare Australe Detectio: facta laboriosissimo et periculosissimoitinere a Guilielmo Cornelij Schoutenio Hornano etc.* Amsterdan: Guilielmum Jansonium.

-----1619b. *The Relation of a Wonderful Voyage Made by William Cornelison Schouten of Horne [1615-1617], shewing how southe from the Straights of Magelan, in Terra Del-fuego: he found and discovered a newe passage through the great South Sea, and that way syled round the world.* London: Nathanaell Newbury.

-----1619c. Relacion diaria del viage de Jcobo de Mayre, *y Guillelmo Cornelio Schouten, en que descubieron nuevo Estrechoy passage del mar del Norte al mar del Sur, a la parte Australdel Estrech de Magallanes.* Madrid: Bernardino de Gusman.

-----1619d. "The Relation of a Wonderful Voiage made by William Cornelison Schouten, 1619." In James. A, Burney, *Chronological History of the Voyages and Discoveries in the South Sea or Pacific Ocean. Part II from the year 1579 to 1628.* London, 1806.

-----1619e. *Australian Navigations Discovered by Jacob Le Mairein the Years 1615, 1616, and 1617.* Translated by J.A.J. de Villiers. London: Hakluyt Society, 1906.

Sharp, Andrew. ed. 1968. *The Voyages of Abel Janszoon Tasman*. Oxford: Oxford University Press.

Silverman, Marilyn, and P.H. Gulliver, eds. 1992. *Approaching the Past: Historical Anthropology Through Irish Case Studies*. New York: Columbia University Press.

Spate. O.H.K. 1979. *The Spanish Lake*. Minneapolis: University of Minnesota Press.

----- 1988. *Paradise Found and Lost*. Minneapolis: University of Minnesota Press.

Specht, Jim. 1968. "Preliminary Report on Excavations on Watom Island." *Journal of the Polynesian Society* 77: 117-134.

----- 1974. "Stone Pestles on Buka Island, Papua New Guinea." *Mankind* 9: 324-328.

Strathern, Andrew. 1991. "Struggles for Meaning." In *Clio in Oceania: Towards a Historical Anthropology*. Aletta Biersack, ed. Washington: Smithsonian Institution Press.

Symcox, Geoffrey. 1972. "The Wild Man's Return: The Enclosed Vision of Rousseau's Discourses." In *The Wild Man Within An Image of Western Thought* From *The Renaissance to Romanticism*. Edward Dudley and Maximillian E. Novak, eds. Pittsburgh: University of Pittsburgh Press.

Tasman, Abel Janszoon. 1968 [1642]. *The Voyages of Abel Janszoon Tasman*. Andrew Sharp, ed. Oxford: Clarendon Press.

Thorsley, Peter L. Jr. 1972 "The Wild Man's Revenge." In *The Wild Man Within: An Image in Western Thought from the Renaissance to Romanticism*. Edward Dudley and Maximillian E. Novak, eds. Pittsburgh: University of Pittsburgh Press.

Threlfall, Neville. 1975. *One Hundred Years in the Islands. The Methodist/United Church in the New Guinea Islands Region 1875-1975*. Rabaul, Papua New Guinea: Taksave na Buk Dipatnab.

Tryon, D.T. 1982. "Austronesian Languages." In *Melanesia: Beyond Diversity*. R.J. May and H. Nelson, eds. Canberra: Research School of Pacific Studies, Australian National University.

Villiers, Alan. 1931 *Vanished Fleets*. New York: Charles Scribner's Sons.

Wachtel, Nathan. 1977. *The Vision of the Vanquished: The Spanish Conquest of Peru Through Indian Eyes, 1530-1570*. Ben and Siăn Reynolds, trans. Hassocks, [Eng.]: Harvester Press.

Wagner, Roy. 1986. *Asiwinarong: Ethos, Image and Social Power Among the Usen Barok of New Ireland*. Princeton: Princeton University Press.

------ 1991. "New Ireland is Shaped Like a Rifle and We Are at the Trigger: The Power of Digestion in Cultural Reproduction." In *Clio in Oceania: Towards a Historical Anthropology*. Aletta Biersack, ed. Washington: Smithsonian Institution Press.

Wawn, William T. 1893. *The South Sea Islanders and the Queensland Labour Trade*. London: Swann Sonnenschein & Co.

White, Hayden. 1972. "The Forms of Wildness: Archeology of an Idea." In *The Wild Man Within: An Image in Western Though from the Renaissance to Romanticism*. Edward Dudley and Maximillian E. Novak, eds. Pittsburgh: University of Pittsburgh Press.

White, J. Peter. 1972. "Carbon Dates from New Ireland." *Mankind* 8(4): 309-310.

White, J. Peter and Jim Allen. 1980. Melanesian Prehistory: Some Recent Advances. *Science* 207: 728-734.

White, J. Peter, and J.E. Downie. 1980. "Excavations at Lesu, New Ireland." *Asian Perspectives* 23: 193-220.

White, J. Peter, J.E. Downie, and W.R. Ambrose. 1978. "Mid-recent Human Occupation and Resource Exploitation in the Bismarck Archipelago." *Science* 199: 877-879.

White, J. Peter and J.R. Specht. 1971. "Prehistoric Pottery from Ambitle Island, Bismarck Archipelago." *Asian Perspectives* 14: 88-94.

White, Richard. 1991. *The Middle Ground: Indians, Empires, and Republics in the Great Lakes Region, 1650-1915.* Cambridge & New York: Cambridge University Press.

Whiteman, Darrell L. 1985. "Missionary Documents and Anthropological Research." In *Missionaries, Anthropologists and Culture Change.* Darrell L. Whiteman, ed. Studies in Third World Societies, Publication #25.

Williams, Ronald G. 1972. *The United Church in Papua New Guinea and the Solomon Islands,. The Story of the Development of an Indigenous Church on the Occasion of the Centenary of the LM Sin Papua 1872-1972.* Rabaul: Trinity Press.

Wurm, S.A., ed. 1975. *Papuan Languages and the New Guinea Linguistic Scene.* Pacific Linguistic Series C - No. 38, New Guinea Area Languages and Language Study. Vol.1 Australian National University, School of Pacific Studies.

-----1982. *Papuan Languages of Oceania.* Ubingen: Guntherr Narr.

Zwinge, Hermann. 1932. "Die Missionierung: Guantuna (Kanaken der Gazellehalbinsel)," In *Pioniere Der Sudsee.* Hiltrup: Missionarevom Hlst. Herzen Jezu.

INDEX

Anthropological history, 9, 10, 14, 16
Australia, 19, 20, 33, 87, 99, 107, 121, 131, 145, 149, 173, 175, 184, 186, 187, 188, 192, 201, 219, 250, 264, 296, 298, 303, 305, 312, 321, 343
Big Men, 16, 112, 160, 162, 168, 169, 197, 231, 255, 263, 285, 294, 314
Boluminski, Franz, 229, 230, 234, 235, 244, 245, 248, 251, 254, 255, 258, 277, 300, 315
Brown
  New Irelanders' views of, 344
Brown, Reverend George, 40, 48, 218, 344
  New Irelanders' views of, 205
Buying a church, 216
Cannibalism, 2, 50, 62, 70, 71, 72, 73, 82, 152, 154, 193, 197, 201, 206, 271, 318
Capitalism, 2, 10, 30, 33, 121, 122, 136, 141, 142, 144, 167, 173, 256, 258, 294, 297, 308, 311, 313

Catholic Mission, 274, 275, 276, 277, 278, 279, 280, 282, 319
Checkerboard pattern enemies and allies, 49, 127, 152, 169, 228, 315, 316
Chiefs and "kings", 16, 37, 38, 48, 49, 112, 128, 129, 134, 144, 156, 160, 168, 169, 182, 195, 196, 199, 213, 228, 230, 231, 234, 288, 294, 301, 302, 314
Chinnery, E.W. Pearson, 45, 46, 64, 339, 345
Clans, 44, 45, 49, 50, 51, 52, 53, 54, 62, 172, 227, 239, 257, 282, 289, 294, 313
Clay, Brenda Johnson, 3, 61, 329
collecting and museums, 22, 76, 77, 83, 114, 136, 141, 154, 159, 241, 268
Collecting and museums, 207
Copra, 27, 141, 144, 149, 150, 153, 167, 168, 171, 173, 184, 193, 236, 239, 242, 244, 247, 251, 252, 254, 288, 293, 296, 297, 298, 302, 304, 305, 308, 310, 311, 313, 314, 316

Corvee labor, 234, 249, 258, 317
d'Urville, M.J. Dumont, 111, 119, 134
Districts, establishment of, 49, 214, 229, 230, 232, 233, 237, 252, 280
dukduk, 57, 117, 205, 208, 216, 244
Duke of York Islands, 26, 58, 133, 142, 143, 144, 149, 154, 155, 156, 174, 175, 193, 195, 199, 204, 210, 211, 212, 218, 219, 230, 252, 262, 265, 271, 287
Enemies and allies, 49, 50, 51, 62, 103, 109, 127, 152, 166, 169, 170, 188, 197, 198, 201, 203, 217, 222, 223, 225, 226, 227, 228, 231, 232, 235, 236, 282, 291, 315, 316
Exchange, 43, 53, 60, 90, 91, 122, 146, 147, 165, 167, 252, 258, 308, 310
Fijian catechists, 197, 201, 202, 204, 206, 274, 318
Fijian teachers, 154, 195, 198, 199, 200, 201, 206, 207, 209, 210, 211, 212, 220
Forsayth, Emma, 149, 150, 181, 240, 241, 242, 246, 300, 304, 337
Groves, William, 45, 48, 66, 339, 351

Hernsheim, 41, 65, 143, 159, 160, 167, 182, 225, 259, 315
Iron, 36, 95, 101, 103, 105, 106, 110, 115, 116, 117, 118, 119, 120, 122, 123, 125, 129, 130, 131, 132, 133, 134, 137, 138, 145, 146, 147, 148, 165, 226, 308, 309, 315
Kavieng/Nusa, 33, 147, 229, 234, 235, 244, 245, 246, 266, 267, 269, 277, 278, 279, 287, 290, 291, 295, 296, 300, 303, 304, 305, 315, 316, 339, 340
Laborers
  payments to, 173, 175, 176, 179, 188, 209, 239, 243, 247, 249, 250, 257, 264, 275, 291, 296, 299, 304, 310, 312, 313, 314, 316
Land, acquisition of, 18, 21, 44, 46, 53, 72, 80, 86, 87, 99, 102, 107, 110, 124, 125, 129, 133, 135, 138, 142, 143, 146, 147, 154, 155, 164, 167, 168, 169, 172, 180, 181, 203, 206, 207, 208, 209, 214, 219, 232, 235, 239, 240, 244, 245, 246, 247, 248, 249, 254, 259, 267, 284, 碑 289, 296, 297, 298, 304, 308, 313, 314, 324, 325, 326, 327, 337

INDEX

Lapita, 36, 37, 63, 325, 326, 328, 330, 331, 332, 333, 335, 341, 351, 354
Lesu, 44, 46, 48, 50, 64, 65, 232, 247, 272, 282, 318, 327, 328, 330, 332, 334, 363
Ligeramaluoga, 34, 53, 66, 271
Lihir, 26, 38, 64, 93, 101, 133, 149, 171, 175, 177, 178, 180, 203, 279, 289, 315, 328, 339, 340
lotu, 201, 208, 210, 216, 282, 285
luluai, 36, 230, 231, 235, 236, 255, 301
malanggan, 25, 40, 44, 47, 52, 54, 60, 65, 144, 147, 268, 285, 317, 318
Marquis de Rays, 17, 155, 161, 162, 163, 165, 168, 172, 182, 243, 273, 274, 341
Marriage, 45, 46, 47, 48, 52, 53, 61, 64, 65, 81, 204, 272, 299, 318
masalai, 239, 264, 284
Melanesians, as perceived by Europeans, 111, 121, 135, 165
Methodists, 143, 155, 170, 174, 192, 193, 194, 209, 210, 213, 214, 217, 218, 221, 261, 262, 263, 264, 265, 266, 267, 268, 269, 270, 274, 275, 276, 277, 278, 279, 280, 281, 282, 283, 284, 285, 319, 362
Moieties, 44, 45, 50, 51, 52, 53, 55, 56, 61, 62, 218, 261, 282, 283, 319, 321
Money (shell, stone, other), 43, 48, 51, 55, 64, 65, 128, 142, 144, 159, 160, 167, 176, 177, 216, 249, 252, 263, 288, 294, 309, 310
Mouton, Jean Baptiste, 44, 45, 160, 161, 162, 163, 165, 225, 226, 243, 244, 254, 264, 292, 293, 303, 316, 343, 356
Nakedness, 12, 13, 38, 70, 91, 111, 208
New Britain, 26, 36, 58, 103, 105, 121, 142, 145, 147, 150, 153, 154, 157, 160, 166, 170, 184, 187, 194, 200, 201, 207, 208, 211, 212, 218, 219, 220, 225, 229, 239, 240, 241, 242, 243, 244, 245, 246, 247, 251, 253, 264, 266, 273, 274, 275, 276, 287, 316, 324, 325, 329, 330, 331, 332, 337, 344, 346, 347
Noble Savage, 70, 71, 72, 74, 77, 81, 82, 83, 84, 103, 109, 111, 114, 121, 134, 136
orong, 47, 48, 49, 55, 66, 216
Parkinson, Richard, 40, 57, 61, 64, 150, 170, 171, 241, 242, 243, 244, 264

Polynesia, 16, 32, 37, 120, 136, 138, 160, 165, 191, 307, 335, 342, 346, 347, 351, 355, 359

Powdermaker, Hortense, 42, 46, 51, 64, 65, 232, 272, 282, 283, 321

Queensland plantations, 173, 174, 179, 187

Rituals and ceremnies, death, 51

Rituals and ceremonies, boys' and girls' initiations, 52, 54

Rituals and ceremonies, death, 25, 40, 53, 57, 61, 205, 318

Rituals and ceremonies, taboo of crops for, 104, 255, 295

Sahlins, Marshall, 16, 24, 138, 189, 360

Schouten, Willem, 10, 38, 78, 86, 87, 88, 89, 90, 91, 92, 93, 94, 95, 100, 101, 110, 112, 114, 125, 360, 361

Science, 2, 76, 370

Sexual intercourse, 55, 60, 61, 62, 65, 138, 299

Solomon Islands, 16, 86, 92, 111, 150, 153, 173, 184, 220, 241, 296, 309, 344, 346

Tanga, 26, 38, 46, 47, 48, 49, 51, 52, 53, 58, 64, 93, 97, 102, 113, 175, 177, 178, 228, 279, 283, 289, 315, 339, 342, 343, 350

Translation of Christian texts to local languages, 265, 266, 285

Warfare, 49, 50, 60, 84, 91, 109, 127, 135, 170, 188, 193, 206, 216, 226, 227, 229, 231, 233, 235, 236, 239, 282, 302, 316, 317

Weapons (cannons, guns, rifles), 91, 96, 100, 106, 110, 118, 126, 127, 155, 158, 160, 166, 167, 170, 176, 184, 188, 205, 214, 222, 223, 226, 227, 298, 301, 315, 316

Wild men, 72, 73, 76

Women, 25, 42, 43, 45, 48, 49, 50, 51, 52, 54, 57, 59, 60, 61, 65, 69, 75, 78, 124, 138, 140, 153, 165, 176, 177, 178, 182, 184, 187, 189, 195, 196, 204, 205, 208, 211, 212, 214, 243, 263, 271, 298, 340

ABOUT THE AUTHORS

Paula G. Rubel and Abraham Rosman in 2004
(Suzanne Hanchett photo)

Paula G. Rubel (1933-2018) was an anthropologist with a Ph.D. from Columbia University. She taught at Barnard College, retiring as a Professor in 1998. She engaged in several research projects, starting with her Ph.D. research on Kalmyk Mongol immigrants to the United States and continuing in collaboration with Abraham Rosman to pursue their common interests in comparative social structure and historical analysis in multiple locations over a period of more than 50 years.

Professor Rubel was the Principal Investigator for the National Science Foundation grant (No. BNS8605676) which funded the 1987 ethnographic fieldwork in New Ireland, which is referred to in this book.

Abaham Rosman (1930-2020), a Yale University Ph.D. anthropologist, also was a Professor at Barnard College and retired in 1998. His original research was with the Kanuri of northern Nigeria. After finishing their collaborative work on potlatches in the Northwest Coast of North America, he and Paula Rubel pursued their comparative and structuralist interests, combining field research with historical studies in Iran, Afghanistan, New Guinea, and New Ireland.

www.ingramcontent.com/pod-product-compliance
Lightning Source LLC
Chambersburg PA
CBHW051542010526
44118CB00022B/2548